'Ponte is able to draw on rich empirical insights from multiple sectors to illustrate his story. He does not merely point at generic key similarities across industries and commodities—he knows these industries and commodities like the back of his hand. He is therefore able to both do justice to context and the particulars, while developing a persuasive broader argument about where corporate sustainability practices and sustainability governance are headed, and why.'

Luc Fransen, Associate Professor of International Relations, University of Amsterdam

'In the face of an ever growing range of threats to our planet, businesses are under pressure to green their corporate strategies. Building on 15 years of empirical research across different sectors and regions and informed by a multi-disciplinary theoretical approach, Ponte shows not only how sustainability management is a key feature of contemporary capitalism, but also why pursuing "just sustainabilities" is so imperative. I strongly recommend the book.'

Professor Peter Newell, University of Sussex, author of *Globalization and the Environment and Global Green Politics*

'Since the 1980s, the main question has been how to leverage foreign direct investment and GVC engagement for economic development. Now, with the habitability of the planet in question, this book shifts the lens toward sustainability. Very timely!'

Timothy J. Sturgeon, Ph.D. Senior Researcher, MIT Industrial Performance Center (IPC)

D1320272

BUSINESS, POWER AND SUSTAINABILITY IN A WORLD OF GLOBAL VALUE CHAINS

ABOUT THE AUTHOR

Stefano Ponte is Professor of International Political Economy and Director of the Centre for Business and Development Studies at Copenhagen Business School. He is primarily interested in transnational economic and environmental governance, with focus on overlaps and tensions between private authority and public regulation. His research, fieldwork, teaching and policy work are informed by international political economy approaches, global value chain analysis and convention theory. He analyses business–government–civil society interactions, economic development and environmental upgrading trajectories in global value chains – especially in Africa and in the Global South. Stefano is particularly interested in how sustainability labels, certifications and codes of conduct shape power relations in global value chains, and in how different forms of partnerships affect sustainability outcomes. Finally, he is involved in projects critically examining the role of celebrities and branding in these processes, new forms of development aid, changing corporate social and environmental responsibility practices, and cause-related marketing. Stefano is the author or editor of 9 other books, including *Brand Aid: Shopping Well to Save the World* (with Lisa Ann Richey), *Trading Down: Africa, Value Chains and the Global Economy* (with Peter Gibbon) and *The Coffee Paradox: Global Markets, Commodity Trade and the Elusive Promise of Development* (with Benoit Daviron).

BUSINESS, POWER AND SUSTAINABILITY IN A WORLD OF GLOBAL VALUE CHAINS

Stefano Ponte

ZED

Business, Power and Sustainability in a World of Global Value Chains was first published in 2019 by Zed Books Ltd, The Foundry, 17 Oval Way, London SE11 5RR, UK.

www.zedbooks.net

Typeset in Plantin and Kievit by Swales & Willis Ltd, Exeter, Devon
Index by ed.emery@thefreeuniversity.net
Cover design by Kika Sroka-Miller

A catalogue record for this book is available from the British Library

ISBN 978-1-78699-258-1 hb
ISBN 978-1-78699-257-4 pb
ISBN 978-1-78699-259-8 pdf
ISBN 978-1-78699-260-4 epub
ISBN 978-1-78699-261-1 mobi

Printed by CPI Group (UK) Ltd, Croydon CR0 4YY

To Peter Gibbon, for mentorship and inspiration

CONTENTS

FIGURES

TABLES

ABBREVIATIONS

2BSvs	Biomass Biofuels voluntary scheme
4C	Common Code for the Coffee Community
AAA	Nespresso AAA Sustainable Quality Program
AAG	Association of American Geographers
ABLC	Advanced Biofuels Leadership Conference
ADM	Archer Daniels Midland
Aireg	Aviation Initiative for Renewable Energy in Germany e.V.
ASTM	American Society for Testing and Materials
bbl/d	barrels per day
BCI	Better Cotton Initiative
BEE	Black Economic Empowerment
BP	British Petroleum
BRC	British Retail Consortium
BWI	Biodiversity and Wine Initiative
CAAFI	Commercial Aviation Alternative Fuels Initiative
C.A.F.E.	Starbucks Coffee and Farmer Equity Practices
CCWG	Clean Cargo Working Group
CDP	Carbon Disclosure Project
CEO	chief executive officer
CGIAR	Consultative Group for International Agricultural Research
CO_2	carbon dioxide
CORSIA	Carbon Offsetting and Reduction Scheme for International Aviation
COSA	Committee on Sustainability Assessment
CSI	Clean Shipping Index
CSER	corporate social and environmental responsibility
CSR	corporate social responsibility
DoE	United States Department of Energy
EC	European Commission
EEDI	Energy Efficiency Design Index
EPA	Environmental Protection Agency
ESI	Environmental Ship Index

ETS	Emissions Trading Scheme
EU	European Union
FAA	Federal Aviation Authority
FFU	Danish Ministry of Foreign Affairs Consultative Research Committee for Development Research
FLEGT	Forest Law Enforcement, Governance and Trade
FLO	Fairtrade Labelling Organizations International
FQD	Fuel Quality Directive
FSC	Forest Stewardship Council
FSE	Danish Social Science Research Council
GBEP	Global Bioenergy Partnership
GCCs	global commodity chains
GDP	gross domestic product
GE	General Electric
GHG	greenhouse gas
GiFAS	French Aerospace Industries Association
GLAD	Global Aviation Dialogue
GM	genetically modified
GPN	global production network
GTAS	Gafta Trade Assurance Scheme
GTZ, now GIZ	German Agency for Technical Development and Cooperation
GVC	global value chain
H&M	Hennes & Mauritz AB
HVO	hydrotreated vegetable oil
IATA	International Air Transport Association
IBM	International Business Machines Corporation
ICA	International Coffee Agreement
ICAO	International Civil Aviation Organization
ICO	International Coffee Organization
IDH	Sustainable Coffee Program
IFOAM	International Federation of Organic Agriculture Movements
IFP	French Institute of Petroleum
IFS	International Featured Standards
IGO	intergovernmental organization
ILO	International Labour Organization
ILUC	indirect land use change
IMO	International Maritime Organization

IO	international organization
IPW	Integrated Production of Wine
IRENA	International Renewable Energy Agency
ISA	International Studies Association
ISCC	International Sustainability and Carbon Certification
ISEAL	International Social and Environmental Accreditation and Labelling
ISO	International Organization for Standardization
IWAY	IKEA standards on sustainability
JDE	Jacobs Douwe Egberts
LCA	life-cycle analysis
LEED	Leadership in Energy and Environmental Design
M&A	mergers and acquisitions
M&S	Marks & Spencer
MARPOL	International Convention for the Prevention of Pollution from Ships
MASBI	Midwest Aviation Sustainable Biofuel Initiative
MBM	market-based measure
MDGs	Millennium Development Goals
MEAs	Multilateral Environmental Agreements
ML	million litres
MRV	Monitoring, Reporting, Verification
MSC	Marine Stewardship Council
MSI	multi-stakeholder initiative
MT	metric ton
NGO	non-governmental organization
NISA	Nordic Initiative for Sustainable Aviation
NOx	nitrogen oxides
NSMD	non-state market-driven
OIV	International Organization of Vine and Wine
PC	personal computer
pkm	passenger-kilometre
QWAY	IKEA standards on quality
R	South African rand
R&D	research and development
RBSA	Abengoa RED Bioenergy Sustainability Assurance
RED	Renewable Energy Directive

RFS	Renewable Fuel Standard
RIMPAC	Rim of the Pacific
RIN	Renewable Identification Number
RSB	Roundtable on Sustainable Biomaterials
RSPO	Roundtable on Sustainable Palm Oil
RTRS	Roundtable on Responsible Soy
SAFN	Sustainable Aviation Biofuels Northwest
SAFUG	Sustainable Aviation Fuel Users Group
SCAA	Specialty Coffee Association of America
SCM	supply chain management
SDGs	Sustainable Development Goals
SEAT	Sustaining Ethical Aquaculture Trade
SEEMP	Ship Energy Efficiency Management Plan
SME	small and medium-sized enterprises
SOx	sulphur oxides
SQC	Scottish Quality Farm Assured Combinable Crops Limited
SSCM	sustainable supply chain management
SSI	Sustainable Shipping Initiative
SWSA	Sustainable Wine South Africa
TASCC	Trade Assurance Scheme for Combinable Crops
UCC	Ueshima Coffee Co.
UFAS	Universal Feed Assurance Scheme
UK	United Kingdom
UN	United Nations
UNEP	United Nations Environment Programme
UNFCC	United Nations Framework Convention on Climate Change
UNGC	United Nations Global Compact
UNICA	Brazilian Sugarcane Industry Association
US	United States
USD	United States dollar
USDA	United States Department of Agriculture
USLP	Unilever Sustainable Living Plan
WBCSD	World Business Council on Sustainable Development
WEF	World Economic Forum
WIETA	Wine and Agricultural Ethical Trade Association

WOSA	Wines of South Africa
WPCI	World Ports Climate Initiative
WSB	Wine and Spirit Board
WTO	World Trade Organization
WWF	World Wildlife Fund
WWF-SA	World Wildlife Fund South Africa

PREFACE AND ACKNOWLEDGEMENTS

This book is the result of 20 years of research carried out through individual and collective projects. It is written as a monograph but is based on numerous collaborations. It does not arise from a predetermined set of research questions and methods – it is rather a bricolage of research efforts that varied in terms of objectives, focus, sectoral coverage, and size and type of funding. The book is a reflection on what these efforts mean when combined and contrasted with each other. It does not provide a neat set of findings that address a set of hypotheses. It is an exercise of sensemaking on how sustainability governance operates through global value chains and what kinds of regulatory, political and activist instruments can help to address some of the global sustainability crises humanity is facing.

The different projects that are the backbone of this book were based on different designs and methodologies. My main contribution to them was mostly based on key informant interviews carried out during fieldwork or through participation at industry conferences – normally as part of the process of following a global value chain from production (often in Africa) to consumption (often in Europe and the US). In addition to in-depth interviews, I carried out focus groups, surveys, informal conversations and participant observation with a variety of actors along global value chains – from smallholder coffee farmers and artisanal fishers to managing directors of export companies; from logistics officers and CEOs of international trading companies to operations managers of large buyers; from board members of multi-stakeholder sustainability initiatives to journalists rating wines; and from NGO and development cooperation officers to radical activists.

In this 20-year period, I carried out over 1,000 interviews with producers, transporters, processors, providers of inputs and services, bankers, government officials, officials of international organizations, standard makers, certifiers, experts and practitioners, traders, branded manufacturers, retailers, labour organizers, NGO representatives, social activists, and 'tastemakers'. I researched value chains especially in the agro-food sector (coffee, wine, fish, aquaculture products, biofuels), but also more recently in capital industries with mobile assets (aviation and shipping). I worked closely with researchers and supervised PhD students who worked in labour-intensive manufacturing (clothing, furniture), knowledge-intensive industries (pharmaceuticals, 3D printing) and other agro-food industries (spices, cut flowers, fresh fruit and vegetables, cotton, cocoa). I gained very useful insights from policymakers, business leaders and civil society groups while coordinating the Sustainability Platform at Copenhagen Business School, and while supervising many MSc theses in the International Business and Politics programme and the Business and Development Studies programme, on all sorts of value chains and different sustainability issues. Finally, I took training courses to be able to research these value chains with enough knowledge of the technicalities of production, processing and quality – including training in viticulture, wine production and wine tasting at the Cape Wine Academy in South Africa.

In relation to sustainability, my research has been mostly concerned with multi-stakeholder initiatives and especially those that offer a consumer label and/or third-party certification. I studied the social aspects of sustainability (e.g. Fairtrade certification and South Africa's Black Economic Empowerment initiatives); I also researched labels, certifications and cause-related marketing initiatives that combine social and environmental aspects (UTZ, Rainforest Alliance, various aquaculture certifications, ProductRed). More recently, I have also worked on the environmental aspects of sustainability (the Marine Stewardship Council label, various biofuel sustainability certifications, 'green' shipping and aviation initiatives), which are the focus of this book. In some of this research, I drew connections between sustainability initiatives and governance and upgrading in GVCs, but other contributions were more specifically targeted to scholars and practitioners interested in sustainability regulation and governance per se. This book stems from a desire to draw lessons across various experiences of GVC governance and sustainability governance, and across different sectors.

Chronologically, the first phase that ignited this process started in 1999 – when I began carrying out a project focused on issues of governance and upgrading in the coffee GVC, with a strong interest in understanding how 'quality' is negotiated, arbitrated and used to shape value addition, capture and redistribution along this value chain, often at the detriment of smallholder producers in the Global South (Daviron and

Ponte, 2005; Giovannucci and Ponte, 2005; Ponte, 2002a, 2002b). The coffee project was part of the research programme 'Globalization and Economic Restructuring in Africa', which examined a series of agro-food GVCs originating in Africa. This led to several collaborative theoretical and empirical contributions to the GVC literature with my main mentor and collaborator Peter Gibbon (Gibbon and Ponte, 2005, 2008; Gibbon et al., 2008; Ponte and Gibbon, 2005), and later on with Tim Sturgeon and Mark Dallas (Dallas et al., 2017, 2019; Ponte and Sturgeon, 2014). A second phase, which included individual and collective components as well, took me to study the wine GVC in South Africa and the fish GVC in Uganda and South Africa, this time with a focus on quality and sustainability standards (Ponte, 2007a, 2009, 2012; Ponte and Cheyns, 2013; Ponte and Ewert, 2009). This research project was part of a larger programme (Standards and Agro-Food Exports) that examined standards as tools of trade governance (Gibbon et al., 2010; Ponte et al., 2011).

A third phase, just concluded, was based on several collaborative projects that run more or less in parallel: a project with Lisa Ann Richey critically examining the role of celebrities and consumption in attempting to stimulate development (Richey and Ponte, 2014) and make the world a more sustainable place (Richey and Ponte, 2008, 2011); a large EU FP7 project on ethical and sustainable aquaculture GVCs in South East Asia (Sustaining Ethical Aquaculture Trade – SEAT) (Jespersen et al., 2014; Ponte et al., 2014) and related collaborations (Bush et al., 2013; Vandergeest et al., 2015); a project focused on sustainability certifications in biofuels (Ponte, 2014a, 2014b; Ponte and Daugbjerg, 2015); a collective effort reflecting critically on the 'green economy' in the Global South (Brockington and Ponte, 2015); and a project dedicated to emerging sustainability initiatives in aviation and shipping (Henriksen and Ponte, 2018; Lister et al., 2015; Poulsen et al., 2016, 2018). The various designs, methods and data sources behind these efforts are available in the individual works cited here and throughout this book.

Given that the first seed for these efforts was planted in 1999 when I moved from North Carolina to Copenhagen to join the then Centre for Development Research, it is virtually impossible to list and acknowledge the contribution of all the people who made this book possible. However, a few individuals stand out: Peter Gibbon, my mentor and colleague for many years; Lisa Ann Richey, my partner in life and work; our children Sasha, Arianna and Zeno, who put up with our travels, obsessions and dinner conversations that counted as 'work' in their eyes; and Covarec, Gherison, Papo and Tonev – for being there at any time. A special thanks to Sasha Neema Ponte for fixing all my graphs and tables.

In connection to the actual writing of this book, I am particularly indebted to Neil Coe and Henry Yeung, who hosted me at the Global Production Network Centre, National University of Singapore in May 2016. Their feedback at the very beginning of the writing process saved me from taking all sorts of tangential directions that would have made it even more difficult to finish the book – not to speak of their social companionship and shared love of good wine and food. At the other tail end of the process, I am very grateful to Mike Hensen and Gary Gereffi for hosting me at the Duke University Global Value Chains Centre in 2017/18, and to the Otto Mønsted Fund for financial support during my sabbatical there.

Various people read and provided helpful comments and feedback on draft chapters and related papers at various points in time: Ken Abbott, Graeme Auld, Jenn Bair, Stephanie Barrientos, Michael Bloomfield, Simon Bush, Lars Buur, Ben Cashore, Emmanuelle Cheyns, Neil Coe, Mark Dallas, Peter Dauvergne, Frank de Bakker, Valentina De Marchi, Eleonora Di Maria, David Levi Faur, Luc Fransen, Susanne Freidberg, Mai Fujita, Gary Gereffi, Pieter Glasbergen, Janina Grabs, Lars Gulbrandsen, Elizabeth Havice, Lasse Folke Henriksen, Martin Hess, Matthew Hoffmann, Rory Horner, John Humphrey, Jonkoo Lee, Jane Lister, Peter Lund-Thomsen, Raphie Kaplinsky, Aarti Krishnan, Alex Marx, Fritz Mayer, Will Milberg, Arthur Mol, Jeremy Moon, Mette Morsing, Jim Murphy, Khalid Nadvi, Stefan Ouma, Florence Palpacuer, Nicola Phillips, John Pickles, René Taudal Poulsen, Gale Raj-Reichert, Andreas Rasche, John Ravenhill, Stefan Renckens, Lisa Ann Richey, Mari Sako, Philip Schleifer, Greetje Schouten, Len Seabrooke, Duncan Snidal, Cornelia Staritz, Tim Sturgeon, Meenu Tewari, Peter Vandergeest, Paul Verbruggen, Lindsay Whitfield, Henry Yeung, Jonathan Zeitlin and Fariborz Zelli.

I also benefited from feedback from Zed Books editors and reviewers, and from audiences at various conferences, workshops and seminar series where I presented this work from 2016 to 2018: the Association of American Geographers (AAG) annual conference (2016, 2018); the annual convention of the International Studies Association (ISA) (2016, 2018); the annual conference of the African Studies Association (2017); the Conference on Global Production, National University of Singapore (2017); the annual conference of the Society for the Advancement of Socio-Economics (2018); the international workshop on 'Private Authority and Public Policy in Global Context', Yale University (2018); the Centre of African Economies annual conference, Roskilde University (2018); the African Studies Center, University of North Carolina at Chapel Hill (2018); the Duke University Global Value Chain Center (2017); the Department of Geography, University of North Carolina at Chapel Hill (2017); the Department of Business and Politics, Copenhagen Business School (2016, 2017); the Global Production Network Centre and the Department of Geography, National University of Singapore (2016); the Faculty of Management, Bogor University of Agriculture, Indonesia (2016); and the Centre for Competition, Regulation and Economic Development, University of Johannesburg, South Africa (2018).

I would like to acknowledge the various funding sources for the research projects that informed this book: the Social Sciences and Humanities Research Council of Canada for the research partnership grant 'Green Shipping: Governance and Innovation for a Sustainable Maritime Supply Chain' (2017–2023) and the research grant 'The Hidden Costs of Supply Chains' (2018–2024); the EU FP7 for the research programme 'Sustaining Ethical Aquaculture Trade' (2009–2014); the Danish Ministry of Foreign Affairs Consultative Research Committee for Development Research (FFU) for the research and capacity building programme 'Standards and Agro-Food Exports' (2005–2010); and the Danish Social Science Research Council (FSE) for the research projects 'Standards as a Trade Passport' (2004–2006) and 'Globalisation and African Agriculture' (1999–2002). During this time, I was employed at three institutions that provided essential support and excellent intellectual environments: the Centre for Development Research, Copenhagen (1999–2003), the Danish Institute for International Studies (2003–2012) and Copenhagen Business School (2012–present).

A section of Chapter 1 ('Multi-Stakeholder Initiatives on Sustainability') was originally written together with Frank de Bakker and Andreas Rasche as part of a much longer and comprehensive literature review on MSIs. The ideas that underpin the section on 'Approaches to GVC Governance' in Chapter 2 were developed throughout the years in collaboration with Peter Gibbon, Tim Sturgeon and Jenn Bair. The section 'Four Types of Power in Global Value Chains' in the same chapter was developed jointly with Mark Dallas and Tim Sturgeon, including Tim's original graphics. Some of the issues related to environmental upgrading in Chapter 5 were originally examined in joint work with Valentina De Marchi and Eleonora Di Maria. In Chapter 5, the analysis of orchestration in the shipping industry was carried out together with René Taudal Poulsen and Jane Lister, while the study of aviation biofuels was carried out in collaboration with Lasse Folke Henriksen and Nicholas Haagensen. All material drawing from these collaborations has been adapted, further analysed and/or applied in different empirical settings in this book – however, the intellectual roots of this effort remain collective. Throughout the years, I carried out fieldwork in Brazil, Denmark, Ethiopia, Indonesia, Italy, Kenya, Malaysia, South Africa, Tanzania, Uganda and the US. The insights of this book have been made possible only because many people dedicated their time and effort to teach me how the world works. Errors, misinterpretations and omissions remain my own.

INTRODUCTION

Business, Sustainability and the Global Economy

Our business model drives growth that is consistent, profitable, competitive – and responsible. It is why we created the Unilever Sustainable Living Plan (USLP) ... The USLP is driving growth through brands with purpose, taking out costs and reducing risk – helping us build trust.

Statement by Unilever, www.unilever.com/
sustainable-living/values-and-values/

I have a wall covered with sustainability certificates. I had to hire an extra person to take care of all these procedures. I need to do it to keep buyers happy. Do they pay better prices for my product? No, it is just one more thing I have to do for them.

Author's interview with a wine producer,
South Africa

Green growth, corporate social responsibility and sustainability management have become part of the lexicon of business. Sustainability competitions and prizes showcase the 'good work' that some corporations are doing to address social and environmental concerns, from the global to the local levels. Many firms regularly publish sustainability reports to document their commitment to a better future, while reassuring investors that they can achieve positive financial results too. They also require their suppliers (often based in the Global South) to improve their own social and environmental practices. Given this picture, do we need different or additional regulatory interventions and activism to push business to further improve its practices?

Climate change, rampant deforestation in some parts of the globe, loss of biodiversity, and ocean acidification suggest that current business practice is not enough, that current regulatory instruments are falling short, and that social movements and activism still have a long way to go. In this book, I argue that the roles of public authority and civil society are still key for improving environmental sustainability, but that their strategies and approaches need to be informed by an understanding of how powerful firms govern global value chains (GVCs).

Sustainability has become a mainstream concern in the operation of the global economy and its regulatory structure. The reframing of the international development agenda from the Millennium Development Goals (MDGs) to the Sustainable Development Goals (SDGs) is one example. Furthermore, the 2015 Paris Agreement on Climate Change will have important implications on economic activity as it seeks to limit greenhouse gas emissions. But the SDGs and Paris Agreement goals will have to be attained in a world that over the past century has seen a true trans-nationalization of economic activity. Global trade has not only grown exponentially (far outpacing GDP growth), but has also undergone a major transformation, following the restructuring in the organization of production away from market exchange and vertical integration within transnational corporations – and towards the operation of GVCs (Gereffi, 2014; Ponte and Sturgeon, 2014).

Parallel to this reorientation, a rapid proliferation of corporate, industry-level and multi-stakeholder initiatives and partnerships (MSIs) focused on sustainability has taken place – at the transnational, national and local levels. These have led to significant shifts in the way powerful firms in GVCs approach sustainability and leverage it to create and capture value. As transnational MSIs on sustainability continue to extend their influence, there has been increased interest in understanding how they contribute to sustainability governance – together with different forms of government regulation, international agreements and direct action by activist groups and international NGOs. Previous research has shown that regulation and support from governments and international organizations still play an important part in facilitating sustainability governance (Bush et al., 2013; Foley, 2013; Gale and Haward, 2011; Gulbrandsen, 2014), both directly (e.g. through regulation, partnerships, facilitation and endorsement) and indirectly (e.g. through changing the institutional context of sustainability transitions). Therefore, the interaction of sustainability governance and GVC governance is not only of interest to an academic audience, but has important implications for public policy, business strategy and social activism.

In the rest of this chapter, I will first introduce the reader to what it means to be in a 'world of global value chains', followed by a discussion of the different challenges faced in governing sustainability in this context. Next, I will explain that environmental sustainability has become a business and has entered the mainstream of business strategy and operations. I will then argue that the current practices corporations put in place to address sustainability issues are facilitating a process of 'green capital accumulation', also by squeezing value out of suppliers through sustainability-driven demands. In the final two sections, I include a short rendition of the main arguments and key questions addressed in the book, and a guide for different audiences on how to read it. In the rest of the book, the term 'sustainability' is used narrowly to refer to its environmental aspects, unless otherwise stated. This choice was made to both provide a feasible focus and address an aspect of sustainability that the existing GVC literature has relatively neglected, given its predominant attention to social and labour issues.

A World of Global Value Chains

Global Value Chains and Their Governance

Technological and organizational changes have been crucial in transforming the way in which production is organized across time and space. The steam engine in the nineteenth century made transportation and manufacturing economic in ways that allowed the spatial separation of production from consumption (Baldwin, 2016), but for much of the twentieth century production was still organized mostly along vertically integrated firms. By the late 1970s, however, a more flexible and spatially dispersed mode of production had taken hold – based on slicing up production into specific tasks and moving some of these out of the boundary of the firm through external contracting (Piore and Sabel, 1985). Information and communication technology in the latter part of the twentieth century further facilitated the global outsourcing and offshoring of manufacturing activities (Dicken, 2007). This has led to the organization of economic activity in GVCs that are dispersed globally but governed centrally by 'lead firms' (Bair, 2009a; Cattaneo et al., 2010; Gereffi, 1994; Gereffi et al., 2005; Ponte and Sturgeon, 2014).

The term GVC refers to the full range of activities that firms, farmers and workers carry out to bring a product or service from its conception to its end use, recycling or reuse. These activities can include design, production, processing, assembly, distribution, maintenance, disposal/

recycling, marketing, finance and consumer services. In a 'global' value chain, these functions are distributed among many firms in different places around the world. In this context, 'lead firms' are groups of firms that operate at particular functional positions along the chain and that are able to shape who does what along the chain, at what price, using what standards, to which specifications, and delivering in what form and at what point in time (Gereffi, 2019; Gereffi et al., 2005; Humphrey and Schmitz, 2001; Ponte and Sturgeon, 2014).

Understanding the changing dynamics of the global economy requires knowledge of how GVCs are governed. The original concept of GVC governance is based on the observation that value chains are rarely coordinated spontaneously through market exchange (Gereffi, 1994; Gereffi et al., 2005; Gibbon et al., 2008). Instead, they are governed as a result of strategies and decision-making by specific actors, usually large firms that manage access to final markets, but also at regional and national/local levels. In deciding how to manage trade and production networks in global industries, lead firms are faced with a number of choices. First, whether to make components in-house, procure them on the market, or adopt hybrid solutions involving various kinds of longer-term relationships with suppliers. And second, if they decide to buy, they need to specify the characteristics of the good or service (such as price and volume) as well as identify the qualifications or attributes that suppliers should possess – including those related to sustainability. From this perspective, GVC governance is thus the set of concrete practices and organizational forms through which a specific division of labour between lead firms and other actors arise and is managed (Gibbon et al., 2008). Examining GVC governance then means studying the content and the management of these decisions across all suppliers and sub-suppliers, the strategies behind the decisions taken, the management methods chosen to implement them, and the systems through which their outcomes are monitored and reacted on (Ponte and Sturgeon, 2014).

From a broader perspective, however, GVC operations are also shaped by actors that do not directly produce, transform, handle or trade products and services – such as civil society organizations, social movements, consumer groups, networks of experts and policymakers, and multi-stakeholder initiatives for sustainability (Bair, 2017; Bair and Palpacuer, 2015; Nickow, 2015; Ponte and Sturgeon, 2014). Finally, states and international organizations play a key role in constructing and maintaining GVCs through facilitative, regulatory and distributive interventions (Mayer and Phillips, 2017; Nadvi and Raj-Reichert, 2015; Neilson and Pritchard, 2011). States can act as intentional architects of GVCs, regulate (or deregulate) their functioning, and choose to (not) redistribute the extra wealth generated through GVCs. States can also be important direct actors in GVCs, for example through state-owned enterprises and public procurement (Horner, 2017). In other words, states make active choices in a 'GVC world', and only a comprehensive analysis of all these actors can aptly explain the changing dynamics of sustainability governance and related processes of capital accumulation.

GVCs, the 'New' Global Economy and Capital Accumulation

The rise of GVCs is redrawing 'the international boundaries of knowledge. The contours of industrial competitiveness are now increasingly defined by the outlines of international production networks rather than the boundaries of the nations' (Baldwin, 2016: 6). Production of goods and services is fragmented and spatially dispersed, and is governed by lead firms that coordinate the activities of a myriad of supplies and sub-suppliers (Coe and Yeung, 2015; Dicken, 2007; Gereffi, 2014; Gibbon and Ponte, 2005). In other words, 'GVCs have become the world economy's backbone and central nervous system' (Cattaneo et al., 2010: 7). Lead firms have progressively focused on the specific tasks they excel in, while outsourcing and offshoring others – a movement that opened up possibilities for suppliers in new locations (and especially in the Global South) to specialize in specific tasks without necessarily needing their countries to build back-to-front industrial systems (Gereffi, 2019).

The advent of the Internet has facilitated further restructuring in GVCs, with outsourcing dramatically expanding into services (Low, 2013). This, parallel to a dramatic increase in the trade of intermediate products, has led some scholars to talk about the 'servitization' (Vandermerwe and Rada, 1988) or 'servicification' (Low, 2013) of the global economy, and the rise of 'manuservices' (Bryson and Daniels, 2010). The digitization of value chains and the growth of automated manufacturing technologies are currently fuelling new restructuring dynamics, which may facilitate the virtual movement of labour through telepresence and telerobotics, and a partial reshoring of production activities in the Global North, for example through 3D printing (Baldwin,

2016; Rehnberg and Ponte, 2017). Artificial intelligence, robotics, and what is now known as the Industry 4.0 model more generally, are likely to change the world of work and the sustainability of production (Husain, 2017; McAfee and Brynjolfsson, 2017; Schwab, 2017, 2018), but also to push large groups of people off employment, necessitating some form of basic income provision for social peace (Bregman, 2017). These transformations will entail new economic geographies of production, divisions of labour, regionalization dynamics, and perhaps a shortening of the distance between production and consumption – but they may also consolidate existing patterns and power dynamics.

Vertical specialization in GVCs has entailed that capital accumulation for lead firms increasingly takes place through carrying out multiple tasks at the two ends of a value chain – in pre-production activities (such as design and R&D) and post-production activities (such as marketing, branding and aftersales services) – where much of the value added is currently being created or captured (see Figure 0.1). In the past three decades, we have indeed observed a movement away from a relatively balanced distribution of value added along various functions in the value chain, to a situation where most value is added in pre- and post-production activities, reflecting a 'smiling curve' in the distribution of value added (Ali-Yrkkö and Rouvinen, 2015; Baldwin, 2013; Low, 2013; Shin et al., 2012). New technological and organizational innovations, however, may reshape this curve in the future (see Figure 0.1). For example, research on one of these new technologies (3D printing) (Laplume et al., 2016; Rehnberg and Ponte, 2017) highlights two possible scenarios: a *complementarity* scenario of 3D printing and traditional manufacturing overlapping, which would reproduce power relations in GVCs and the current distribution of value added along a 'smiling curve'; and a *substitution* scenario of 3D printing partly or fully superseding traditional manufacturing, which would have more transformational effects – in terms of 'rebundling' of activities, regionalization or localization of GVCs, and a flattening of the smiling curve into a 'smirk'.

In order to continue extracting value and maximizing capital accumulation, lead firms in GVCs seek to reduce cost/capability ratios in dealing with their suppliers (Coe and Yeung, 2015). Rather than simply minimizing costs, they aim at finding the most *capable* suppliers to carry out a specific task at a competitive cost. Lead firms are also sourcing from fewer, larger suppliers and transferring the costs of inventory to

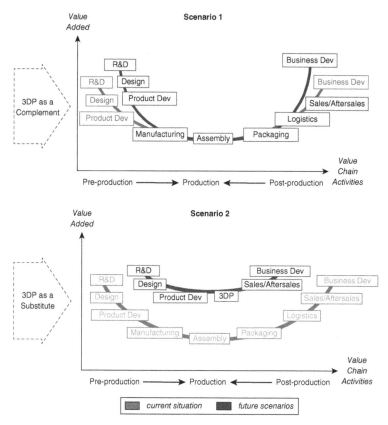

Figure 0.1 Possible Modifications in the 'Smile Curve' of Distribution of Value Added along GVCs

Source: Adapted from Rehnberg and Ponte (2017: 4)

them (Gereffi, 2014; Gibbon and Ponte, 2005). Because they operate in a global economy that is ever-more uncertain and unpredictable, due to fast technological change, financial instability and climate variability, lead firms need to actively manage risks – including those arising from sustainability demands placed by regulation, consumers and civil society groups. This requires not only cleaning up their own operations, but also those of their suppliers – through codes of conduct, mandatory reporting, supplier monitoring and/or requiring suppliers to deliver certified 'sustainable' products. This involves varying combinations of hands-on strategies (related to suppliers' operations and supply specifications) and hands-off strategies (such as third-party certification) that allow the externalization of responsibility for sustainability.

Last but not least, lead firms seek to become more 'financialized' through outsourcing their operations and minimizing productive capital investment and inventory – to better deliver 'shareholder value' (Coe and Yeung, 2015; Engelen, 2008; Froud et al., 2000; Gibbon and Ponte, 2005). This entails more focus on short-term reorganization of their finances than on long-term investment in productive activities, but also the 'optimization' of their tax liabilities and wealth through active management of their 'global wealth chains' (Seabrooke and Wigan, 2014, 2017). Lead firms thus do not only disaggregate production activities around the globe; they also disaggregate themselves legally and financially to place profit and (non-tangible) assets in tax haven jurisdictions.

As sustainability becomes a central concern in business conduct and strategy, and in approaches to value creation, capture and distribution, this book addresses several questions regarding GVCs that remain unanswered. How is the new shape of sustainability governance transforming GVC governance, and vice versa? Are lead firms in GVCs strengthening their power positions vis-à-vis other actors, or is their power being diluted by the emergence of a global sustainability agenda? How are sustainability concerns threatening, consolidating or transforming capital accumulation? Are sustainability solutions adopted by lead firms solving, reinforcing, or making no difference in terms of tackling environmental problems? Will even the most successful sustainability initiatives in GVCs be sufficient to tackle these challenges, or are they providing distractions from adopting more radical solutions?

Governing Sustainability

The term 'sustainability' has been known for at least two centuries, and was first coined in reference to forest management in Europe (Scoones, 2016). But it was not until the 1970s and 1980s that sustainability became a widespread concern, with activists calling for radical change and governments adopting harder regulation approaches to shape business conduct. With the publication in 1987 of the Brundtland Report, the notion of 'sustainable development' started to take shape, defined as 'development that meets the needs of the present without compromising the ability of future generations to meet their own needs' (Brundtland Commission, 1987: 45). Sustainable development thus introduced the idea that economic growth and environmental protection can both be achieved. This view was solidified at the 1992 UN Conference on Environment and Development in Rio de Janeiro, and the follow-up Rio+20 conference in 2012. The latter placed particular weight on the promotion of multi-stakeholder partnerships for sustainability, now enshrined in the Sustainable Development Goals as goal 17.

Definitions of, and approaches to, *environmental* sustainability (the focus of this book) are critically discussed in a variety of disciplines (see Scoones, 2016): from neoclassical economics' use of the concept of natural capital (which is either substitutable with human capital, or needs to be maintained at a certain level) (Coffey, 2016) to ecological economics' more dynamic linking of economic activity and ecological systems (through life-cycle analysis, footprint evaluations, cradle-to-cradle approaches) (Finnveden et al., 2009; McDonough and Braungart, 2010); from earth system approaches arguing that environmental (and more recently also social) 'planetary boundaries' need to be sustained (Biermann, 2014; Rockström et al., 2009a) to analyses of natural hazards and climate change (Turner et al., 2003); and from political ecology approaches linking politics, political economy and natural resource use (Newell, 2012; Peet et al., 2010) to the delineation of discursive and material pathways to sustainability and their distributional effects (Clapp and Dauvergne, 2011; Leach et al., 2010; Scoones, 2016; Scoones et al., 2015). In this book, I take a pragmatic approach to the definition of sustainability – accepting anything that is labelled by GVC actors as environmentally sustainable as such, but critically approaching these definitions and related operationalizations. At the same time, this broad take on sustainability is adapted to different analytical needs, translating into the following definitions:

- *Sustainability management* indicates the strategic actions taken by 'lead firms' in GVCs in relation to environmental issues; this is one of the elements of *GVC governance*, the set of concrete practices and organizational forms through which lead firms shape a specific division of labour between them and other actors along the chain.
- *Sustainability governance* refers to the cumulative efforts by public sector actors, corporations and business associations, NGOs and other civil society groups to address environmental challenges.

- *Orchestration* relates to the specific efforts of public actors in attempting to shape environmental processes and outcomes; this is essentially a public sector entry point to sustainability governance that goes beyond the traditional tools of government regulation.

Business can do much in reducing the environmental footprint of its own operations. But the fact that production is increasingly fragmented, both geographically and organizationally, poses extra challenges in transmitting sustainability requirements to other value chain actors. The many scandals that have touched branded companies have led them to devise sustainability strategies for their own operations and for those of their suppliers to minimize reputational risk, and to participate in multi-stakeholder initiatives addressing sustainability issues in GVCs (Nadvi, 2008; Vurro et al., 2010; Wahl and Bull, 2014).

Environmental improvements that corporations can implement on their own include those affecting production, processing, distribution, consumption and disposal or recycling. These processes can lead to net cost reductions for operators due to, for example, increased efficiency or reduced energy consumption. In other instances, they lead to net value addition, for example through the creation and certification of new environmental qualities that become embedded in products selling at premium prices. Other times, they impose net costs in the short term that can only be recouped in the long term. If the net additional costs are permanent, firms will carry out environmental improvements only if their major competitors do so, either through regulation or through industry-wide voluntary standards (Orsato, 2009), or only if consumers are available to pay higher prices for goods produced with better environmental standards. Given the range of factors involved, it is no surprise that corporations, even within the same sector, follow a variety of paths and have diverging environmental performance (Gunningham et al., 2003).

Many environmental impacts, such as the greenhouse effect, have transnational dimensions and require transnational governance. They may be non-tangible and have time-delayed effects. In these cases, national regulation, even in key polluting countries, can only provide partial solutions. At the same time, truly global environmental governance is very hard to attain through international legally binding agreements. International organizations and agencies, such as UNEP, and Multilateral Environmental Agreements (MEAs) have important roles to play. MEAs with a relatively narrow focus, such as the Convention on International Trade in Endangered Species, the Stockholm Convention on Persistent Organic Pollutants, and the International Stratospheric Ozone Regime (1987 Montreal Protocol), have been relatively successful. But broader multilateral negotiations, such as the 1992 United Nations Framework Convention on Climate Change (UNFCC), are prone to deadlock. The 1997 Kyoto Protocol took only two years to negotiate (with rules of implementation finalized in 2001), but the negotiations to replace it have been very complex and time-consuming, finally leading to the Paris Agreement of 2015. Even after these agreements are signed, however, they are still vulnerable to changes in political climate, as President Trump's declaration that the US will retract from the Paris Agreement attests.

A number of governance solutions have emerged alongside national regulation, MEAs and voluntary business action. These include the United Nations Global Compact (UNGC), many forms of public–private partnerships, and an increasing number of multi-stakeholder initiatives for the sustainability of agro-food and forestry products, minerals, chemicals, electronics, and many others. Thus, sustainability governance includes components of intergovernmental negotiation, private action and hybrid public–business–civil society interaction. But how can it be orchestrated so it delivers positive sustainability outcomes, and not just green capital accumulation? Existing research on transnational sustainability governance can provide some answers, but, as we will see in Chapter 1, these are of limited value without the insights of how GVCs operate.

One of the main tenets of transnational sustainability governance is that actors and institutions involved in it are constantly seeking to assert political and rule-making authority – the decision-making power over particular environmental issues that is accepted as legitimate from specific audiences (Cashore, 2002; Fransen, 2012). This is because they cannot rely on the exclusive authority of the state or a global institution. The emergence of private authority has not led to a wholesale retreat of the state, but to new overlaps between the public and private spheres. While private authority has been on the rise, it often applies to areas that were never regulated by the state to begin with. When private authority addresses transnational problems, it can actually enhance state capacity by allowing the state to escape innate constraints placed by territorial borders and to focus more effectively on other areas of regulation. Finally, private authority often needs public authority to establish legitimacy. This suggests that what is normally conceived as private authority, in contrast to public authority, actually has salient hybrid features (Ponte and Daugbjerg, 2015).

These hybrid dynamics can provide alternative and more flexible venues to address environmental problems – as shown by the rich variety of transnational experiments and entrepreneurial governance initiatives that are being carried out by industry associations, alliances of cities, individual corporations, international and local NGOs, and other non-state actors (Andonova et al., 2009; Bäckstrand, 2008; Hoffmann, 2011). Hybrid instruments can also overcome two of the main problems that have plagued intergovernmental treaty formation, such as path dependence and institutional inertia. Yet they can also facilitate self-interest for individual actors to achieve particularistic goals. And state capacity and intergovernmental action remain crucial in facilitating the emergence, implementation and enforcement of sustainability governance.

Some of the challenges of sustainability governance relate to how to create some coherence in the fragmentation of governance instruments in the environmental field and how to build meta-governance instruments (Derkx and Glasbergen, 2014; Zelli and Van Asselt, 2013). Thus, much attention is now being dedicated to the possible mechanisms and strategies that nation states and international organizations can use to shape environmental outcomes. The concept of *orchestration* provides a useful tool to address the perceived transnational governance deficit. It refers to a wide set of mechanisms, some 'directive' and others 'facilitative', that public authorities can put in place (see examples in Chapter 5). Directive orchestration relies on the authority of the state and international organizations, and seeks to incorporate private initiatives into its regulatory framework, for example through mandating principles, transparency, and codes of conduct. Facilitative orchestration relies on softer instruments that are often carried out behind the scenes – such as the provision of material and ideational support, in order to kick-start new initiatives and/ or to further shape and support them (Abbott and Snidal, 2009a; Abbott et al., 2015; Hale and Roger, 2014; Henriksen and Ponte, 2018; Lister et al., 2015; Schleifer, 2013).

Orchestration happens when states or intergovernmental organizations initiate, guide, broaden and/or strengthen transnational governance by non-state and/or sub-state actors. It can combine a variety of instruments, including intermediation, regulatory hierarchy, collaboration and delegation. Orchestrators may thus combine straight regulation (or the threat of future/stronger regulation) with collaboration, delegation, intermediation and other hybrid mechanisms – such as placing their own representatives in key positions in intermediary organizations (Henriksen and Ponte, 2018) or harnessing civil society pressure and consumer influence to achieve specific environmental benefits. What we lack so far in existing orchestration approaches is an understanding of the GVC factors that shape sustainability governance, and of how this knowledge can be used strategically and with what limitations. This book seeks to shed light on these questions.

Green Is the New Black: The Business of Sustainability

The role of business in sustainability governance has changed quite dramatically in recent times. Until the 1990s, lead firms in GVCs operated mainly reactively to emerging sustainability concerns. They only had limited power in actively shaping the early sustainability agenda, which was driven mainly by civil society groups and social movements, sometimes in coalition with cities and states. When business exercised influence, it was commonly targeted to slowing down or defeating attempts at environmental regulation it perceived as threatening. In the 1970s and 1980s, corporations were mostly reacting to activist and NGO campaigns and environmental regulation. Sustainability commitments among large corporations tended to be public relation campaigns or reactive measures that followed the exposure of their deleterious practices by NGOs, the media and consumer groups. At that time, companies whose image and product offerings were built on sustainability (e.g. Ben & Jerry's, Patagonia, The Body Shop) tended to target niche markets, although they were growing healthily (Dauvergne, 2016; Dauvergne and Lister, 2013).

However, the deregulation and liberalization processes that took place starting in the 1980s provided the basic conditions for a major transformation. Some environmental NGOs, such as the WWF, started to collaborate with corporations, attracted by the resources they can mobilize and the speed of change they can impart. Lead firms in GVCs became more active in positively shaping sustainability discourses and practices, first by becoming engaged in self-regulatory and market-based initiatives aimed at improving the environmental impact of their operations, and then by identifying ways in which value could be created and captured through sustainability management. By the mid-2000s, a new wave of sustainability initiatives within major corporations (e.g. Danone, General Electric, IKEA, McDonald's, Nestlé, Nike, Unilever, Walmart) started to emerge (Bregman, 2017). These initiatives are based on the expectation that they enhance profitability and brand reputation, and thus generate additional value. Lead firms in GVCs are now actively using sustainability to help mitigate reputational risk, add to the bottom line, create new product lines, enhance brand loyalty, and increase their power. Sustainability is thus becoming mainstream in business strategy and operations (Humes, 2011) and is likely to remain a strategic concern – as long as it can be leveraged for capital accumulation and to ensure competitive advantage. Corporations continue to lobby against stricter environmental regulation and fund parties and politicians that could deliver the same, but this now tends to take place as part of a wider portfolio of corporate sustainability actions. In other words, corporations are turning sustainability into a business.

The gradual mainstreaming of sustainability has been driven by cost-cutting and eco-efficiency efforts that provide corporations with a 'business case' for applying environmental improvements. Eco-efficiency processes such as decreasing energy and water use, optimizing packaging, and improving recycling often lead to net cost reductions in operations, and thus allow a focus on the bottom line – something that became even more urgent following the economic downturn of the late 2000s. Companies such as IKEA and Walmart have applied substantial cost-cutting measures on energy consumption, packaging and transport in their own operations, while showcasing these as examples of their 'commitment to sustainability'. Collecting carbon and other sustainability information has also allowed corporations to let possible investors better assess risk in investment decisions, thus facilitating access to finance (Dauvergne and Lister, 2013: 57–59). The fact that it pays to be green for business is also confirmed in much of the research on socially responsible investment, which suggests that there is no harm in market capitalization performance for lead firms that have a higher sustainability reputation, except at times of stock market spikes (Belghitar et al., 2014: 61; Delmas and Blass, 2010).

Shifting consumer preferences are obviously a factor in shaping what kinds of products lead firms sell and with what sustainability features.

However, consumer agency (both individual and collective in relation to consumer group pressure) should not be overstated. IKEA did not start demanding more sustainable packaging solutions from its suppliers as a result of consumer dissatisfaction, and Walmart did not move aggressively into organics because its customers were clamouring for it. They took strategic steps in areas where they perceived a potential for better value creation and capture. Brand risk management (to avoid negative media exposure and/or adverse NGO campaigns) is more central to sustainability management practices than consumer demand (Richey and Ponte, 2011).

Whether the motivation is strategic and/or related to consumer demand, corporations are seeking to develop new product lines with 'green' or 'ecological' features to diversify their portfolio, and/or create new or improved green goods and services, such as photovoltaic cells, smart thermostats, and wind turbines. This allows them to avoid the saturation of established markets in the Global North by diversifying into new, green products and to open up new markets in emerging economies. The latter is especially feasible when corporations can leverage increasing concerns with food safety and quality among the burgeoning middle classes in the Global South through claiming that their products are 'green' or 'healthy'. Furthermore, large corporate groups have aggressively sought the acquisition of smaller, 'sustainability oriented' companies to diversify their brand and product portfolios (e.g. the acquisitions of Ben & Jerry's by Unilever and Green Mountain Coffee Roasters by Keurig Dr Pepper).

The emergence of the sustainability agenda has also led to a true explosion of partnerships, coalitions and multi-stakeholder initiatives. This has implied an increasing need for lead firms in GVCs to participate in, or at least monitor the development of, these initiatives. Corporate involvement in sustainability partnerships with governments, NGOs and civil society groups has softened the latter's regulatory and political demands, deflecting more radical solutions and policy options (Dauvergne, 2016). Furthermore, hardcore corporate strategies are themselves being embedded into the practices of multi-stakeholder initiatives on sustainability. The market for sustainability certifications has become as competitive as the market for the goods upon which these labels are affixed (Ponte, 2014b). As a result, we are witnessing a proliferation in the number and scope of certifications and labels in the sustainability marketplace

(International Trade Centre, 2017); increased competition within the same realms of sustainability concern (e.g. the breaking off of Fair Trade USA from Fairtrade International in 2011); and the first signs of classic corporate dynamics, such as merger and acquisition activity (e.g. in 2017, two of the main sustainability certifications in agro-food products – Rainforest Alliance and UTZ – announced a merger).

Some of these sustainability initiatives have been created within industry and business associations, such as Vision 2050 of the World Business Council on Sustainable Development (WBCSD) and the Sustainability Initiative of the World Economic Forum (WEF). Others have taken the form of consortia of like-minded corporations (such as the Business for Innovative Climate and Energy Policy, the Sustainable Food Laboratory, the Sustainability Consortium and the Sustainable Agriculture Initiative Platform). Bilateral partnerships between business and civil society groups have also emerged (e.g. between Unilever and Greenpeace, Procter & Gamble and WWF, and Unilever and Fairtrade's certification arm). Finally, we observe the growth of multi-stakeholder initiatives that were initiated by lead firms in collaboration with civil society organizations (e.g. Unilever was a key player in the formation of the Marine Stewardship Council) and the formation of alliances of sustainability organizations (e.g. the Sustainable Food Laboratory, ISEAL Alliance). In the next section, I explain how the mainstreaming of sustainability facilitates the capital accumulation strategies by lead firms in GVCs – also through squeezing value from their suppliers in the Global South under the mantle of sustainability management.

Sustainability Management, Green Capital Accumulation and the Sustainability-Driven Supplier Squeeze

What do these trends mean for the structure and operation of GVCs and the global economy more generally? As Coe and Yeung (2015: 4–7) have argued, the organizational dynamics of global value chains and production networks have been driven by three important capitalist dynamics in the past three decades: (1) cost minimization; (2) flexibility; and (3) speed. The drive for ever-lower costs has led to 'spatial fixes', with lead firms, for example, seeking lower-cost but competent suppliers in new locations – in other words, trying to minimize cost/capability ratios. The other two dynamics have led to 'organizational fixes' (e.g. outsourcing to independent suppliers and/or seeking flexibility through the casualization of labour and the weakening of labour unions) and 'technological fixes', such as seeking new solutions to improve lead time and adaptability (see also Dicken, 2007). Both sets of fixes in turn have tended to facilitate vertical specialization in segments of GVCs where lead firms have the greatest core competences and have allowed capital accumulation to continue and strengthen – as new technologies, deregulation and globalization transform the institutional framework within which corporations operate.

In this book, I argue that we are currently witnessing the emergence of a *fourth capitalist dynamic*: *sustainability management*. Sustainability management relates to the practices that corporations put in place to address sustainability issues in ways that facilitate continuous capital accumulation. Sustainability management is reshaping existing spatial, organizational and technological fixes in various ways: (1) some products are increasingly sourced from locations that can deliver sustainability certifications and specifications in larger volumes and at lower cost, or with lower material and energy use (Auld, 2014; Gulbrandsen, 2010; Ponte, 2012); (2) multi-stakeholder initiatives are playing an important role in governing sustainability and, indirectly, in reshaping the organization of GVC operations (Barrientos et al., 2010; De Marchi et al., 2013b; Hassan and Lund-Thomsen, 2016); (3) labour regimes in supplier operations are put under pressure from the need to meet new environmental sustainability demands of lead firms (Riisgaard, 2011); and (4) the need to monitor and document sources and processes of sustainability compliance is bringing into play new technologies, such as value chain traceability, sustainability auditing of suppliers, and new metrics and instruments of compliance assessment (Freidberg, 2013, 2014; Giovannucci and Ponte, 2005). These technologies are themselves being leveraged to obtain more information from suppliers that can be used to better manage value chains without necessarily resorting to vertical integration (Dauvergne and Lister, 2013). This is especially important in view of managing procurement risk due to natural disasters (e.g. the severe disruptions caused in 2011 by the tsunami in Japan and floods in Thailand). As value creation and capture possibilities constantly change, sustainability management is offering new venues of *green capital accumulation*.

While from the mid-1990s to the mid-2000s the tendency had been for lead firms to move away from hands-on engagement with suppliers in view of tackling sustainability challenges, for example through third-party certifications (Gibbon and Ponte, 2005), in the past decade or so this tendency has partially reversed. Lead firms are now re-engaging more directly with (fewer) suppliers within systems of sustainability metrics that they either control internally or develop in cooperation with international NGOs (such as IKEA's IWAY, Nescafé's Better Farming Practices, Unilever's Sustainable Agriculture Code, Mondelēz's Cocoa Life, or Barry Calebaut's Cocoa Horizons). They ask their suppliers to apply life-cycle analysis, undertake audits, comply with standards and certifications, and/or provide sustainability reporting (Freidberg, 2013). Sustainability demands are often couched in ideational terms under the business school mantra of 'shared value' (Porter and Kramer, 2011). In many industries, first-tier suppliers are encouraged to do the same with their own suppliers, either by implementing lead firms' standards or by creating their own, which they then offer to companies as an alternative to third-party certification (Grabs, 2017).

Closer interaction with suppliers, in view of monitoring energy and resource use along value chains, provides lead firms with more information about and control over their suppliers – allowing them to leverage additional cost information, extract value, and push the extra cost of sustainability compliance and its related risks upstream towards producers (see Chapters 3 and 4). This raises entry barriers for smaller, less organized and/or more marginalized actors – especially in the Global South. Extra environmental compliance costs can also create incentives to actually further undermine social and labour conditions of production among suppliers. Under the mantle of achieving environmental sustainability, lead firms in GVCs capture value for themselves, while extracting more demands from their suppliers and promoting a further consolidation of their supply base. This is what I term the *sustainability-driven supplier squeeze*, which is part of a wider 'cost squeeze' dynamic aptly documented by Milberg (2008) and Milberg and Winkler (2013).

Devising their own sustainability standards and procedures also allows lead firms in GVCs to seek further diversification – as the market for certified sustainable products grows, it is more difficult to leverage these certifications as a unique selling point. On the one hand, the risk of reputational loss in internal sustainability systems is higher because compliance problems are more easily related to the brand, rather than the certification logo. On the other hand, lead firms can set internal standards at lower levels than for certifications and employ a discourse of 'continuous improvement', thus mitigating the probability and impact of compliance failure.

Several other benefits for lead firms in GVCs arise from addressing sustainability concerns: (1) they gain better control over product quality and logistics without having to vertically integrate or invest in fixed assets; (2) they can stabilize and monitor the availability of resources and thus reduce the risk of negative impacts deriving from possible disruptions; (3) closer engagement with suppliers grants them better access to resources at times of supply shortages – this has been the case not only for rare earths for electronics, but also for high-quality cocoa or unique coffee origins; and (4) the multiplication of sustainability, training and other 'development' initiatives, which allows lead firms to package their supply concerns under the veneer of 'doing good' for local communities and farmers (e.g. Mars' Cocoa Development Centres and Cocoa Village Clinics, Nestlé's Rural Development Framework, Starbucks' Kahawa Bora in collaboration with the Eastern Congo Initiative).

By leveraging sustainability management strategically, lead firms in GVCs can now actually afford to be *less* concerned with shaping the broader sustainability governance agenda beyond their corporate boundaries. Granted, collective initiatives on sustainability that are industry-driven are still important (Fransen, 2012), and corporations are still either participating in, or closely monitoring, NGO-driven sustainability initiatives. However, recent social network analyses have shown that lead firms do *not* currently play a central role in multi-stakeholder initiatives (Fransen, 2015; Henriksen, 2015; Henriksen and Ponte, 2018). Some lead firms played important roles in early phases of institutionalization but are now taking a more hands-off approach (e.g. Ahold stepped out of UTZ, Unilever is no longer formally part of the MSC). In other words, lead firms have been active in implementing a particular interpretation of the sustainability agenda for their own benefit, but are not currently dominant, or even central, in shaping it (Fransen et al., 2018). They do not need to concern themselves too much with it because they have found ways to make specific operationalizations of sustainability management profitable; and when addressing some aspects of sustainability that are not profitable in the short term, lead firms can still use sustainability instruments to externalize risk, widen product portfolios, improve information about and control over suppliers, and manage brand reputation. Although lead firms are no longer directly involved in multi-stakeholder initiatives, they can still use them to diffuse responsibility away from themselves, promote ideas of continuous improvement to defer accountability, and ultimately portray that they can marry two otherwise incommensurable goals – achieving sustainability while constantly stimulating growth in global production and consumption (Bowen, 2014; Kendra, 2012; Newell and Paterson, 2010).

In sum, the business of sustainability is not sufficient as a global solution to pressing climate change and other environmental problems. It is doing enough for corporations seeking to acquire legitimacy and governance authority. This legitimacy is further enhanced through partnerships with governments and civil society groups. Some of this engagement is used strategically to provide 'soft' solutions to sustainability concerns and to avoid more stringent regulation. While the business of sustainability is leading to some environmental improvements in some places, and better use of resources in relative terms in some industries, the overall pressure on global resources is increasing. The green capital that business accumulates through sustainability management accrues at the cost of brown environments. Green capitalism and the unsustainable exploitation of nature continue to go hand in hand.

In the rest of this book, I will show the importance of GVC dynamics in informing the orchestration of sustainability by public actors and civil society, but also indicate the limitations of business-driven solutions as the goal of green capital accumulation trumps the achievement of sustainability improvements. Therefore, I will also reflect on a larger set of ideas on the systemic rethinking that is needed to reorganize the global economy towards 'just sustainabilities'.

Main Arguments and Novel Contributions

The book is structured along two main arguments. The first argument is that sustainability management is becoming an additional feature of contemporary capitalism, together with the minimization of cost/capability ratios and the maximization of flexibility and speed – contributing to the consolidation of 'green capitalism'. It will show that sustainability management is leading to new configurations of existing spatial, organizational and technological 'fixes' that facilitate continuous capital accumulation. Despite suppliers having undergone impressive economic and environmental upgrading trajectories in many

GVCs, they have achieved only limited economic gains. Suppliers offer sustainability certification or verification often to simply keep participating in GVCs, leading to lower margins unless productivity gains can more than compensate for higher costs. When suppliers do manage to receive higher prices from buyers as part of economic and environmental upgrading, it is usually in the context of much larger gains that buyers capture in the same GVC. Thus, the sustainability-driven supplier squeeze goes hand in hand with green capital accumulation by lead firms in GVCs. This is the main analytical contribution of the book.

The second argument is that, even within the confines of green capitalism, public actors at all jurisdictional levels can still put in place orchestration strategies seeking to improve the achievement of sustainability goals, rather than simply green capital accumulation. Likewise, activists and civil society groups can identify and leverage pressure points to strengthen the effectiveness of orchestration. But these strategies have to be informed by the realities of the daily practices, power relations and governance structures of a world economy that is organized in global value chains. In Chapter 5, I will show that orchestration is more likely to succeed when a combination of directive and facilitative instruments is used; when sustainability issues have high visibility in a GVC; when private and public sectors' interests are aligned; and when orchestrators are aware of the kinds of power that underpin GVC governance and act to reshape these power configurations accordingly. Orchestration thus entails choices about possible combinations of directive and facilitative instruments that reinforce each other, ways of improving issue visibility, and approaches and incentives that facilitate the alignment of private and public sector interests – through measures that recognize the different forms and combinations of power exercised by lead firms in GVCs. Therefore, this book seeks to provide novel insights on how to ask the right questions, rather than providing a neat but ultimately flawed general model of orchestration.

Tackling the combination of green capital accumulation and limited sustainability gains demands approaches that: span from the micro to the macro level; examine the day-by-day micro-practices and incentives for and against environmental sustainability and how they are transmitted along supply chains; and explain how they aggregate and coalesce or clash with the myriad of regulations, initiatives and experiments at various geographical scales that make up sustainability governance. Yet the 'sustainability strategy' literature in business studies is exclusively focused on what happens inside the firm (Orsato, 2009), and especially within transnational corporations. The 'sustainable supply chain management' literature provides relevant entry points on supply relations (Seuring and Gold, 2013; Seuring and Müller, 2008; Seuring et al., 2008) but remains descriptive and focused on achieving competitive advantage. And the large literature on transnational sustainability governance in the social sciences more generally provides a rich source of analysis of the complexity of sustainability instruments and overlap of actors, but downplays how these interact with the day-by-day governance dynamics in the main organizational feature of the contemporary global economy – the global value chain. At the same time, existing GVC research has not satisfactorily incorporated environmental concerns in its effort to explain governance and upgrading dynamics.

On the basis of 20 years of theoretical engagement and field research, in this book I draw especially from three case studies of labour-intensive value chains in the agro-food sector (wine, coffee and biofuels), but also from the experiences of capital-intensive GVCs where mobile assets are important (shipping and aviation). The various roles of governments, civil society organizations, business and business associations, multi-stakeholder initiatives, and other groups are integrated organically in the analysis in sustainability governance, but their role is 'read through' the framework of GVC analysis, and in particular its power dynamics.

Ultimately, I seek to make three main analytical contributions to the fields of sustainability governance and GVC analysis in this book: (1) provide an approach to understanding processes and outcomes of sustainability governance *through* the lenses of GVC analysis (Bush et al., 2015); (2) further develop current efforts aimed at embedding sustainability in GVC governance theory through the lenses of power (Dallas et al., 2019); and (3) expand the analysis of GVC upgrading by further exploring its environmental dimensions.

Organization of the Book

In Chapter 1, I review relevant literatures that can provide useful insights on the complexity of governing sustainability in a world of global value chains. In Chapter 2, I discuss the foundational bases for understanding the governance of global value chains (GVCs) from a sustainability perspective. I then inject sustainability issues into a typology of power in GVCs (bargaining, demonstrative, institutional and constitutive) to provide an analytical framework for the empirical analysis carried out in the following chapters. In Chapter 3, I examine the dynamics of governance, power and sustainability in three GVCs in the agro-food sector: wine, coffee and biofuels. I trace the evolution of various combinations of power and how sustainability factors play into them – in view of providing a nuanced and dynamic picture of GVC governance. In Chapter 4, I examine how sustainability factors are shaping the interlinked processes of economic and environmental upgrading – distinguishing between upgrading as *process* and upgrading as *outcome* (for lead firms, suppliers and the environment). Empirically, I continue the analysis of the wine, coffee and biofuels GVCs, but also draw from other GVCs in labour-intensive and capital-intensive manufacturing. In Chapter 5, I discuss to what extent orchestration by public authorities and international organizations can facilitate environmental upgrading trajectories in GVCs. I assess the role of four possible enabling factors of orchestration: combinatory measures of directive and facilitative instruments, issue visibility, interest alignment, and regulatory uncertainty. I draw empirically from the same three agro-food GVCs, but also from detailed work on orchestration efforts in two capital-intensive GVCs – aviation and maritime shipping. In the Conclusion, I explore the potential role and limitations of orchestration and activism in a world of global value chains and green capitalism.

This book is targeted to two main audiences. The first is a general audience interested in how the global economy is changing and in how business manages sustainability issues. This audience includes undergraduate and graduate students, practitioners, policymakers, journalists, and whoever may care about the environment and inequality. To this audience, I seek to provide a general picture of whether and to what extent business can help solve global environmental issues, what redistributions are entailed in the mainstreaming of sustainability, and the potential and limits of orchestration and activism within the confines of green capitalism. These readers are likely to be especially interested in the empirical parts of Chapter 2 (on power, sustainability and governance), Chapter 3 (on environmental upgrading processes and outcomes), Chapter 4 (on the role of public actors in orchestrating change) and the Conclusion (on 'just sustainabilities' in a world of GVCs).

The second audience is comprised of scholars and researchers interested in green capitalism, global environmental issues, transnational sustainability governance, multi-stakeholder initiatives on sustainability, corporate strategy and organization, and the governance of global value chains and production networks. The book will be more appealing to those who work across disciplines in the social sciences – rather than exclusively inside one – and who contribute to debates relevant to economic geography, industrial organization, international and transnational relations, environmental policy and planning, political ecology, international political economy, international development, corporate social responsibility, and business studies more generally. These readers are likely to be particularly interested in the review of the relevant literatures included in Chapter 1 and in the analytical framework on power, sustainability and governance developed in Chapter 2. Those interested in how global value chains and production networks are being reconfigured through sustainability management will be particularly interested in Chapters 3 and 4. Those interested in transnational sustainability governance, sustainability transformations and environmental policy will be particularly interested in Chapter 5.

1 | WHAT WE KNOW ABOUT SUSTAINABILITY GOVERNANCE

Until fairly recently, much of the existing work in international political economy that deals with environmental issues was focused narrowly on international agreements, institutions and regimes. This included research on how international economic regimes and institutions (such as the WTO) addressed environmental issues, and research on the economic provisions of international environmental governance initiatives (such as carbon markets). But research on the rise of private and hybrid governance initiatives has now emerged, addressing its political, economic and environmental interfaces (Clapp and Helleiner, 2012). In this chapter, I highlight the main features of key literatures that can help unpack the mutual relations between sustainability governance and the sustainability elements that shape the governance of GVCs. I start with a review of the transnational sustainability governance literature, followed by a more detailed analysis of research on multi-stakeholder initiatives (MSIs) on sustainability. Then I reflect on the business school literatures on self-regulation, strategy and corporate social (and environmental) responsibility. These reviews highlight that current understandings of the multilayered and complex nature of sustainability governance are limited by a lack of mutual engagement between researchers embedded in political science, environmental politics and international political economy, on the one side, and business studies, on the other side. In Chapter 2, I will build upon these reflections to construct a framework that embeds sustainability issues in the analysis of power, governance and upgrading in GVCs.

Transnational Sustainability Governance

Transnational sustainability governance consists of 'transnational actors operating in a political sphere in which public and private actors interact across borders and political jurisdictions' to address environmental concerns (Andonova et al., 2009: 69). It is fragmented, multilayered, characterized by a hybrid of private and public authority, and takes place through different kinds of partnerships – frequently involving the steering of networks to achieve public policy goals (Andonova, 2010; Andonova et al., 2009; Bäckstrand, 2008; Haas, 2004). Numerous transnational experiments and entrepreneurial governance initiatives are being carried out by cities and their networks, industry associations and individual corporations, international and local non-governmental organizations (NGOs), and other non-state actors at different spatial levels and across jurisdictions (Abbott et al., 2016; Bulkeley et al., 2012; Dingwerth and Pattberg, 2009; Green, 2013, 2017a; Hoffmann, 2011; Overdevest, 2010; Overdevest and Zeitlin, 2014, 2018; Ponte and Daugbjerg, 2015).

The changing shape of transnational sustainability governance has been a key academic and policy concern in the past two decades, as part of a wider debate on the putative advance and limitations of 'private authority' in governing economy, society and the environment (Bartley, 2018; Cutler et al., 1999; Hall and Biersteker, 2002). Many contributors have highlighted the emergence of market-based forms of authority (Bartley, 2007; Büthe and Mattli, 2011; Cashore et al., 2004; Pattberg, 2007) and have shown that this development has not led to a withering away of the state (Auld, 2014; Bartley, 2014; Gale and Haward, 2011; Gulbrandsen, 2010, 2014). Rather, we are witnessing the birth of hybrid governance forms where business, civil society and public actors interact at different levels, in parallel and intersecting arenas where domestic and international legal orders can also apply (Abbott and Snidal, 2009a; Andonova et al., 2009; Bäckstrand, 2008; Bair, 2017; Levy and Newell, 2005; Ponte and Daugbjerg, 2015)

Part of the existing literature suggests that private regulation started strengthening from the 1980s onwards as a result of the retreat of public authority from regulating pressing social and environmental challenges – especially those with a transnational or global character – eventually leading to a crowding out of public regulatory instruments by private regulation (Bartley, 2007; Cutler et al., 1999; Vogel, 2008). An alternative argument is that public authority remains key not only in providing legitimacy to private regulation, but also in facilitating its compliance (Black, 2003; Foley, 2013; Gale and Haward, 2011; Gulbrandsen, 2014; Mills, 2016; Nadvi and Raj-Reichert,

2015; Verbruggen, 2013). A main focus in existing work has been the interplay of government, civil society and business (Avant et al., 2010) to understand how they compete and/or cooperate to shape rule systems and achieve legitimacy (Bernstein and Cashore, 2007; Black, 2008; Eberlein et al., 2014; Fransen, 2012). Particular attention has been paid to the effects of alignment and misalignment of interests between industry and the state (Auld, 2014; Gulbrandsen, 2014; Verbruggen, 2013). This vast body of literature has provided important insights in unpacking the complexity of transnational governance fields variously conceptualized as 'hybrid governance' (Andonova et al., 2009; Bäckstrand, 2008; Ponte and Daugbjerg, 2015), 'multilevel governance' (Hooghe et al., 2001), 'ensemble regulation' (Perez, 2011), 'partnered governance' (Hale and Roger, 2014), 'co-regulation' and 'smart regulation' (Gunningham, 2002, 2009; Gunningham et al., 2003; Holley et al., 2013; Sinclair, 1997), 'transnational neopluralism' (Cerny, 2010), and 'responsive regulation' (Abbott and Snidal, 2013; Ayers and Braithwaite, 1992).

There has also been growing attention paid to understanding how interests can be (and have been) made to align – in other words, whether and how public authority can or should work to bridge possible gaps between different groups of public, private, and civil society actors and/or work to realign established positions. This literature examines how public authorities can steer an existing variety of private and hybrid governance instruments to promote desired outcomes. Examples of related concepts employed for this purpose are 'enrolment' (Black, 2008; Braithwaite and Drahos, 2000), 'steering' (Hale and Roger, 2014), and 'benchmarking' through the lenses of 'experimental governance' (Overdevest and Zeitlin, 2014, 2018).

Common to the endeavour of understanding sustainability governance lays a fundamental concern with the sources of legitimacy and authority that blend into governance processes. The existing literature on transnational governance examines the fragmentation of governance instruments, the reconfiguration of regulation, various forms of institutional design, and the dynamics of legitimacy for different types of governing mechanisms (Biermann et al., 2009; Zelli and Van Asselt, 2013). It often seeks to identify 'best institutional designs' to achieve their putative sustainability objectives (Overdevest, 2010; Tamm Hallström and Boström, 2010), and examines how government, civil society and business compete and/or cooperate to shape institutions and rule systems (Dingwerth and Pattberg, 2006; Fransen, 2012). Existing work also highlights that sustainability governance can be counterproductive, as actors may navigate its complexity to achieve individualistic goals (Alter and Meunier, 2009; Schleifer, 2013). At the same time, it suggests that some of its instruments can provide alternative, experimental and more flexible venues to solve sustainability issues where more comprehensive international regimes have so far failed to emerge (Hoffmann, 2011; Keohane and Victor, 2011; Overdevest and Zeitlin, 2014).

An influential approach that emerged in recent years has been that of 'orchestration'. While not diverging substantially from the concerns of experimentalist governance and from the concept of 'steering', orchestration has provided a useful analytical device (Abbott and Snidal, 2009a, 2009b, 2010, 2013; Abbott et al., 2015, 2017; Hale and Roger, 2014; Schleifer, 2013). In Chapter 5, I will use the term orchestration to explicitly signal a concern with tools and a combination of instruments that public regulatory bodies can use to shape sustainability governance. These tools can involve indirect tools and soft power in view of steering industries and citizens towards addressing global problems, but also more direct regulatory tools, regulatory threats, and/or incentives – including instruments that nudge actors towards self-regulation and those who seek public and private sector co-regulation (Adger and Jordan, 2009; Albareda, 2008; Delmas and Young, 2009; Gunningham, 2002, 2009; Héritier and Eckert, 2008; Lyon and Maxwell, 2004). Although more recent literature has focused on international organizations as possible orchestrators, in regulatory fields or industries lacking an effective international organization that handles environmental concerns, key national/regional governments can play key roles as orchestrators of sustainability governance (Abbott et al., 2015; Henriksen and Ponte, 2018).

The tendency so far in the orchestration literature has been to analyse regulatory tools in isolation, along a matrix distinguishing between *direct* and *indirect* tools, and *hard* and *soft* power (Abbott et al., 2015; Green, 2013). Less work has been dedicated to how public authorities can use specific *combinations* of these and other tools, such as regulatory threat or hybrid delegation/intermediation (e.g. embedding public policy actors in intermediary institutions) (see Chapter 5). Recent work has also highlighted the importance of orchestrators embedding themselves within networks of experts and other stakeholders (Fransen, 2015; Fransen et al., 2016, 2018; Henriksen, 2015; Henriksen and Ponte, 2018; Henriksen and Seabrooke, 2016; Seabrooke and Henriksen, 2017). These networks can be used to stay informed on what industry is doing and to communicate signals to business on where policies are headed.

The literature reviewed so far suggests a series of key features of transnational sustainability governance: (1) it is carried out by national and transnational actors operating in a political sphere in which public and private actors interact across borders and political jurisdictions to address sustainability concerns; (2) it is fragmented and lacks a central authority; (3) it is multi-scalar and multi-jurisdictional (operates at local, national, regional, transnational and international levels); (4) it is a hybrid of private and public forms of governance; and (5) it can be orchestrated by public actors through various combination of direct and indirect, hard and soft instruments. Although there are many examples of historical analysis, this literature often lacks explicit reflections on the politics and pathways of change. Research on sustainability transitions and transformations can provide helpful insights in this realm, as it highlights at least four overlapping transformation processes and associated politics (Scoones, 2016; Scoones et al., 2015):

(1) *Technology-led* transformations, which are focused on the potential of new technologies to help achieve sustainability, for example through large-scale adoption of solar energy.

(2) A broad spectrum of *state-led* transformations, which include those that see a key role played by a 'green entrepreneurial state' picking winners and funding research and innovation for green technologies (Bäckstrand and Kronsell, 2015; Death, 2016b; Eckersley, 2004; Mazzucato, 2015a, 2015b) and those seeking 'ecological modernization' processes (Mol, 2003) where economy and ecology are seen as fruitfully combined by an enlightened state.

(3) *Civil society-led* transformations, relying on the role of grassroots innovation and community mobilization in the promotion of alternative technologies (Gibson et al., 2000; Martinez-Alier, 2003).

(4) *Market-led* transformations, which are explored in debates on whether the right incentives, systems and prices can promote

sustainability, for example through markets for carbon offsets (Leach and Scoones, 2015), payments for ecosystem services (Corbera et al., 2009) and/or multi-stakeholder initiatives (Bäckstrand, 2006; Fransen, 2012), and whether they lead to the commodification of nature and related processes of dispossession (Büscher et al., 2012). Much of the debate on the 'green economy', both supportive (Pearce et al., 1989) and critical (Brockington and Ponte, 2015; Death, 2015; Kenis and Lievens, 2015), as well as more radical contributions calling for 'steady-state economies' or even 'de-growth' (D'Alisa et al., 2014; Jackson, 2009), revolve around these sets of issues.

According to Scoones (2016), governing sustainability requires exploring the political space available at the intersection of three 'regimes' (drawing from Watts and Peluso, 2014): (1) *regimes of truth*, governing 'which transformations occur and in which directions ... [by shaping] who understands what and in which frame' (Scoones, 2016: 305); (2) *regimes of rule*, governing 'who controls what and through which forms of governance' (Scoones, 2016: 305); and (3) *regimes of accumulation*, shaping 'who gets what and how it is distributed' (Scoones, 2016: 306). The research agenda attached to this approach is promising, but so far has dedicated little attention to the everyday practices of lead firms and their suppliers in the operation of GVCs. Much has been written on the environmental damage caused by multinational corporations and on the ecological and social disasters of unfettered capitalism at the macro level, and on specific, local-level consequences. But approaches that can bridge macro and micro elements are lacking, thus the need to 'connect empirically, and account for theoretically, the ways in which "macro" social and economic forces in the global economy configure the "micro" practices of environmental politics' (Newell, 2012: 58).

The GVC approach taken in this book can usefully contribute to this agenda as it bridges macro, meso and micro dimensions of economic activity and sustainability. Furthermore, it implicitly addresses: 'regimes of rule' through its analysis of GVC governance and the intersections with public regulation and civil society pressure; 'regimes of accumulation' through its focus on value creation, capture and redistribution, and linked processes of green capital accumulation; and 'regimes of truth' through its analysis of what is considered 'best practice' and 'sustainable' in GVC operations and corporate conduct.

Multi-Stakeholder Initiatives on Sustainability

One of the fastest-growing streams within the broad literature on transnational sustainability governance has focused on multi-stakeholder initiatives on sustainability (MSIs), such as the Forest Stewardship Council (FSC), the Marine Stewardship Council (MSC) or Rainforest Alliance. This literature is particularly relevant for the key empirical case studies included in this book – the wine, coffee and biofuels GVCs. It has so far focused mostly on how MSIs develop, gain and manage legitimacy among different audiences and stakeholders, given that these initiatives cannot lean exclusively on the sovereign authority of the state (Bernstein and Cashore, 2007; Black, 2008). Much of this work shows that in order to be effective, MSIs need to achieve a balance of input legitimacy (inclusion, stakeholder representation), process legitimacy (governance procedures, participatory mechanisms, accountability, transparency) and output legitimacy (results achieved).

Some of the literature shows that increasingly complex governance structures may undermine MSI efficacy (Auld and Gulbrandsen, 2010; Fransen and Kolk, 2007; Gulbrandsen, 2010, 2014; Ponte, 2014b; Quack, 2009; Tamm Hallström and Boström, 2010). The governance set-up of MSIs is often meant to ensure (if not just signal) a degree of professionalization, participation of relevant stakeholders in key decision-making processes, and transparency. As a result, sustainability MSIs are becoming ever-more sophisticated in how they facilitate formal participation of relevant stakeholders, manage deliberation and use technologies that ensure *some* provision of input even from more marginalized actors. Yet there are serious gaps between being part of deliberation and being able to shape outcomes for marginal actors (Cheyns, 2011).

MSIs that develop sustainability standards are supposed to 'have participants from both business and societal interest groups as members and governance structures allowing for an equal possibility of input among the different partners in steering the initiative' (Fransen, 2012: 166). This differentiates MSIs from other forms of private regulation such as firm-specific codes of conduct or business-driven initiatives.

MSIs also differ from rules set by international standard-setting bodies, such as the International Organization for Standardization (ISO). While some MSIs are created around certification systems (e.g. the Forest Stewardship Council), others promote broader principles without certification procedures (e.g. the UN Global Compact) (see Rasche et al., 2013). MSIs can thus be seen as voluntary rule systems for sustainability that are governed by stakeholders who cross the profit/non-profit and state/non-state boundaries (Fransen, 2012; Fransen and Kolk, 2007; Gilbert et al., 2011).

Three thematic areas of research arise from a review of MSIs (de Bakker et al., 2019). A *first thematic area* relates to discussions about how MSIs are created and managed. This commonly focuses on mapping actors (Abbott and Snidal, 2009a), explaining input legitimacy (e.g. see Bernstein, 2011; Partzsch, 2011; von Geibler, 2013) and examining the politics of standard development (e.g. see Gale, 2014; Klooster, 2010; Levy et al., 2016). The mapping of actors involved in MSIs and their characteristics in this literature is often descriptive and provides useful background information on specific initiatives. Other work maps social networks at both the institutional level (relations between organizations) and at the individual level (multiple membership, relations between individuals, board membership), and use different social network analysis measures of centrality to assess power and influence (Fransen et al., 2016, 2018; Henriksen and Ponte, 2018; Henriksen and Seabrooke, 2016).

Discussions of input legitimacy have also been prominent, especially in relation to whether MSI governance is open to public scrutiny and stakeholder participation (Bäckstrand, 2006; García-López and Arizpe, 2010). Much existing research delineates the criteria for assessing the input legitimacy of MSIs, and examines how input legitimacy and process legitimacy relate to each other (Mena and Palazzo, 2012), how input legitimacy shapes credibility of claims (Miller and Bush, 2015), and/or how lack of inclusiveness in standard-setting affects input legitimacy (e.g. Gilbert et al., 2011; Miller and Bush, 2015; Pichler, 2013; Ponte, 2014b). Many MSIs have set up governance structures that are supposed to enable equal participation of stakeholder groups (Auld and Renckens, 2017). Yet these structures can also be enacted in manipulative ways to reinforce the power of dominant stakeholders and marginalize others (Cheyns, 2014; Elgert, 2012; Schouten et al., 2012).

The politics of standard development, and how struggles over power and representation are conceptualized, also feature in this thematic area of research, focusing especially on the politics involved in the early stages of institutional development of MSIs (e.g. Bartley, 2014; Büthe, 2010; Ponte, 2008; Vellema and van Wijk, 2015; Verbruggen, 2013), and on how their development has been challenged by the creation of business-driven initiatives (e.g. Fransen, 2012; Manning et al., 2012; Ponte, 2014b). This literature shows that some business-driven initiatives have incorporated notions of multi-stakeholder governance without changing their official institutional structures, while other business-driven initiatives have made changes to their governance structure without fundamentally altering their business-driven nature (de Bakker et al., 2019).

A *second thematic area* is built around issues of how MSIs are turned into stable and partly taken-for-granted institutions, and focuses especially on three aspects: business motivations in adopting MSIs; mainstreaming and diffusion processes; and the dynamics of competition, collaboration and parallelism (de Bakker et al., 2019). In terms of motivation to adopt MSIs, the literature often shows that corporations, especially those that are consumer-oriented and hold important brands, are interested in adoption to develop their markets (Cashore, 2002). Approaches interested in diffusion mechanisms examine the importance of early institutionalization phases and processes of isomorphism. They examine the role of small groups of early movers, the legitimacy of specific institutional designs, and mimicry processes, often highlighting path dependence (Auld, 2014; Fransen, 2012; Gulbrandsen, 2008; Ponte, 2008). Early phases of institutionalization and path dependence are also important to understand the *failures* of MSIs (Bloomfield and Schleifer, 2017). The literature focused on the mainstreaming of sustainability highlights the adoption of MSIs by large-scale buyers and the certification of big suppliers (Fortin, 2013; Klooster, 2010; Ponte, 2012) – showing that it can drive market creation and may change the practices of powerful actors (Pattberg, 2005), but also negatively affect MSI governance structures, with more resourceful actors (not necessarily business) capturing multi-stakeholder processes (Ponte, 2014b). More recent contributions are exploring whether mainstreaming of sustainability is also moving to the Global South, and report encouraging signs in some places, such as China, but not in others, such as India (Schleifer and Sun, 2018).

Much attention has also been paid to the dynamics of competition, collaboration and parallelism among MSIs (Fransen, 2011; Fransen and Burgoon, 2014; Manning et al., 2012; Riisgaard, 2011; Turcotte et al., 2014). Some scholars (Reinecke et al., 2012) argue that MSIs coexist because standard-setters are able to differentiate themselves despite the existence of similarities, for instance by stressing distinctive features of sustainability, by targeting different producer groups, or by offering different levels of stringency. They also point out that these interactions are leading to a 'modular governance architecture' (Manning and Reinecke, 2016), where MSIs develop semi-independent modules through local experimentation (e.g. on soil conservation, integrated pest management, forest cover), embed and adjust these modules in certification processes, and create linkages between these modules that bridge differences between areas of concern and levels of stringency.

The majority of contributions, however, view the coexistence of MSIs as a problem in that increased competition may cause confusion among consumers and a regulatory 'race to the bottom'. Such a race undermines institutionalization processes as markets for sustainable products become scattered among a number of niche players (Bloomfield, 2012; Fortin and Richardson, 2013; Hospes et al., 2012; O'Rourke, 2006; Ponte, 2012). Other work, however, shows that some industries have managed a 'race to the top' with a convergence around higher standards (Cashore and Stone, 2014; Overdevest, 2010; Overdevest and Zeitlin, 2014; Riisgaard, 2011), that the creation of a community of MSIs with shared interests increases the potential for learning and co-evolution (Manning et al., 2012), and that competition makes different initiatives increasingly resemble each other, and hence facilitates mutual adjustment (Clark and Hussey, 2016). Finally, Fransen (2012) highlights two other possible trajectories beyond the 'race to the bottom' versus 'race to the top' distinction: a 'decoupling' trajectory, where MSIs signal the adoption of higher standards but as a form of window dressing; and a 'paradox of empty promises' trajectory, where the pressure of expectations raised in a decoupling approach eventually leads to upward revisions (for further detail, see de Bakker et al., 2019).

A *third thematic area* concerns the impact of MSIs, measured in terms of outputs (e.g. numbers of issues covered, market share, number of certified facilities, area or quantity certified) and in terms of outcomes (e.g. improvements in working/production conditions and/or the environment) (de Bakker et al., 2019). One immediate output of MSIs is their own rules and standards, which tend to be stricter when they are set up with a strong role played by independent organizations rather than by industry (Darnall et al., 2017). Some authors argue that MSI rules are often perceived as weak because they are too closely aligned with Western values (Hatanaka, 2010; Moog et al., 2015; Pattberg, 2006; Ponte, 2012) and/or are undercut by the political-economic constraints that shape the relevant market environment. Other studies focus on outcomes for the final beneficiaries of MSIs (including impacts on local communities), highlighting that it has proven difficult to measure them (Fuchs et al., 2011), and that even when they can be measured, it is unclear whether changes in environmental conditions are causally linked to MSI implementation. Furthermore, it has been suggested that MSIs often address only selected manifestations of such problems without addressing their root causes, and may even create additional problems. Much of the literature claims that MSIs facilitate selective or only marginal positive outcomes for final beneficiaries (Gulbrandsen, 2009; McCarthy, 2012; Pattberg, 2006), or have no positive outcomes at all (Barrientos and Smith, 2007; Hatanaka, 2010; Marx, 2008; Selfa et al., 2014).

In relation to outcomes, the literature shows that failure to achieve them often arises from adopters not implementing MSIs despite formally embracing them (Fransen, 2012). Adopters can also comply with formal policies but fail to achieve the intended goals (Wijen, 2014). The MSIs that are financially dependent on certification fees need to 'sell' an initiative, thus creating incentives to lower standards in order to attract clients or water down audit procedures on the ground (Fortin and Richardson, 2013; Gulbrandsen, 2009; O'Rourke, 2006; Ponte, 2012; Schepers, 2010). Finally, important trade-offs emerge between comprehensive and specialized MSIs. Specialized MSIs focus on a specific problem, usually with lower internal cost and a higher probability of impact, but may neglect other important co-causational aspects. Comprehensive MSIs are better at attempting to address multiple and complex problems, but have higher internal costs and are more likely to partially or wholly duplicate other initiatives attempting to cover the same ground (Auld, 2014).

Overall, the MSI literature suggests that legitimacy, institutionalization processes, design features, and factors shaping trajectories of cooperation and competition among different initiatives are important elements for understanding how sustainability governance works and with what results. But a common assumption in this work is that institutional features and developments in sustainability governance can be explained independently from the characteristics and strategies of the main business actors who produce, process, transport, package, and sell products and services. There is no space in these frameworks for business to shape sustainability governance and affect sustainability outcomes beyond engaging in MSIs and lobbying regulators. These are, of course, important elements, but pertain mostly to the shaping of the sustainability agenda rather than its application through everyday practices. In other words, what is still missing in the literature on transnational sustainability governance is an account of how it is operationalized within corporations and along GVCs.

Self-Regulation, Strategy and Corporate Social and Environmental Responsibility

Contributions from business studies that examine how corporations govern sustainability within their boundaries and along their supply chains are concerned with how lead firms seek to improve their financial performance through sustainability efforts from a managerial perspective. These contributions analyse various forms of self-regulation, corporate social (and environmental) responsibility (CSR/CSER) and corporate strategy. Self-regulation can be of different kinds: *pure* self-regulation, when specific behaviour is recommended by an organized group (often a business association) to its members through the stipulation of codes of conduct, best practices and, sometimes, externally audited standards; *mandated* self-regulation, when public authority mandates an industry to regulate its own behaviour; and *hybrid* self-regulation, when public authority sets the framework conditions for self-regulation, but leaves much of the detail to be specified by industry associations (Gunningham et al., 1998).

CSER instead is based on individual firms taking steps on a *voluntary and unilateral* basis. CSER can include: wholly individual initiatives at the firm level to address environmental externalities beyond what is mandated in regulation; being part of industry-level initiatives without coercion; entering into initiatives where public authority only plays a coordinating or facilitating role; producing environmental reports; voluntarily releasing relevant information to affected communities and the wider public; and signing up to international initiatives such as the UN Global Compact (Gunningham et al., 1998, 2003; Shearing et al., 2013). Finally, efforts towards environmental improvements in business operations can take place through *strategic choices* that can be proactive, reactive or inactive (inaction can also be a strategic choice). They can relate to internal operations but also extend to the functioning of the supply chain. These issues are extensively covered in the business literatures on sustainable and/or green supply chain management (SSCM), CSER and sustainability strategy, to which I turn next.

The SSCM literature is an extension of the business studies technical discipline of supply chain management (SCM). Sustainability issues started being examined in this field with some regularity from the mid-1990s, with a remarkable growth in the 2000s (e.g. see Lindgreen et al., 2013; Seuring and Gold, 2013; Seuring et al., 2008). Several reviews have mapped the now burgeoning SSCM literature (Ahi and Searcy, 2013, 2015; Gold et al., 2010; Lund-Thomsen and Lindgreen, 2014; Seuring and Müller, 2008). They highlight how the SSCM literature so far has focused on environmental issues, rather than on social issues, and that the triggers leading SCM managers to address sustainability issues have usually been linked to external pressure (especially by customers, regulators and NGOs). These reviews also identify two of the main strategies adopted in SSCM: first, focusing on the greening of processes for optimizing risk and performance of suppliers; and second, developing or improving the green credentials of products (Seuring and Müller, 2008). In terms of pros and cons of embedding sustainability in SCM, they highlight: the importance of blending sustainability tools without losing sight of profit and market share objectives; the potential for cost savings, improved efficiency and better synergy among partners; and the need to consider both short-term costs and long-term benefits (Ahi and Searcy, 2013).

One of the main conclusions arising from the SSCM literature overall is the need for more cooperation among partner companies to smoothen the flow of sustainability-related information and improve the efficiency of SCM. Indeed, one of the most popular definitions of SSCM frames it as 'the management of material, *information* and capital flows as well as cooperation among companies along the supply chain while taking goals from all three dimensions of sustainable development ... into account' (Seuring and Müller, 2008: 1700, emphasis added). Given that SCM is meant to optimize operations along supply chains, it is no surprise that this literature does not take into consideration the strategic value of information sharing, especially in the context of uneven power relations. It is also silent on how value is created, distributed or appropriated along supply chains in the process of 'greening' SCM. While information sharing can indeed improve operational performance, it can also be used by lead firms in GVCs to extract concessions and squeeze margins out of suppliers, without necessarily improving the environmental outcomes of these operations.

The literatures on corporate social and environmental responsibility, eco-innovation and sustainability strategy have some traits in common: they generally focus on the internal operations of firms and their effects on immediate suppliers/buyers and other stakeholders, rather than following the whole supply chain as in SSCM; they aim at identifying best practices in sustainability management and strategy for firms to follow, which can deliver both positive sustainability outcomes (or at least positive stakeholder perceptions) and improve the bottom line; and they seek to find solutions to sustainability issues that can enhance the credibility, reputation and/or brand value of the firm. Often these reflections are couched in a discourse of leveraging sustainability for competitive advantage (Esty and Winston, 2009; Orsato, 2009; Rennings, 2000). Empirical analyses of different industries in these literatures suggest that trust and long-term relationships are important factors in facilitating the greening of suppliers – along with stable demand and technical support (De Marchi et al., 2013b). Meyer and Hohmann (2000), for example, argue that partnerships are key in developing 'green products'. Seuring (2004) also indicates that cooperation is needed to overcome transaction costs, because they are generally higher in the organization of green production. As more systemic approaches to environmental management are developed (e.g. life-cycle analysis – LCA), relational networks become even more important (De Marchi and Grandinetti, 2013).

These insights show that firms can employ strategic push factors to foster environmental innovation proactively, both in-house and by placing demands on their immediate suppliers. They can benefit from environmental improvements when they heighten their competitiveness, open new markets for their products, decrease costs, and/or improve the commitment and productivity of their workforces. Four environmental innovation strategies are commonly identified among firms (Orsato, 2009), which combine two sources of competitive advantage (lower cost, differentiation) and two competitive foci (on organization and procedures, on products and services): (1) *eco-efficiency*, based on lowering costs through organizational and procedural improvements (e.g. lowering energy costs by allowing natural light into stores) both in-house and along the value chain; (2) *environmental cost leadership*, based on lowering costs while improving the environmental qualities of products or services (e.g. using cheaper but more environmentally friendly materials, or lighter packaging); (3) *beyond compliance leadership*, based on differentiation through organizational and procedural improvements (e.g. building company reputation for environmental excellence, even though it increases operational costs); and (4) *eco-branding*, based on differentiating the products and services offered to customers (e.g. through environmental certification or a 'green' brand) (Orsato, 2009). Other sustainability strategies include: better *ex ante* management of ecological risk to minimize regulatory punishment, legal liability and reputational damage, and Blue Ocean Strategies, which involve creating completely new marketplaces (Esty and Winston, 2009). Blue Ocean Strategies can be achieved through servitization (e.g. leasing appliances instead of owning them, which tends to increase their lifespan), by creating novel 'green' products (e.g. such as electric cars, solar panels), and by leveraging sustainability management through the Internet of Things (e.g. saving energy use through remote control and monitoring devices) (McAfee and Brynjolfsson, 2017).

These literatures are mainly focused on finding the best strategies that place firms in a better competitive situation and maximize their growth or their chances of survival. However, there is considerable variation in the literature on how to balance the bottom line and actual environmental improvements. The literature on CSER is generally more concerned with the latter, or at least with the implications of failing to address sustainability issues in terms of corporate reputation and credibility (Epstein and Buhovac, 2014; Levy and Newell, 2005; Matten and Moon, 2004, 2008; McWilliams et al., 2006; Meckling, 2015). More hardcore strategy contributions see positive environmental outcomes almost as a side effect of capital accumulation and business success. Esty and Winston (2009: 11), for example, are mainly concerned with 'the gold that smart companies mine from being green'. They argue that green strategies can improve innovation, create value, build competitive advantage, create new products, ensure the future supply of natural resources, inspire employees, help recruit a better labour force, enhance credibility and improve brand trust. Companies such as GE, Walmart, BP and Toyota are now pro-actively weaving environmental strategy into overall corporate strategy, rather than exclusively reacting to pressing regulation or NGO campaigns. These 'green innovators' argue that they are not driven by a moral imperative, but by the necessity of ensuring a social licence to grow. Esty and Winston (2009: 132) see expanding production and consumption as the keys to achieving sustainability, in a world where power dynamics and distributional issues do not appear to matter. Value, according to them, is always created and not extracted from other value chain actors, yet they warn suppliers against expecting price premiums for matching the new environmental standards set by buyers (Esty and Winston, 2009: 132). Capturing data and creating metrics along the whole value chain becomes an important aspect of corporate strategy to turn 'green into gold'. But this is often framed in the business strategy literature within a discourse of 'cooperation', 'partnering' and information sharing with suppliers, which need to be promoted across the board – even though they may result in lower margins and less bargaining power for suppliers, especially in the Global South. Finally, 'partnering for advantage' with civil society groups and NGOs becomes a way of reducing the risk of reputational exposure and allows a form of 'brand inoculation', providing a firm with extra defences against attacks (Esty and Winston, 2009: 186). These approaches assume that sustainability strategy (whether inside the corporation or along its supply chains) works in a power vacuum, and often if not always leads to win–win situations (for an exception, see Sako and Zyberberg, 2017). In the next chapter, I will show that GVC analysis can provide a critical and power-aware approach to business strategy, but it is still at an early stage of development when it comes to sustainability factors. Therefore, a new analytical framework is needed to push it forward.

Discussion and Next Steps

The literatures reviewed in this chapter provide important insights into understanding sustainability governance, its actors and its mechanisms. However, the literature on transnational sustainability governance, including that on MSIs, often assumes that institutional features can be understood separately from the characteristics and strategies of GVC actors beyond their engagement in regulatory lobbying and participation in MSIs. On the contrary, the business literature on sustainability is concerned narrowly with identifying the best strategies and approaches that can improve the competitiveness of individual firms, build corporate reputation and minimize risk – with little regard for the actual impacts on the environment. This is often embedded in a power-blind discourse of cooperation and partnering. The GVC approach adopted in this book can usefully contribute to pushing our understanding of sustainability governance further, as it brings together all relevant actors, bridges macro, meso and micro dimensions of economic activity and sustainability, and seeks to explain power dynamics and changing layers of inequality. In the next chapter, I will start this process by developing an analytical framework that can help explain how sustainability issues are embedded in power dynamics that underpin governance and upgrading trajectories in GVCs.

2 | POWER IN GLOBAL VALUE CHAINS

Global value chain analysis has been widely used in international political economy, development studies, economic geography and economic sociology to explain the transnational organization of economic activities. It examines discrete 'value chains' (the full range of value-adding activities that firms, farmers and workers carry out to bring a product from its conception to its end use, disposal or recycling) that are explicitly governed by one or more groups of 'lead firms' (such as retailers or branded food processors) (Gereffi, 1994). Lead firms can be seen as the global economy equivalent of 'keystone species' in ecosystems, which have a disproportionate influence on their structure and function (Österblom et al., 2015).

Three dimensions of GVC analysis are especially relevant for the purposes of this book (Ponte et al., 2019). A first dimension concerns various forms of *GVC governance* (Cattaneo et al., 2010; Gereffi, 1994; Gereffi, 2019; Gereffi et al., 2005; Gibbon and Ponte, 2005; Milberg and Winkler, 2013; Ponte, 2014a; Ponte and Gibbon, 2005), which will be analysed in this chapter. A second dimension concerns the *institutional framework* within which GVCs operate. This aspect, less prominently covered in the existing literature, refers to the mutual interactions between governance processes carried out by lead firms within GVCs and those executed by external actors and regulatory processes (Jespersen et al., 2014; Ponte, 2014a). In this chapter (and in Chapter 5 on orchestration), I will embed these considerations under the analysis of 'institutional' power, thus linking the institutional framework directly to GVC governance. A third dimension, often coupled with reflections on economic development in the Global South, refers to *GVC upgrading* – the paths for value chain actors to add value and extract more rent, eventually moving up the value chain to more sophisticated and skill-intensive operations (Gereffi, 1999,

2014; Humphrey and Schmitz, 2004). I will examine these paths in Chapter 4 and highlight their environmental components.

In relation to GVC governance, the literature underscores the role played by powerful corporations, especially those that exert 'buyer power' by placing large orders in their value chains. But instead of focusing on how they influence governments or international organizations to obtain favourable rules, these lead firms are mainly of interest in GVC analysis as core actors in transnational business networks. These networks are both internal to the (multinational) firm and linked to independent suppliers and customers in increasingly elaborate and spatially extensive systems of sourcing, production, distribution and consumption. The idea of governance in GVCs rests on the assumption that while both disintegration of production and its reintegration through inter-firm trade have recognizable dynamics, they do not occur spontaneously, automatically or even systematically (Gibbon et al., 2008). Instead, these processes are driven by the strategies and decisions of specific actors. Earlier work focused principally on the governance dynamics internal to a GVC, and thus on lead firms, but more recent research has examined the role of other actors, such as governments, social movements and international NGOs. In this book, I take this broader approach to GVC governance, and thus define it as 'the actions and norms that shape the conditions for inclusion, exclusion and mode of participation in a value chain, which in turn determine the terms and location of value addition and capture' (Dallas et al., 2019: 3).

In this chapter, I push this research agenda forward in two ways. First, I seek to unpack the role of power in shaping GVC governance. In most GVC research (e.g. Gereffi et al., 2005), power has been understood as manifested in the uneven bargaining relationships between firms, and especially between 'lead' firms and suppliers. It is explicitly tied to rents (Davis et al., 2017; Kaplinsky, 2005) or implicitly related to different degrees of 'drivenness' or 'driving', but with little explicit insight on what other kinds of power may support or hinder bargaining power. Second, I examine the role of sustainability issues in shaping power relations, and thus GVC governance, something that has not been researched yet. In the next section, I unpack three approaches to GVC governance: 'governance as driving', 'governance as linking' and 'governance as normalizing' (drawing from Gibbon et al., 2008; Ponte and Sturgeon, 2014), and highlight other emerging directions in this field. In the following section,

I build on Dallas et al.'s (2017, 2019) typology of power in GVCs to provide an analytical framework for the empirical analysis of power and governance in selected GVCs from a sustainability perspective – including some features of their 'institutional framework' through one of the four kinds of power.

Approaches to GVC Governance

Governance as 'Driving'

The early approach to governance developed by Gereffi (1994) related to what he then called global commodity chains (GCCs) as the process of organizing activities along a value-adding chain. Because some activities have higher entry barriers and are more profitable than others, this division of labour influences the allocation of resources and distribution of gains among chain actors (firms and workers). A group of 'lead firms' play a critical role in governance by defining the terms of supply chain membership, incorporating or excluding other actors, and allocating where, when and by whom value is added (Gereffi, 1994; Gibbon and Ponte, 2005; Kaplinsky, 2005).

In Gereffi's GCC framework, there are two types of lead firms: buyers and producers. The producer-driven variant is akin to the internal and external networks emanating from large multinational manufacturing firms, such as General Motors and IBM. Although these firms had long been a focus of research and debate among scholars of the global economy, the GCC framework brought a novel aspect in its attention to a set of global buyers that had been largely ignored in previous research. Global buyers include large retailers, such as Walmart, Tesco, Target and Carrefour, as well as branded merchandisers and agro-food processors, such as Nike, H&M, Nestlé and Kraft. Gereffi's (1994) research, initially focused on the apparel industry, found that global buyers often do more than placing orders; they actively help to create, shape and coordinate their supply chains, sometimes directly from headquarters or 'overseas buying offices' and sometimes through intermediaries, which can include a wide range of actors, such as international trading companies. While global buyers typically own few, if any, of their own factories and processing plants, the volume of their purchases gives them great power over suppliers. Global buyers sometimes specify in great detail what, how, when, where and by whom the goods they sell are produced. But even when explicit coordination is not present, extreme market power has allowed global buyers to extract price concessions from their main suppliers. Suppliers have responded by locating more of their operations in low-cost locations and by extracting labour cost and price reductions from their own workers and upstream suppliers (Feenstra and Hamilton, 2006).

Gereffi (1994) showed that producer-driven chains are usually found in capital- and technology-intensive industries, such as electronics and autos, while buyer-driven chains are more common in labour-intensive industries such as apparel and consumer goods. Because innovation in buyer-driven chains lies more in product design and marketing than in manufacturing know-how, it is relatively easy for lead firms to outsource the manufacturing of labour-intensive products. In more technology- and capital-intensive chains, technology and production expertise are core competences that are generally developed and deployed in-house, or in closely affiliated 'captive' suppliers that can be blocked from sharing them with competitors.

The buyer- and producer-driven GCC typology was thus based on a historical depiction of technology and barriers to entry that was appropriate for a specific set of industries in a specific time period, mainly the 1970s and 1980s. While the buyer- and producer-driven lead firm categories are still useful, technological change, firm- and industry-level learning, and the emergence of new norms and standards constantly reshape the features of GVC governance. The chain governance shifts of the 1990s led to a multiplication of efforts in explaining changes in the organization of global industries over time (see the following sections). They also led to the adoption of the term 'value' to replace 'commodity' because of the common understanding of the latter as pertaining only to primary products. The term 'value' also captures the concept of 'value added', which fits well with the chain metaphor (Sturgeon, 2009).

Governance as 'Linking'

Moving beyond the historically-based typology of buyer-driven versus producer-driven governance, Gereffi et al. (2005) constructed a theory that could, absent other factors, account for observed changes and anticipate future developments in how inter-firm linkages are governed in GVCs. They identified five generic ways that firms set up and govern linkages in value chains (see Figure 2.1): (1) simple *market* linkages, governed by price; (2) *modular* linkages, governed by standards, where complex information regarding the transaction is codified and often digitized before being passed to highly competent suppliers; (3) *relational* linkages, governed by trust and reputation, where tacit information is exchanged between buyers and suppliers with unique or at

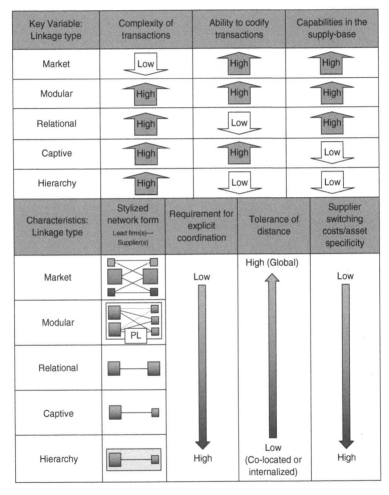

Figure 2.1 Global Value Chain Linkage Mechanisms and Network Characteristics

Note: PL = platform leader. The shaded box denotes corporate ownership and control
Source: Ponte and Sturgeon (2014: 204), as modified from Gereffi et al. (2005) and adapted by Dicken (2007: 158). Reproduced with permission from Taylor & Francis.

least difficult-to-replicate capabilities; (4) *captive* linkages, governed by buyer power, where less competent suppliers are provided with detailed instructions by very dominant buyers; and (5) linkages within the same firm, governed by management *hierarchy*.

Gereffi et al. (2005) argue that these five linkage types arise from predictable combinations of three variables: the *complexity* of information exchanged between value chain tasks; the *codifiability* of that information; and the *capabilities* resident in the supply base relative to the requirements of the transaction. So, while 'governance' in Gereffi's (1994) formulation referred to the role played by powerful firm-level actors, or chain 'drivers', Gereffi et al. (2005) focus on the determinants of make-or-buy decisions in transactions and the characteristics of linkages between firms at individual nodes in the chain. Therefore, theirs is a theory of linkages rather than of governance along GVCs, as firms may form different types of linkages with different business partners, and linkages typically differ between different segments of the value chain (see also Sturgeon et al., 2008).

Governance as 'Normalizing'

The approach to 'governance as normalizing' explores the discursive and normative dimension that frame buyer–supplier relations and transmission mechanisms along the chain. The term 'normalizing' does not mean 'making things normal', but rather how a given practice is aligned with dominant standards, expectations or norms (Gibbon et al., 2008). While the focus on standards resonates with the governance as linking approach just discussed (especially the modular form), much of the existing work on GVC governance as normalizing has drawn on convention theory (Ouma, 2010; Ponte, 2009, 2016; Ponte and Gibbon, 2005). Convention theory builds upon the seminal work of Boltanski and Thévenot (1991), who argue that establishing equivalence between different people, firms or objects is often based on a form of judgement drawn from some 'higher principle'. They identify six ideal-type 'orders of worth', drawn from philosophical texts, and illustrate how they are used to frame the justification of human interaction and economic practice, including the organization of firms (see also Boltanski and Chiapello, 2000). To illustrate how these orders of worth are used as justificatory devices in practice, they examine a set of action-oriented manuals for business managers, showing that multiple and competing orders of worth may coexist within organizations. Even when one is dominant at one particular time, it may be challenged, thus leading to clarification, adaptation, compromise and/or demise over time.

Convention theory has been used not only to explain internal firm organization (see a review in Jagd, 2011), but also how coordination takes place among firms via the establishment of product quality conventions (Eymard-Duvernay, 1989, 2006; Gibbon and Ponte, 2005; Ponte, 2009; Thévenot, 1995; Wilkinson, 1997). While quality conventions typically overlap, one or a specific combination often form a dominant underpinning for linkages in a value chain node at a particular time. However, conventions and their combinations also evolve, are subjected to testing, and are adjusted or give way to different conventions or combinations over time. Convention theory has allowed researchers to ask questions about the normative nature of coordination that go beyond the three GVC linkage variables of complexity, codifiability and supplier competence. At the same time, examination of the conventions underpinning GVC linkages can contribute to a deeper understanding of how commonly agreed notions of 'quality' (including its environmental components) in a transaction actually take shape – and thus how transactions can become more or less codified as products, business practices and technologies change (an issue addressed by Gereffi et al., 2005). Repeating the exercise of examining GVC linkages across several nodes of a value chain (see an empirical application in Ponte, 2009) has allowed researchers to highlight whether dominant conventions 'travel' along a chain, what makes them travel, and which actors have the normative power to impose one convention over another beyond a single value chain node.

Supplier Power, Governance Polarity and Strategic Disarticulations

Many GVC contributions have sought to tame some of the inevitability of 'buyer power' in the earlier literature by showing how key suppliers in some industries have been able to establish increasingly powerful positions (Kawakami, 2011; Raj-Reichert, 2015; Sturgeon, 2002, 2009; Tewari, 2006), or by highlighting paths and strategies that suppliers can follow to not only create value, but also to retain it (Kaplinsky, 2004, 2005; Ponte and Ewert, 2009; Sako and Zylberberg, 2017). Others have sought to highlight the increasing power of lead firms based in the Global South, often facilitated by state support (Horner, 2017; Horner and Nadvi, 2018; see also various contributions to Ponte et al., 2019).

Much of the existing GVC literature has focused on *unipolar* value chains (Gereffi, 1994; Gibbon, 2001) – where lead firms in one functional position of the chain play a dominant role in shaping it. Some scholars have explored the dynamics of governance in GVCs characterized as *bipolar*, where two sets of actors in different functional positions both drive the chain, albeit in different ways (Fold, 2002; Islam, 2008). Research on the notebook PC and mobile phone handset industries by Imai and Shiu (2011) and Kawakami (2011) also showed the important roles 'platform leaders' can play. Ponte and Sturgeon (2014) expanded this direction further to suggest examining governance across a unipolar to *multipolar* continuum, and called for analyses identifying the main drivers of these GVCs, and the different degrees and mechanisms of driving (see also Davis et al., 2017; Jespersen et al., 2014; Ponte, 2014a; Poulsen et al., 2016). Multipolarity can involve other actors outside the value chain, such as international NGOs, trade unions, governments and multi-stakeholder initiatives (Nadvi and Raj-Reichert, 2015), thus aligning with the concerns of the GPN approach, which highlights the complexity and variety of non-firm actors in shaping the organization of economic activity (Coe and Yeung, 2015; Coe et al., 2008; Henderson et al., 2002; Hess and Yeung, 2006; Lund-Thomsen and Lindgreen, 2018; Yeung and Coe, 2015).

Another set of contributions broadening the approach to governance in GVCs beyond 'internal' factors has highlighted processes of disarticulation and counteraction. What brings these theoretically diverse approaches together is a general movement away from an interest in buyer-determined governance dynamics, and towards: (1) highlighting the strategic logic of suppliers exiting from GVCs in specific situations; (2) the processes of suppliers clawing back power from lead firms; and/or (3) the important role of actors not directly involved in value-adding activities (Bair and Werner, 2011a; Bair et al., 2013; Werner, 2016). Bair and Werner (2011a) in particular call for a disarticulation perspective on GVCs in order to consider the dynamics of exclusion or expulsion from GVCs. Building on earlier work by Bair (2009a), this perspective calls for a return to the long-range, macro-historical roots of earlier work on commodity chains, but with a focus on disjunctions, fragmentations and disarticulations.

Disarticulation scholars argue that the GVC literature has developed a bias on inclusion dynamics and that attention should be paid to *how* links in the chain are forged, not only in material terms, but also ideologically and in relation to the creation of subjectivities. They examine the set of social relations that secure commodity production and related processes of exclusion (Bair and Werner, 2011b); highlight the social and spatial contours of production through everyday practices and struggles over the creation and appropriation of value (see also Neilson and Pritchard, 2011); and lament the instability inflicted on regions as GVCs rapidly enter and exit places and regions. Their implicit take on governance shifts attention from integrative efforts (participation in value chains) to a more nuanced picture that includes the agency allowing less powerful actors to disarticulate and disentangle themselves from uneven and exploitative GVCs relations, or to refuse participation (Berndt and Boeckler, 2011; Goger, 2013; Havice and Campling, 2013; Nickow, 2015).

Sustainability, Power and GVC Governance

This brief review of approaches to GVC governance highlights three main issues of relevance for the analysis carried out in the rest of this book. First, existing research does not normally examine whether and how sustainability issues shape GVCs. Bush et al. (2015) provide a useful distinction that can help solve this issue – that between governing sustainability *in*, *of* and *through* GVCs (see also Bush and Osterveer, 2019). From their perspective, governing sustainability *in* value chains means researching how lead firms tackle sustainability issues within their organizational boundaries and how they can improve their competitive advantage through strategy (e.g. see Sako and Zylberberg, 2017). This approach has been dominant in the business strategy and organization literatures (see Chapter 1). Governing the sustainability *of* value chains means paying attention to how sustainability demands travel along a value chain, what incentives and punishments are imparted by lead firms on suppliers that meet or do not meet their demands, and what consequences these processes have for the geography of production and the distribution of value added, the nature and organization of production activities, and the actual impacts on environmental outcomes. So far, most of this relatively small literature within the GVC tradition has framed these dynamics under the mantel of 'environmental upgrading', examining also to what extent this kind of upgrading is driven by lead firms and with what consequences for suppliers and the environment (Bolwig et al., 2010; Boström et al., 2015; De Marchi et al., 2013a, 2013b; Goger, 2013; Khattak et al., 2015; Riisgaard et al., 2010).

But the transmission of sustainability mechanisms along GVCs has important implications for GVC governance as well, a relationship that has not yet been duly examined (Poulsen et al., 2016). For this reason, in this book I fold these concerns within what Bush et al. (2015) call 'governing sustainability *through* value chains'. This involves looking at 'a set of normative and regulatory practices that use the chain as a conduit for influencing the social and environmental conditions of production and consumption' (Bush et al., 2015: 13). This approach 'captures the interaction between the chain and its firm actors with a wider set of networked actors and activities that collectively steer sustainable production and consumption practices' (Bush et al., 2015: 13; see also Bush and Osterveer, 2019), and thus implicitly accommodates two key dimensions in my analysis: power (see Chapter 3) and orchestration (see Chapter 5).

Second, the GVC literature has mainly focused on bargaining power between lead firms and suppliers when attempting to explain governance dynamics, when it considers power relations at all. As the analytic lens of GVCs has expanded, different applications of the concept of power have implicitly emerged, running the gamut from formal to informal (Dallas, 2014). For instance, firms and other actors come to agreement over explicit and formal industrial standards and certifications, but also over more informal conventions, best practices and norms (Nadvi, 2008; Ponte and Gibbon, 2005). Likewise, the social movements that seek to shape GVCs also vary in their degree of formal organization (Bair and Palpacuer, 2015). Various levels of state action and authority have important structuring effects on GVCs as well (Horner, 2017; Jespersen et al., 2014; Neilson and Pritchard, 2011). While these socio-economic structures might include elements of cooperation and collective action, they can also be highly contentious, and when fully consolidated, embody and fix power relationships in ways that systematically create winners and losers (Dallas et al., 2019). In other instances, power can be exerted in even more 'diffuse' ways (e.g. through demonstration effects) and collective outcomes can arise unintendedly (Dallas, 2014). This suggests that GVC research should reach beyond the analysis of power as exerted by clearly defined 'lead firms' and other powerful firm-level actors. An emerging literature has indeed started to examine how NGOs and social movements (both transnational and local) contest existing power dynamics in GVCs (Bair and Palpacuer, 2012; Bartley, 2007; Bloomfield, 2014,

2017a; Levy, 2008; Schurman and Munro, 2009). Nickow (2015), for example, highlights different kinds and combinations of activist strategies (protest campaigns, promotion of certification, and the shaping of standards and market facilitation) and their outcomes.

Third, new contributions are drawing attention to how the expansion of capitalist production is necessarily based on the appropriation of nature (Baglioni and Campling, 2017; Havice and Campling, 2017) and to how power relations change among value chain actors when environmental issues arise and/or when natural resources are brought to the centre stage of analysis (Baglioni and Campling, 2017; Havice and Campling, 2013, 2017). Contributions that have taken this approach often apply commodity frontier theory (Moore, 2015) and argue that 'the ability of lead firms to govern GVCs cannot be disjointed from the appropriation of nature, strategies to control the labour process and firms' associated ability to capture surplus value' (Baglioni and Campling, 2017: 4), not only in relation to resource extraction, but also to non-material 'green commodities', such as carbon credits (Neimark et al., 2016). This literature highlights that environmental conditions of production are key to how different kinds of firms reshape or contest power dynamics in GVCs, and that failures in sustainability governance often arise because the targets of improvement are considered independently from the GVC dynamics and pressures they are embedded in.

To build upon these insights, in the rest of this chapter I draw from Dallas et al. (2017, 2019) to construct a stylized typology of power in GVCs that goes beyond bargaining power and that includes specific sustainability features.

Four Types of Power in Global Value Chains

Two Dimensions of Power

Dallas et al. (2017, 2019) categorize two dimensions of power: a *transmission mechanism* and an *arena of actors*. The *transmission mechanism* of power is anchored by two ideal types: direct and diffuse. On the one end are circumstances where GVC actors (individually or collectively) seek to exert direct forms of influence over other actors or actor groups. On the other end are more diffuse forms of power where the actors or collectives and the objects of power may be less clearly identifiable, and actions less intentional. The *arena of actors* specifies whether power is wielded in dyads or collectives. To date, much of the GVC literature has been concerned with dyadic relations between individual buyers (lead firms) and suppliers (Gereffi et al., 2005), but more collective approaches to power and governance in GVCs have also emerged, looking at the role of government, business associations and social movements. Combining these two dimensions yields a four-category typology that incorporates the types of power normally observed in GVCs: *bargaining*, *demonstrative*, *institutional* and *constitutive* (see Figure 2.2).

The Transmission of Power – Direct and Diffuse

The GVC and cognate literatures have started to differentiate (at least implicitly) between different kinds of power in GVCs by highlighting whether its transmission is more direct (Coe and Yeung, 2015; Gereffi, 1994; Gereffi et al., 2005) or more diffuse (Dallas, 2014; Gibbon and Ponte, 2005). In *direct* forms of transmission, the actor or collective wielding power and those who are objects of it are relatively easy to identify by all parties. This form of power is relatively unambiguous: actors can clearly identify each other; their actions are intentional and goal-oriented; and specific actors 'possess' power and the tools and methods of exerting it. Transmission mechanisms tend to be formal and explicit, and can be quite specific in their detail. The exertion of direct power is most often intentional and the goals of powerful actors are well known. Direct power also generally inheres within actors or collectives (including the state) in the sense that they possess material or ideational resources or can leverage their structural or network position within a GVC (Dallas et al., 2019). The utilization of these resources and the mechanisms of transmission by influential actors are also more likely to be explicit and precise, in the sense that the exercise of control includes specific, measurable and monitorable requirements, including those on environmental impact. Examples of the direct exertion of power include the relative bargaining power between two transacting firms, lead firm-specific sustainability requirements and protocols for suppliers, government regulation, rules set by a business association for its members, or environmental protection standards set by third-party certifications (Davis et al., 2017).

But power transmission can also be *diffuse*, with mechanisms that are based on more demonstrative processes, follow broader societal trends, or are based on taken-for-granted or emergent best practices (e.g. on corporate conduct and organization) or dominant quality conventions (Gibbon and Ponte, 2005). While diffuse power can sometimes result in unintended but substantively important outcomes, the locus of power may reside outside the organizational boundaries of any well-defined set of actors. The transmission mechanisms for diffuse power can be imprecise, such as those emerging from social movements or through the uncodified 'best practices' that tend to propagate with new managerial models (Gibbon and Ponte, 2005), or the interplay of hegemonic and counter-hegemonic forces. Power can also be diffuse when individual actors or collectives fail to realize the unintended consequences of their actions, even when they have real and material impact on their interests. The actions of powerful actors may have an influential demonstration effect on other actors, leading the latter to change their behaviour in ways beneficial to the former even without the knowledge of the powerful, without their intention to have such an effect, or without a clear sense of who will or will not follow the 'demonstrator'. Power is also diffuse when groups of actors behave in a manner akin to social movements. In the GVC literature, such dynamics can be present in diffusion mechanisms such as the creation or demise of sustainability standards, quality conventions and environmental best practices. In these circumstances, actors wield little direct power by themselves, but when substantial numbers of actors alter their behaviour in rapid succession, they exert power through diffuse mechanisms, even though they do not belong to a formal organization or participate in a common network (Dallas et al., 2017, 2019).

Diffuse power is also at work when best practices are propagated, for example by consulting firms or pressure from financial markets for companies to conform to normative modes of behaviour in which agreement about best practices are collectively determined. For example, over the 1990s and early 2000s, sustainability in business circles was mainly discussed in relation to establishing a 'business case' for it. At the time, it only populated corporate strategy as long as it led to cost reduction strategies, but only rarely in relation to market valuation or overall corporate identity and branding. By the late 2000s, sustainability had become much more integrated into corporate strategy, but the early normative dialogue generated a threshold level of acceptability that in many corporate environments led to slower and more timid approaches to sustainability management.

The Arena of Actors – Dyads and Collectives

A second dimension that differentiates power in the GVC literature is the 'arena of actors'. An arena is where specific actors or collectives engage with other actors. Dallas et al. (2017, 2019) propose two categories of actor arenas – dyads and collectives. In GVC and some related literatures (e.g. theories of the firm, strategic management), the focus on the inter-firm dyad is well established. This was the arena studied in Gereffi's (1994) research on lead firms and their links to suppliers or intermediaries that managed detailed contracting relationships and translated buyer requirements for factories. A dyadic arena is even more the focus in Gereffi et al.'s (2005) governance theory, where power asymmetry is seen to decrease as one moves from hierarchy towards market forms of linkages, and where the power exerted between a dyadic pair is shaped by relative bargaining positions rooted in purchasing power and competence power (Sturgeon, 2009).

The second arena of actors in GVCs, less explicitly researched and theorized, involves *collectives* of actors. The locus of power in this case is a function of the collective behaviours of multiple players acting simultaneously (intentionally or not) and/or of more institutionalized collectives such as business associations, multi-stakeholder sustainability initiatives or states. I avoid using the term 'institutions' here because not all collective arenas have obvious institutional or organizational traits. Therefore, I reserve the term 'institutional power' for cases where the collective arena is combined with direct power transmission (one of our four combinations in Figure 2.2). In an institutionalized collective, a focal organization (such as the state) sets more or less transparent rules for all, or for specific groups of actors (e.g. in industrial policy).

While a collective may appear to be a unitary actor with uniform and coherent rules, leadership or organization, it might also be more loosely organized and coordinated. Some collectives may have developed a degree of formal organization, explicitly codified rules, and may imbue certain actors with leadership who exert direct power – though not enough to consider them full institutional actors. In other collectives – such as collective behaviour coalescing around quality conventions, social movements, and in looser networks, where no single or clear organization can be identified, few codified rules exist, and a sense of leadership is lacking (e.g. Occupy Wall Street, the *gilets jaunes* movement in France). These are more likely to exert diffuse power and characterize situations where the boundaries of those included and excluded in the arena are not clearly knowable, sometimes not even for the actors themselves.

Four Types of Power

Combining the two types of transmission mechanisms and the two arenas of actors explained in the previous section yields four ideal types of power in GVCs: *bargaining*, *institutional*, *demonstrative* and *constitutive* (see Figure 2.2). It is worth noting that these four types of power are *combinatory* in specific GVCs, meaning that they are not mutually exclusive, and thus can become mixed, layered and linked together in complex ways and in different combinations over time. This can happen because one

	Direct	Diffuse
	Bargaining Power	**Demonstrative Power**
Dyadic	• Operates on a one-to-one basis • Exhibits different degrees in different kinds of value chain linkages • Is shaped by the relationship between lead firm requirements and supplier competences, including those on sustainability	• Operates through informal transmission mechanisms along GVCs between individual actors, (e.g. buyers and suppliers or aspiring suppliers) • Is shaped by conventions and best practices, including those on sustainability management, implicitly accepted by the parties of a dyadic transaction
	Institutional Power	**Constitutive Power**
Collective	• Operates through government regulation and/or multi-stakeholder sustainability initiatives or other institutionalized forms • Can be leveraged through collective standards or codified 'best practices', including those on sustainability	• Is based on broadly accepted norms, conventions, expectations and best practices, (e.g. financialization, just-in-time supply chain management, environmental stewardship) • Shapes what is systemically acceptable and desirable, (e.g. green capital accumulation, sustainability-based value extraction from suppliers)

Figure 2.2 Four Types of Power in Global Value Chains
Source: Adapted from Dallas et al. (2017, 2019)

kind of power may be partly derived or dependent upon another kind, such as when the (dyadic) bargaining power of one firm over another derives from its positional power in a collective, or when a supplier uses its dyadic competence power to encapsulate valuable assets formerly held by a collective (e.g. a corporation adapting a collective sustainability standard for its internal use). Furthermore, one type of power can transform into another type, for instance when vaguely defined best practices are codified as a de facto standard or even maintained and enforced as a *de jure* standard – representing a shift from diffuse to more direct power within collectives. This suggests that it is important to carry out evolutionary analyses of how different transmission mechanisms and areas of actors overlap and evolve over time.

'Bargaining' Power – Dyadic and Direct

Bargaining power is clearly the most common form of power found in GVC and related literatures. This is partly because of a focus on linkages between lead firms, often in the Global North, and suppliers, often in the Global South (Gereffi, 1994; Gereffi et al., 2005). The arena of actors has been populated largely by firms, and the analysis of power has been based on a series of firm-to-firm (dyadic) bargaining snapshots. Clearly, the category of bargaining power (where the arena of actors is dyadic and the transmission mechanism direct) is essential. However, it is important to remember that the four categories of power in Dallas et al.'s (2017, 2019) framework are not mutually exclusive, but rather are layered and combinatory. As mentioned above, dyadic power can also be exerted between individual firms and states. And even though bargaining power is exerted directly *between* dyads of firms, power that is *external* to the relationship sometimes undergirds that particular linkage (see different forms of collective power below). For instance, even though 'modular' is a description of a type of dyadic linkage, this form of power often derives from collective diffusion processes – for example, many firms progressively adopt a particular standard.

'Demonstrative' Power – Dyadic and Diffuse

Requirements embedded in a dyadic GVC relationship can shape more than the behaviour and choices of the suppliers involved in a specific transaction. It can also create a demonstration effect among competitor suppliers, would-be suppliers and/or second-tier suppliers and beyond. This may occur through many different mechanisms. For instance, a specific form of environmental upgrading may induce adaptation among competitors, or among suppliers wishing to compete in the future. If suppliers cannot meet these sustainability requirements, they can be excluded from GVCs, and may be forced to downgrade and serve less demanding customers. As I will show in the next chapter, demonstrative power can also be exerted by non-firm actors, such as wine tasters. In other words, the outcome of bargaining within particular dyads can subsequently spread along the value chain and in contiguous industries through demonstration effects, including those related to sustainability management. While this form of power is acknowledged in existing literatures, there is less effort to precisely assess these adaptations and demonstration effects (Dallas et al., 2017, 2019). Yet the dynamics external to (but nevertheless contiguous to) dyadic GVC activities are important to understand the strategic choices available to suppliers and other less powerful firms in GVCs (Sako and Zylberberg, 2017).

'Institutional' Power – Collective and Direct

Institutional power is a form of direct power that is exercised by collectives that are more formally organized (e.g. in business associations, multi-stakeholder sustainability initiatives or within the state). While power in dyadic relationships stems from resources controlled by a single organization, in collective arenas it is at least partly external, in the sense of being dependent upon the strategic actions of groups of actors, or upon the rules set by formally organized collectives. While the GVC literature refers to the 'institutional framework' within which lead firms and suppliers operate, research in this field (including my previous work) has not organically integrated these issues in its analysis of governance, often using regulation and other institutional factors as add-ons to existing frameworks.

The state, when regulating the conduct of a well-defined category of actors, applies institutional power. Multi-stakeholder sustainability initiatives, which are collectives where stakeholders are clearly identified, and which provide voluntary tools for business conduct or the social and environmental conditions of production, also exercise institutional power. When these initiatives end up developing third-party certifications, they can also indirectly shape dyadic relationships – as buyers can require specific certifications from suppliers to meet specific sustainability requirements. As a result, non-firm actors, and especially international NGOs, are receiving more attention in the GVC governance literature.

This does not mean that a collective of actors exists in perfect harmony. There can be, and usually is, substantial contention within any collective, and conflicts may involve many dyadic relationships. Moreover, collectives such as sustainability standard-setting bodies often provide arenas where powerful actors jockey for the inclusion of terms that are especially favourable to them, for example when lead firms are able to shape the definition of minimum standards on environmental impact as a way to lower the costs of compliance. The resources that would give these incumbent firms power in dyadic relationships can be leveraged in collectives as well. What distinguishes institutional power from bargaining power is that it derives from the combined actions of actors that share a clear membership in an initiative or organization, or use a particular standard. As the degree of institutionalization diminishes, 'institutional' power (collective and direct) gradually turns into 'constitutive' power (collective and diffuse) (Dallas et al., 2017, 2019).

'Constitutive' Power – Collective and Diffuse

Constitutive power is manifested when collective arenas do not exhibit clear or formal common membership, and thus power is not embodied in particular actors or an institutionalized locus, even to the point that the outcome of power may be unintended. Some of the literature on 'governance as normalization' has been concerned with these dynamics but has not linked them to other forms of power. Constitutive power emerges when broad-based collective action involves less formal institutionalization or less clear common identity or purpose. Constitutive power is less explicitly codified, is applied through less precise measurement techniques and standards, and requires less direct forms of enforcement. However, actors still know and agree when a general norm or convention has been violated, and sanctions may be collectively imposed, though again enforcement is decentralized and often subtle and nuanced, when compared to the preordained arbiters and judges that may be used to exert institutional power.

On the one hand, constitutive power can become increasingly formalized and codified, and thus evolve into institutional power. On the other hand, institutional power can be challenged, delegitimized and de-codified, and practices and norms may become less formalized and turn into constitutive power. Examples of constitutive power include the slow diffusion of outsourcing or financialization as general best practices against which firms came to become progressively structured (Gibbon and Ponte, 2005), the loose social movement-like diffusion of sustainability concerns (Ponte, 2014b), the normative role exerted by social movements on corporate conduct and transparency (Bair and Palpacuer, 2015), and the general acceptance of green capitalist practices – such as extracting value from suppliers under the aegis of sustainability (Dallas et al., 2017, 2019).

Discussion and Next Steps

Drawing from Dallas et al. (2017, 2019), Figure 2.3 provides a graphic basis for the case-specific applications that follow in the book.

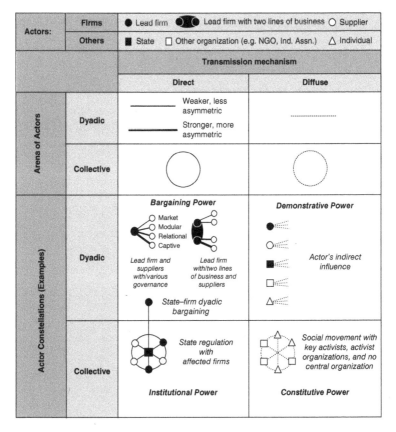

Figure 2.3 Power in GVCs: Key Dimensions
Source: Adapted from design by Sturgeon in Dallas et al. (2017, 2019)

It includes symbols for three types of firm-level actors: lead firms, suppliers, and lead firms with more than one line of business. A few additional actors are specified, including states, non-governmental organizations, industry associations, and influential individuals. Direct power transmission is represented by solid lines, with varying line thickness based on the degree of power asymmetry between actor dyads. Indirect power is represented by dotted lines – showing the diffuse influence of specific actors on others. Collectives are represented by circles that can accommodate any number of actors, with solid or dashed lines to represent direct and indirect power transmission.

The actor constellations section of Figure 2.3 provides a few emblematic, highly stylized examples of power relationships in actor groupings. These include: a lead firm with supplier relationships, where bargaining power is transmitted directly in dyadic linkages that range from low power asymmetry with market linkages to very high with captive linkages following Gereffi et al. (2005); an example of a lead firm with two lines of business, each with its own supplier relationships with various levels of power asymmetry; and a representation of state–firm dyadic bargaining, since powerful firms commonly negotiate terms directly with government agencies, either as one-off agreements or as exceptions to existing regulations. In the category of demonstrative power, Figure 2.3 indicates how transmission mechanisms operate indirectly in dyadic linkages. In institutional power, collectives of actors exert (stronger or weaker) power within groups, for example a state regulating the environmental conditions of production, and thus affecting firms and other institutions. In the category of constitutive power, constellations of actors exert indirect power in collectives, for example an environmental activism movement with more or less coordinated groups of individuals and organizations (Dallas et al., 2017, 2019).

These stylized diagrams by no means represent an exhaustive set of actor constellations. Social movements can involve any type of actor and sometimes evolve to develop more structure, including centralized organizations with selective membership. Multi-stakeholder sustainability initiatives can also involve a range of actors, and exhibit both direct (institutional) and diffuse (constitutive) power relationships among actors. Most importantly, firms, industries, organizations, and social movements both evolve over time and usually involve an interacting set of actors and actor constellations. With this in mind, the distinctions between these four forms of power can be used to trace how organizations and movements copy ideas from actors that exert demonstration power, organize more explicitly or more loosely, and experience spin-offs, extensions and geographic transformations over time. In the next chapter, I apply this framework to examine the historical transformation of power, sustainability and governance in the wine, coffee and biofuels GVCs.

3 | SUSTAINABILITY, POWER AND GOVERNANCE IN THE WINE, COFFEE AND BIOFUELS GLOBAL VALUE CHAINS

Existing research on GVCs has analysed governance dynamics mostly by considering bargaining power as the only kind that matters. This is explicit in the approach to GVC governance as 'linking' (Gereffi et al., 2005), but also in most of the work on GVC governance as 'driving', where bargaining power is equated with 'drivenness' or 'levels of driving' (Gereffi, 1994; Gibbon et al., 2008). By focusing largely on bargaining power, without examining how other kinds of power may undergird or weaken it, existing research has been able to provide only a partial understanding of GVC governance. The approach to understanding power in GVCs devised in the previous chapter suggests a way to organically examine how different forms and combinations of power shape governance. This is important not only analytically to understand how GVCs operate and for whose benefit, but also for policy and activist interventions. So far, these interventions have focused on bargaining power-related 'leverage points' in GVCs – to attempt benefiting (smaller) producers, disadvantaged groups, workers and/or the environment. But when the power of lead firms in a GVC is wielded through a combination of different kinds of power, interventions that focus on bargaining power alone are more likely to have limited or unintended effects (see Chapter 5).

To address these issues, in this chapter I apply the analytical framework developed in Chapter 2 to examine the dynamics of sustainability, power and governance in three GVCs: wine, coffee and biofuels. These GVCs were selected for three reasons: first, they all operate in the agro-food sector, thus allowing some of their features to be kept relatively constant for meaningful comparison; second, I have been carrying out research in all three (since 1999 in coffee, 2005 in wine, and 2010 in biofuels), and thus I can draw from primary as well as secondary material for comparative analysis; and third, there is significant variation in the current importance of sustainability factors in the operation of these GVCs, ranging from relatively low (wine), to fairly important (coffee), to essential (biofuels).

In the wine industry, environmental sustainability factors are becoming more visible in the way wine producers differentiate themselves. Organic and biodynamic production is increasing rapidly, albeit from a low base, and a series of sustainability initiatives and certifications have emerged in the past decade. But sustainability has not yet substantially reshaped value chain operations. The coffee industry, in contrast, has been one of the pioneers in developing verification and certification standards and systems for sustainability. The market share of coffee that is certified or verified under one or another initiative has grown dramatically, leading to a process of sustainability mainstreaming, with important repercussions on value chain operations (Bitzer et al., 2008; Grabs, 2017, 2018, 2019; Kolk, 2013; Millard, 2017; Raynolds, 2009). Finally, the biofuel industry essentially depends on sustainability standards to operate: in the EU, regulation requires biofuels GVC actors to seek third-party sustainability certification to access financial incentives without which biofuels would not be competitive in the market for liquid fuels; in the US, regulation sets minimum sustainability standards that are specified at the level of feedstock/origin combinations.

There are also important differences in product quality differentiation in these three GVCs, which are relevant for the analysis of sustainability, power and governance. In wine, where quality differentiation has been the defining character of the industry for centuries, it is necessary to examine power dynamics within at least three quality strands of the value chain (top-quality, mid-range, and basic wines), and then relate these distinctive characteristics to the emerging need for suppliers to provide broad product quality portfolios to their buyers. In coffee, where quality differentiation is still important but to a lesser extent than in wine, a broader distinction between mainstream and specialty/sustainable coffee suffices for the analytical purposes of this book. In biofuels, where quality differentiation is not visible to consumers, the analysis of power can be carried out without considering product quality differentiation – with the exception of sustainability.

In the next section, I provide some background information on these three GVCs, including a brief comparative profile. In the following section, I apply the framework developed in Chapter 2 to examine the changing constellations and overlaps of four kinds of power in these GVCs (bargaining, demonstrative, institutional and constitutive) and how sustainability factors play into them. I take a simplified evolutionary approach, comparing two broad periods (T1 and T2) that are characterized by distinctive changes in the configuration of power in each GVC. For wine and coffee, I compare constellations of power in the two to three decades before and after 1990, and for biofuels the decade before and after 2007. These years should not be seen as a tipping point, but rather as a reference point of gradual changes over time. In wine, the transition from T1 to T2 relates to the emergence of the figure of the 'new consumer' and related wine styles; in coffee, the transition links to the end of the International Coffee Agreement regulatory system, which lasted from 1962 to 1989; and for biofuels, the two time periods signal radically different norms and perceptions regarding their sustainability, which turned dramatically around after the food shortages and price hikes of 2006/07.

A detailed analysis of how power constellations shape governance at the *local level* is outside of the scope of this book. However, the overall picture emerging here is very much shaped by bottom-up views of GVC governance – arising from fieldwork in Ethiopia, Kenya, Tanzania and Uganda in coffee; South Africa in wine; and Malaysia and Brazil in biofuels. Some of my previous work with more specific geographical coverage delves into local governance issues, but not from the specific perspective of power adopted in this book (Daviron and Ponte, 2005; Jespersen et al., 2014; Ponte, 2002a, 2007b, 2014a). Other useful examples of value chain analyses that 'touch down' in producing countries can be found, inter alia, in Helmsing and Vellema (2011) and Neilson and Prtichard (2011).

The main objectives of this analysis are to: (1) identify the interactions between each kind of power within each GVC – and in particular the roles that demonstrative, institutional and constitutive power play in undergirding, taming or repositioning bargaining power; (2) highlight how different power configurations can explain changes in the governance of GVCs; and (3) assess how and to what extent sustainability plays a role in understanding different kinds of power and how they shape governance.

Global Value Chain Structures and Sustainability Initiatives

Wine

The wine GVC has perhaps the most complex and sophisticated quality infrastructure in the agro-food industry. It has been going through a major process of restructuring in the past few decades, in which the battle lines are drawn along the application, challenge and reinterpretation of different ideas and representations of quality. Recent trends in the geography of wine production, trade and consumption, as well as changes in the quality composition of supply and demand, have been well documented elsewhere (Anderson, 2004; Anderson and Nelgen, 2011; Gilinsky et al., 2015; Hira, 2013; Unwin, 2005). These included, in the last decades of the twentieth century, a dramatic fall in production volumes and per capita consumption in traditional (so-called 'Old World') wine–making and -consuming countries, such as Portugal, Spain, France and Italy; this was partly compensated by growing production and exports in 'New World' producing countries (Argentina, Chile, South Africa, New Zealand, Australia and the US) and by increasing consumption in the UK, the US and in some Asian countries. Table 3.1 indicates the current ranking of the top wine-producing and -consuming countries, including recent trends. The top five producing countries by volume (Italy, France, Spain, the US and Argentina) account for 62 per cent of global supplies. The top consuming countries (the US, France, Italy, Germany and China) account for 48 per cent of global demand.

A period of major consumption growth in 2002–2007 spurred increased interest in applying environmental management systems as part of a multiplication of wine offerings and the search for new differentiation strategies (Atkin et al., 2012; Gilinsky et al., 2015). But the wine industry also suffered a dramatic downturn from 2008, with global consumption starting to decrease. This downturn led to downward pressure on prices and margins and a drop in the introduction of new wine brands and offerings, at least in the US.[1] But by 2015 (the last year for which statistics were available at the time of writing), its global value was back to the level of 2005.[2]

What for centuries was considered a cottage industry, the wine GVC is now characterized by the presence of large multinational companies (Anderson, 2004; Ponte, 2009) and a substantial level of concentration at the wine marketing level. As indicated in Table 3.2, the top four wine

Table 3.1 World Wine Production and Consumption (2015)

Rank	Production				Consumption			
	Countries	Volume (ML)	World share (%)	% change 2015/13	Countries	Volume (ML)	World share (%)	% change 2015/13
1	Italy	4,950	17.4	-8.3	US	3,319	13.4	6.5
2	France	4,759	16.7	12.8	France	2,720	11.0	-3.5
3	Spain	3,720	13.1	-18.0	Italy	2,050	8.3	-5.9
4	US	2,976	10.5	-4.5	Germany	2,050	8.3	1.0
5	Argentina	1,340	4.7	-10.7	China	1,600	6.5	-8.4
Top 5		17,745	62.4			11,739	47.5	
6	Chile	1,290	4.5	0.8	UK	1,290	5.2	1.6
7	Australia	1,190	4.2	-3.3	Argentina	1,030	4.2	-0.4
8	South Africa	1,120	3.9	22.4	Spain	1,000	4.1	2
9	China	1,100	3.9	-6.8	Russia	890	3.6	-14.4
10	Germany	890	3.3	6.0	Australia	540	2.2	0
Top 10		23,335	82.2			16,489	66.8	

Source: Own elaboration of data from www.wineinstitute.org/resources/statistics

merchant groups controlled almost 10 per cent of the global market in 2006, a figure that had decreased only marginally by 2012. It is worth noting that the same three groups, all US-based, rank at the top in both periods. In 2012, the fourth-placed company (based in Australia) was created from a spin-off of the wine division of Foster's into an independent company in 2011. Therefore, there has been little change in the top rankings overall. Wine retail, which was traditionally the domain of small specialist shops, is now in the hands of supermarket chains, especially in Northern Europe, the UK and the US, but increasingly in Southern Europe as well. Although there are fears of homogenization of styles and offerings in the wine market, this is still an industry that produces a phenomenal array of different products, which are sold under a combination of brand names, grape variety, sustainability certifications and/or geographic indications of origin (Ponte, 2009).

Figure 3.1 provides a simplified representation of the wine GVC, focusing on individual functions and on product flows. The main companies listed in Table 3.2 are represented in Figure 3.1 as international traders/marketers/merchants. Many of these are to different degrees vertically integrated – they may also produce wine and may own a number of flagship estates for grape production. The general tendency, however, has been for these conglomerates to concentrate more on value chain functions that require less capital investment and

Table 3.2 World's Top Wine Marketers

Rank	Company	Headquarters	World share (%)
2006			
1	Constellation Brands	US	3.9
2	E&J Gallo Winery	US	2.7
3	The Wine Group	US	1.6
4	Foster's Wine Estates	Australia	1.5
Top 4			9.7
2012			
1	E&J Gallo Winery	US	2.7
2	Constellation Brands	US	2.2
3	The Wine Group	US	1.6
4	Treasury Wine Estates	Australia	1.8
Top 4			8.3

Sources: Own elaboration of data from MarketLine.com (for 2012) and *Impact*, Vol 37, No. 11–12, June 1 and 15, 2007, p. 6 (for 2006)

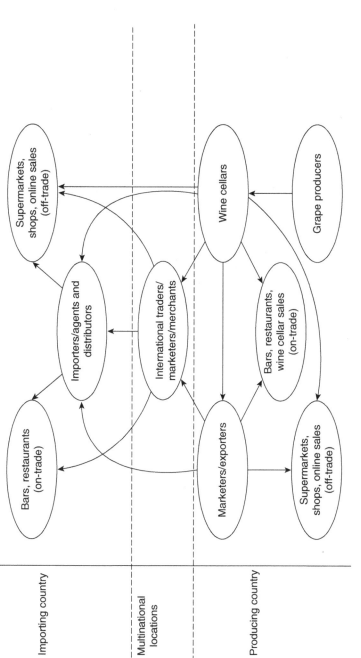

Figure 3.1 Simplified Configuration of the Wine GVC

Source: Adapted from Ponte (2007b)

to find an appropriate equilibrium between own production (usually for top-quality wines) and purchasing from external suppliers (Ponte and Ewert, 2009).

In relation to sustainability issues, organic certification (and fair trade for social issues) has been the early mover in wine, as in many other agro-food GVCs. Although organic grapes for winemaking are still a minor proportion of total production, it has been growing rapidly and has reached 5 per cent of the total area under production in Spain, the leading country in this field (Gilinsky et al., 2015: 42). Organic grape production has grown dramatically in New World producing countries as well, where producers have fewer restrictions on viticulture and winemaking practices. Biodynamic production, whether certified or not, is also spreading worldwide, but remains a small niche. Biodynamic farming practices are based on treating the vineyard as an ecosystem. They draw from astrological influences and lunar cycles, and tap into the vineyard's own natural resources, for example by attracting specific bird species to control specific pests (Flint et al., 2016). In addition to organic and biodynamic certification, in France and Italy small vineyards in traditional wine-producing regions, such as Bordeaux and Chianti, lay claims of 'reasonable' viticultural practices or the production of 'natural wines' based on the characterization that traditional local techniques are similar to those used in organic production.

New World producing countries have spurred a number of broad sustainability initiatives (Borsellino et al., 2016). For example, Sustainable Winegrowing New Zealand, an industry group, introduced its formal environmental management system as early as 1997. It certifies both grape growers and wine producers on the basis of a scorecard and benchmarking. In 2014, it claimed to cover 90 per cent of vineyard areas, of which 7 per cent also hold organic certification (Gilinsky et al., 2015). Similarly, the California Sustainable Winegrowing Program promotes 'green' and 'sustainable' practices, and has developed a certification programme that 'provides verification by a third-party auditor that a winery or vineyard implements sustainable practices and continuous improvement'.[3] By 2017, around one-quarter of vineyard area and two-thirds of wine production in California had gained various forms of sustainability certification or verification.[4] Other programmes of this kind are present not only in other New World producer countries, such as Australia, Chile and South Africa (Flint et al., 2016: 92), but also in Italy (Borsellino et al., 2016).[5]

Programmes for carbon footprint minimization are also starting to be considered in the wine industry. For example, Oregon has set up a 'Carbon Neutral Challenge' and New Zealand has developed a 'carboNZero' label. Practices such as ISO 14001 certification and constructing buildings that are LEED-certified are taking a foothold as well (Flint et al., 2016). Most of the current wine sustainability programmes and certifications focus on environmental issues, rather than social, with the exception of Fairtrade and some South Africa-specific initiatives – such as the Wine and Agricultural Ethical Trade Association (WIETA) and other projects attempting to promote 'Black Economic Empowerment' (BEE) in the wine industry (Du Toit et al., 2008).

Coffee

Coffee goes a long way and changes many hands from bean to cup. For a long period, Brazil and Colombia were the top world coffee producers, but in the 1990s the situation started to change with the fast growth of coffee production in Vietnam – on land previously covered with rainforest. In the new century, Vietnam replaced Colombia as the world second largest producer, with Indonesia and Honduras currently ranking fourth and fifth (see Figure 3.2). The top five producing countries account for about 70 per cent of global production. Production has almost doubled since the early 1990s. Export volume statistics show a similar ranking, with India replacing Honduras in the top five.[6]

The international coffee market is characterized by relatively low price elasticities of supply and demand (Ponte, 2002b). Supply elasticities tend to be low in the short run and higher in the long run because it takes at least two to three years for new trees to be productive and several extra years before they reach full production levels. Therefore, a supply response in the short term is possible only by changing the quantity of resources used for agrochemicals and labour, not by increasing the productive area. Demand elasticity is also low, with coffee demand dropping significantly only at times of large increases of coffee prices. The peculiar characteristics of these price elasticities lead to highly variable prices in the world coffee market. A situation of supply shortage results in high coffee prices without a significant reduction of consumption. Likewise, supply reacts slowly in the short run while new planting efforts take place. In the long run, this leads to a higher

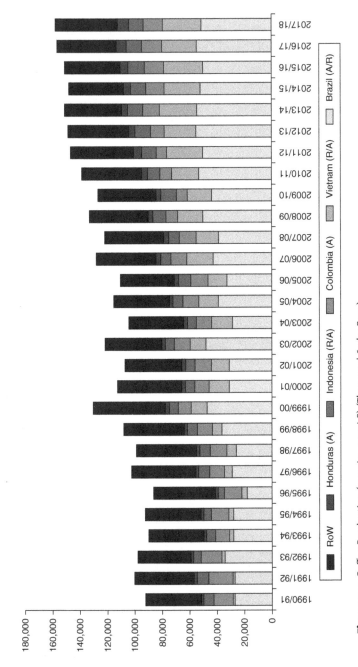

Figure 3.2 Coffee Production (1990/91–2017/18) (Thousand 60 kg Bags)

Source: Elaboration of data available at www.ico.org/trade_statistics.asp

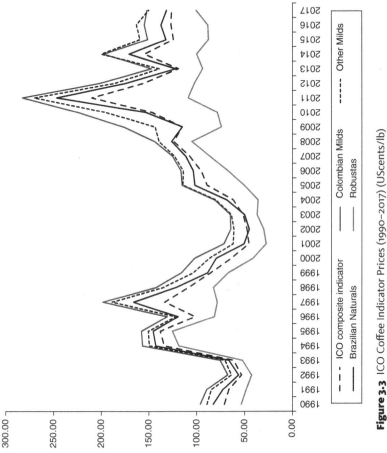

Figure 3.3 ICO Coffee Indicator Prices (1990–2017) (UScents/lb)

Source: Elaboration of data available at www.ico.org/trade_statistics.asp

than necessary supply response as new coffee trees mature. A situation of supply shortage is often followed by one of oversupply and low prices. An opposite bust period then begins, usually lasting longer than the boom period (Daviron and Ponte, 2005).

The International Coffee Organization (ICO) categorizes exports by type of coffee. Figure 3.3 shows the wide swings of international coffee prices in the past two decades, with low prices in the early 1990s and the first half of the 2000s, and price spikes in 1994–1998, 2010–2012 and 2014. Interestingly, the ratio between the average international prices for coffees of the lowest quality (robusta) and the highest (Colombian Milds) has remained on average fairly constant (at around 55–57 per cent between 1990 and 2003 and between 2004 and 2017). This is because higher demand for specialty coffee has been accompanied by higher demand for robusta coffee, which is used for instant and flavoured coffees and in emerging markets where consumption is expanding (Panhuysen and Pierrot, 2014).

The coffee GVC (see Figure 3.4) has been characterized by high concentration at the key nodes of trading and roasting for decades. However, the degree of concentration at the roaster level has decreased in the past two decades. In 1998, the top five roaster groups controlled 69 per cent of roasted and instant coffee markets. By 2014, their share had decreased to 50 per cent (see Table 3.3). This is not surprising, given the ongoing fragmentation of consumption channels and offerings. However, there have been recent signs of increased M&A activity, which are leading to renewed concentration (see details in the next section).

Table 3.3 Top Five Coffee Roasters (% of Global Market Share by Holding Company)

Rank	1998		2014	
1	Philip Morris (US)	25	Nestlé (Switzerland)	22
2	Nestlé (Switzerland)	24	JAB Holdings (Germany)	21
3	Sara Lee (US)	7	Smuckers (US)	2
4	Procter & Gamble (US)	7	Strauss (Israel)	3
5	Tchibo (Germany)	6	Tchibo (Germany)	2
Top 5		69		50

Sources: For 1998, Ponte (2002b: 1108); for 2014, elaboration from Grabs (2017), drawing on www.statista.com/statistics/323254/global-retail-coffee-market-share-by-company/

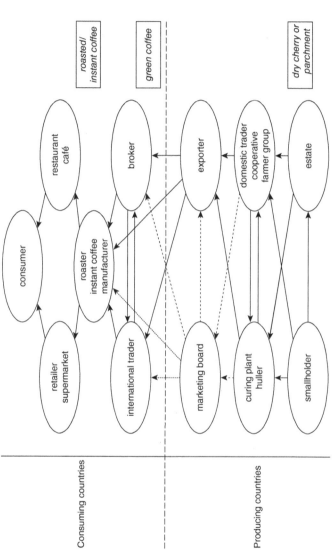

Figure 3.4 Simplified Configuration of the Coffee GVC

Source: Adapted from Ponte (2002b)

Legend: solid line = common transaction
dotted line (one kind only) = historically important but now disappearing

One of the major transformations in the coffee GVC in the past three decades has been the growth of specialty coffee, coffee bar chains and micro-roasters. Another visible development has been an accelerating expansion of the 'sustainable' coffee market (Auld, 2014; Auld and Gulbrandsen, 2010; Giovannucci and Ponte, 2005; Levy et al., 2014, 2016; Manning and Reinecke, 2016; Neilson and Pritchard, 2007; Reinecke et al., 2012). In 2000, sustainable coffee represented only 0.3 per cent of the coffee market by volume and 1.2 per cent by value (Ponte, 2004). By 2013, 40 per cent of total production and 15 per cent of sales of coffee were certified or verified (Panhuysen and Pierrot, 2014). Sustainable coffee can no longer be considered a niche market. However, production of sustainable coffee is highly concentrated geographically, with the top five countries (Brazil, Colombia, Vietnam, Peru and Honduras) representing 81 per cent of global production of standard-compliant coffee (Potts et al., 2014: 159).

A number of certification initiatives operate in the field of coffee sustainability. The oldest are organic certification and Fairtrade labelling (by Fairtrade Labelling Organizations International – FLO), which first emerged in the 1970s and 1980s in the coffee sector. FLO operates a minimum price system plus a social premium that are guaranteed to producer organizations, and now covers some basic environmental standards as well. Organic certification has no price guarantee, but normally attracts a premium – although it has been historically decreasing for coffee (Giovannucci et al., 2008).[7] These two early certification systems were followed by a second wave emerging in the late 1990s and early 2000s, including Rainforest Alliance and UTZ-certified. These certifications may provide price premia, usually linked to higher intrinsic quality rather than sustainability per se, but they are not guaranteed (Kolk, 2013). After a period of multiplication of certification initiatives, there have been recent signs of harmonization (Turcotte et al., 2014) and consolidation in the sustainability market, with Rainforest Alliance and UTZ announcing a merger in 2017.

Other systems of verification have been developed by private companies. Starbucks' C.A.F.E. Practices (Coffee and Farmer Equity Practices) (established in 2004) now account for over 90 per cent of the total volume of coffee purchased by the company. Nestlé's Nespresso AAA Sustainable Quality Program (established in 2003) integrates already existing standards (those forming the basis for Rainforest

Alliance certification), but these are verified internally instead of following third-party certification. Eighty per cent of Nespresso coffee supply complies with the AAA system. More recently, other large coffee buyers (Tchibo, McDonald's) have started to develop their own sustainability verification systems as well (Grabs 2017, 2018). These private, internal systems, like in other commodities, are often implemented by these buyers' main suppliers (international traders) (Freidberg, 2017) – for example, important elements of training, quality control and other service provision related to Nespresso AAA are implemented on the ground by Volcafé and ECOM (Grabs, 2017: 23). Other major traders have followed suit. Olam, for example, has a 'Livelihood Charter' that includes environmental issues, and Neumann developed an initiative (International Coffee Partners) together with some of the main European roasters (Millard, 2017). These systems build systemic links between quality management and sustainable sourcing, focus on safeguarding future supplies of high-quality coffee, and have become part of a 'holistic corporate approach to supply and supply chain management' (Kolk, 2013; Potts et al., 2014: 165).

Industry-level standards and platforms on sustainability have also multiplied. The most important one is the Common Code for the Coffee Community (4C), which operates as a baseline standard and relies on a self-assessment procedure – accompanied by verification every three years. It was originally launched in 2002 as a public–private partnership between the German Agency for Technical Development and Cooperation (GTZ, now GIZ) and the German Coffee Association. This initiative is specifically designed to 'mainstream' sustainability in the coffee industry by providing a basic standard that is not meant to compete with other sustainability initiatives and is not communicated to the consumer with a label (Fairtrade, UTZ and Rainforest Alliance are actually 4C Association members) (Bitzer et al., 2008; Kolk, 2005, 2012, 2013; Neilson and Pritchard, 2007). 4C has grown significantly, and now represents the largest volume of sustainable coffee in the market, with three countries (Brazil, Vietnam and Colombia) providing 90 per cent of 4C-verified production (Potts et al., 2014).

Other important sustainability platforms are the Sustainability Coffee Challenge (supported by Starbucks) and the Global Coffee Platform. The latter absorbed the 4C Association and combined it with the IDH Sustainable Coffee Program, which is supported by Nestlé and Jacobs Douwe Egberts (JDE). Together with several others, these platforms

Table 3.4 Production and Sales of Sustainability Standard-Compliant Coffee (2013) (Thousand Metric Tons)

Certification/ verification system	Production	Sales	Sales/production (%)
Fairtrade	440	145	33.0
Organic	248	133	53.6
Rainforest Alliance	455	168	36.9
UTZ	727	224	30.8
4C	2280	450	19.7
Starbucks C.A.F.E.	170	170	100.0
Nespresso AAA	55	55	100.0
Total	4,375	1,345	30.7

Source: Adapted from Panhuysen and Pierrot (2014: 16)

create a complex institutional infrastructure for sustainability management, where international NGOs, large roasters and international traders play a key role (Grabs, 2017: 24). Table 3.4 shows that only 30 per cent of coffee production that is certified or verified is sold as such. The rest is sold as 'regular' coffee. The gap between production and sales is largest for 4C coffee. Among third-party certification systems, the gap is smallest in organics and highest in UTZ. Own systems of verification are of course tailored to changing demand by the company that runs them; therefore, all produced verified coffee is sold as such.

A final layer of sustainability management is provided by an array of sustainability projects on the ground, usually pairing environmental and/or social concerns with goals related to increasing productivity and improving quality.[8] They are often financed by major roasters (e.g. Tchibo, JDE, Keuring Green Mountain) with matching funds from public sources. They include activities related to extension, access to finance, risk management, value addition and logistics, and are implemented by service organizations such as TechnoServe. Certification organizations are also offering consulting and training services to tap into these new markets – for example, Rainforest Alliance is helping Nestlé to implement projects related to its Nescafé Better Farming Practices (Fransen, 2018; Grabs, 2017, 2018).

When it comes to the largest roasters in the coffee industry (see Figure 3.5 and Table 3.5), the JAB Holdings group purchased sustainable coffee for almost 35 per cent of their total (much of it from

Table 3.5 Purchases of Sustainability Standard-Compliant Coffee by Top Eight Roaster Groups (2013)

	Total coffee purchases (MT)	Standard-compliant (MT)	Standard-compliant (% of total)
JAB Holdings*	958	331	35
Nestlé	880	257	29
Smucker's	300	30	10**
Strauss	230	4	2
Tchibo	180	54	30
Starbucks	180	171	95
UCC	177	25	14
Lavazza	150	2	1
Total top 8	3,055	874	29

* Includes JDE, Mondelez and Keurig/Green Mountain
** Commitment, not actual purchases
Source: Adapted from Panhuysen and Pierrot (2014: 21)

4C, but also from UTZ, Rainforest Alliance and Fairtrade), while almost 30 per cent of coffee purchased by Nestlé in 2014 was certified or verified (much of it by 4C, but also through its own AAA system and purchases of Fairtrade/organic coffees). The highest performer in this ranking is Starbucks, with 95 per cent of its purchases (mostly through its own system). Smucker's and Strauss have not yet seriously entered the sustainability certification market. It should also be noted that two-thirds of certified and verified sustainable coffee is produced in Latin America, where farmers and their cooperatives are more organized. In Africa, certified coffee volumes are much smaller, and mostly concentrated in Kenya and Tanzania (Panhuysen and Pierrot, 2014).

All these systems, to different degrees, seek to address environmental and/or social sustainability issues in the production (and sometimes trade) of coffee. The issue of greenhouse gas reduction, a key component in other sustainability certification systems emerging in the agro-food sector (especially in biofuels, but also budding in wine), has received relatively less attention in coffee certification systems so far, although a range of options to add value to low-emission coffee have been identified (Grabs, 2017).

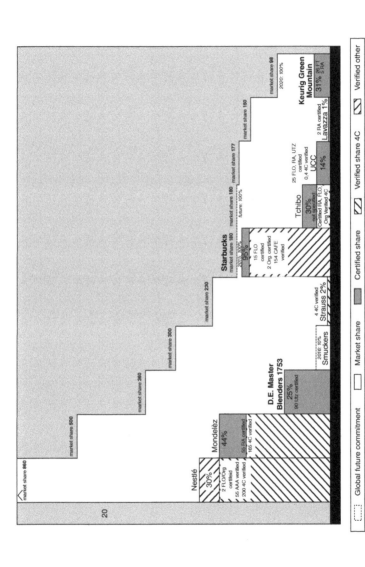

Figure 3-5 Sustainable Certified or Verified Coffee Purchases among Top Roasters (2014)

Source: Panhuysen and Pierrot (2014: 21)

Table 3.6 Biofuel Production and Consumption (2000–2014)

		2000	2001	2002	2003	2004	2005	2006	2007	2008	2009	2010	2011	2012	2013	2014	Top 3 2014
Production																	
US	1,000 bbl/d	106.0	116.0	140.0	184.0	223.0	261.0	335.0	457.0	650.0	747.0	881.5	967.1	921.3	953.6	1018.8	
Brazil	1,000 bbl/d	184.0	198.0	217.0	249.0	252.0	276.0	307.0	396.0	486.0	478.0	467.2	404.1	423.4	494.3	489.5	
EU-28	1,000 bbl/d	17.1	21.2	29.4	39.3	48.6	77.0	123.5	153.8	196.9	233.4	204.0	272.4	266.1	288.0	293.0	
Argentina	1,000 bbl/d	0.1	0.2	0.2	0.2	0.2	0.2	0.7	3.9	14.0	24.0	21.3	31.7	53.4	47.3	61.4	
Indonesia	1,000 bbl/d	0.0	0.0	0.0	0.0	0.0	0.2	0.5	1.2	2.2	5.9	7.3	28.6	34.7	39.8	59.7	
Top 5	(% of total)	97.5	97.6	95.8	94.6	94.5	93.5	91.2	91.7	91.4	91.0	92.8	91.1	90.8	90.3	89.7	
World	1,000 bbl/d	315.1	343.6	403.3	499.3	554.1	657.0	840.6	1103.9	1476.0	1636.2	1704.7	1870.2	1870.1	2019.4	2143.1	

(continued)

Table 3.6 (*continued*)

		2000	2001	2002	2003	2004	2005	2006	2007	2008	2009	2010	2011	2012	2013	2014	Top 3 2014
Consumption																	
US	1,000 bbl/d	108.0	114.7	136.1	184.9	232.7	270.9	375.0	472.4	650.5	741.2	832.7	882.6	900.7	955.4	977.1	977.1
Brazil	1,000 bbl/d	166.9	141.4	160.2	144.0	177.1	182.0	195.2	268.5	355.7	420.3	437.1	341.7	327.3	429.9	470.8	470.8
EU-28	1,000 bbl/d	16.3	18.7	25.8	34.0	48.0	72.0	122.2	172.3	235.6	289.5	332.3	348.3	357.8	326.5	324.0	324.0
China	1,000 bbl/d	0.0	0.1	5.1	13.9	17.3	21.5	32.0	30.7	39.4	47.7	46.2	51.6	59.2	64.9	69.2	69.2
Canada	1,000 bbl/d	4.5	4.5	4.5	4.9	4.9	6.0	5.4	21.6	25.7	27.8	30.2	44.0	51.4	54.9	58.1	58.1
Top 5	(% of total)	62.6	58.1	58.2	50.9	50.9	50.1	47.5	49.8	48.6	49.5	47.8	44.2	43.6	43.9	44.0	44.0
World	1000 bbl/d	299.8	283.6	336.0	386.5	485.5	561.9	747.7	990.3	1349.1	1587.5	1770.0	1777.6	1826.6	1994.7	2096.9	2096.9

Source: Elaboration of data from US Energy Administration Information, www.eia.gov/cfapps/ipdbproject/IEDIndex3.cfm?tid=79&pid=79&aid=2

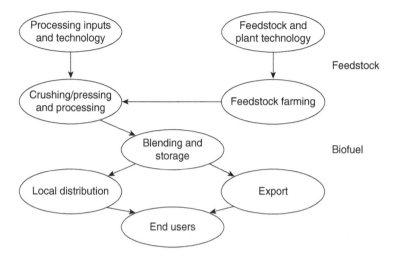

Figure 3.6 Simplified Configuration of the Biofuels GVC
Source: Adapted from Ponte (2014a)

Biofuels

Biofuels are fuels generated by processing specific kinds of biomass, including agricultural crops, for use in transport, electricity production or for domestic use. *Ethanol* accounts for over 90 per cent of biofuel production globally. It is produced by fermenting and distilling sugars from starchy plants (such as sugar cane, sorghum, wheat and corn) into alcohol. So-called 'next-generation' ethanol is under development and is expected to be produced from cellulose contained in forestry products, crop residues, and domestic and industrial waste. Ethanol can be used in low-percentage mixes in regular engines without modification. *Biodiesel* is produced from oily crops or trees (such as soy, oil palm, sunflower and jatropha) and from animal fat and waste cooking oil through the process of trans-esterification. Some kinds of biodiesel can be used in high-proportion mixes or even unblended in modified diesel engines. Next-generation biodiesel and aviation biofuel production is based on inputs from non-fat biomass through thermochemical or biochemical conversion of cellulosic material or other crop residues and waste (Ponte, 2014a).

Three systemically important countries/regions are key in understanding the biofuels GVC: Brazil, the US and the EU. Together with Argentina and Indonesia, they account for 90 per cent of global production, and together with China and Canada for 44 per cent of consumption (see Table 3.6). Global biofuel production and consumption has increased nearly sevenfold since 2000 and has almost doubled since 2007. Much of this growth (both in production and consumption) is accounted by the US, and to a less extent the EU and Brazil. The US and Brazil account for a large proportion of global production of ethanol (mainly from corn in the US and sugar cane in Brazil), with the US and the EU importing substantial amounts. In biodiesel, the EU produces around half of the global volume (mainly from rapeseed in Germany and France), with the US, Argentina and Brazil (mostly from soy oil) and Indonesia and Malaysia (mostly from palm oil) also producing substantial amounts. The EU is the main importer of biodiesel, while Argentina is the main exporter.[9]

National (Brazil, US) and regional (EU) biofuel industries have existed for decades and have operated fairly independently from each other, indicating that until recently there were a variety of loosely coupled biofuel value chains, rather than a global one. In the last two decades, however, we have witnessed a gradual (and still incomplete) establishment of a *global* biofuel value chain (see a simplified representation in Figure 3.6) through a variety of processes of internationalization, cross-regionalization and a few properly global dynamics: (1) increased trade flows and broader geographic dispersion of feedstock production; (2) new international and cross-regional processes taking place mostly through government-led or -facilitated initiatives; and (3) further consolidation among industry actors, the rise of international operations and alliances, and the increased and sometimes completely new involvement in biofuels of global players from agro-food, fuels and agro-processing (Ponte, 2014a). In comparison to wine and coffee, however, the biofuels GVC is still characterized by fragmentation and a large number of actors involved in different kinds of functions, such as specialized feedstock producers and processors, fuel refiners, global agro-food traders, oil companies and fuel distributors, major global airlines, developers of GM crops, research institutions, and venture capital.

The emergence and growth of the biofuels GVC is clearly related to government interventions, first in Brazil, dating back to the 1970s, and then in the US and the EU since the 1990s (for more details, see the section on institutional power below). These policies portrayed biofuels as a possible solution to address climate change, energy security and rural development at the same time (Afionis and Stringer, 2012;

Renckens et al., 2017; Stattman et al., 2013). Currently, 35 countries (counting the EU-28 as one) have biofuel mandates: the largest in proportional terms is applied in Brazil (where ethanol represents 25 per cent of total fuel consumption), with the EU and many other countries setting a 10 per cent mandate, and the US establishing a volume target of 136 billion litres by 2022.[10]

However, following the food crisis of 2006/07, criticism mounted on biofuels for taking away land from food cultivation, and the EU, the US and Brazil devised sustainability standards and regulation for the production, trade and use of biofuels. It also led to a sharper distinction between so-called 'first-generation' biofuels (those based on the processing of feedstock that can also be used for human consumption) and an array of 'next-generation' biofuels (those based on improved and new transformation processes of cellulosic material and other waste, and/or on the development of algae feedstocks). These policies created a large market for 'sustainable biofuels', which facilitated a multiplication of private and multi-stakeholder sustainability certification schemes, both nationally and transnationally (Labruto, 2014; Moser et al., 2014; Partzsch, 2011; Poletti and Sicurelli, 2016; Ponte, 2014a; Scarlat and Dallemand, 2011).

Comparative Elements

Several commonalities and differences characterize the structures of the wine, coffee and biofuels GVCs and their sustainability profiles (see summary in Table 3.7):

(1) The market share of sustainability-certified products over total sales ranges from small in wine to 100 per cent in some key biofuel markets, with coffee placed halfway.
(2) The range of product differentiation follows the same sequence, highest in wine and lowest in biofuels, with coffee in between.
(3) The level of concentration of actors at key GVC nodes also differs, but with a different ranking than above: it is highest in coffee, medium in wine, and lowest in biofuels.
(4) The concentration of the supply base is low but increasing in wine and biofuels, and remains low in coffee.
(5) The geographical base of the top-producing countries ranges from mostly based in the Global North for wine, to exclusively in the Global South for coffee, to a mix of the two for biofuels.

Table 3.7 Comparative Elements of the Wine, Coffee and Biofuels GVCs

	Wine	Coffee	Biofuels
(1) Share of sustainability certification over total market	Small	Medium (40 per cent of production; 15 per cent of consumption, 2013)	High (100 per cent in the EU, 2017)
(2) Product quality differentiation	High	Medium	Low
(3) Concentration at key GVC node	Medium but increasing*	High but decreasing**	Low***
(4) Concentration of the supply base	Low but increasing	Low	Low but increasing
(5) Top-producing countries/regions (by volume)	Italy, France, Spain, US, Argentina (2015) (see Table 3.1)	Brazil, Vietnam, Colombia, Indonesia, Honduras (2017) (see Figure 3.3)	US, Brazil, EU-28, Argentina, Indonesia (2014) (see Table 3.6)
(6) Top five consuming countries (by volume)	US, France, Italy, Germany, China (2016) (www.oiv.int)	EU, US, Brazil, Japan, Russia (2017) (www.ico.org)	US, Brazil, EU-28, China, Canada (2014) (www.eia.gov)
(7) Top processing companies/groups	E&J Gallo, Constellation, The Wine Company, Treasury Wine Estates (2012) (see Table 3.2)	JAB Holdings, Nestlé, Smucker's, Strauss, Tchibo (2014) (see Table 3.3)	n/a
(8) Key environmental concerns	Agrochemical use and run-off; possible biodiversity, habitat and forest loss when new land is cleared for cultivation; energy use in winemaking; processing of solid waste; alternative and lighter packaging materials	Soil erosion and degradation; monoculture (when shade trees are not used); degradation of water supply and quality; agrochemical use and run-off; conversion of primary forest; loss of biodiversity and habitat	Land use change; indirect land use change; land availability; farming intensification; deforestation; loss of biodiversity; insufficient GHG emission reductions in comparison to fossil fuels

	Wine*	Coffee**	Biofuel***
(9) Important international third-party sustainability certifications with environmental content	Organic (IFOAM), biodynamic (Demeter)	Organic (IFOAM), Rainforest Alliance, UTZ, Fairtrade (FLO)	International Sustainability and Carbon Certification (ISCC), Roundtable on Sustainable Biofuels (RSB), Better Sugar Cane Initiative (Bonsucro), Roundtable on Responsible Soy (RTRS), Roundtable on Sustainable Palm Oil (RSPO)
(10) Examples of other sustainability initiatives and verification systems	California Sustainable Winegrowing Alliance; Sustainable Winegrowing New Zealand; SOStain (Sicily, Italy); Sustainable Wine South Africa (SWSA); Biodiversity and Wine Initiative (BWI), South Africa	4C; Starbucks C.A.F.E. Practices; Nespresso AAA; Global Coffee Platform; Sustainable Coffee Challenge	Brazilian Sugarcane Industry Association (UNICA) sustainability reporting; Sustainable Aviation Fuel Users Group (SAFUG); Commercial Aviation Alternative Fuels Initiative (CAAFI); Inter-American Development Bank Biofuels Sustainability Scorecard; Council on Sustainable Biomass Production; Global Bioenergy Partnership (GBEP)

* Wine merchants/marketers
** Roasters
*** Biofuel producers
Source: Own analysis

(6) The geographical base of the top-consuming countries is relatively similar in the three GVCs, with a prevalence of countries in the Global North but also the important presence of China and Brazil.

(7) All the top processors in the GVCs for which we have information on market share are based in the Global North.

(8) Environmental concerns are fairly similar in coffee and wine, while biofuels include additional features.

(9) The sustainability certification market is the most competitive in biofuels in terms of number of initiatives, followed by coffee and then wine; some certification systems operate in both coffee and wine, while biofuels are certified mostly by a dedicated set of certifiers.

These comparative elements will come into play in the rest of this chapter, first in relation to the analysis of power dynamics in each GVC, and then in the analysis of GVC governance.

Changing Constellations of Power

In this section, I apply the typology of power in GVCs as delineated in Chapter 2 to the case studies of the wine, coffee and biofuels GVCs. Combining two types of transmission mechanisms (direct and diffuse) and two arenas of actors (dyads and collectives) yields four ideal types of power in GVCs: *bargaining* (dyadic-direct), *institutional* (collective-direct), *demonstrative* (dyadic, diffuse) and *constitutive* (collective-diffuse). In this section, I examine changes between T_1 and T_2 for each type of power in the three GVCs, highlighting their sustainability dimensions. In the next section, I analyse how these changing power configurations shape the governance of the wine, coffee and biofuels GVCs.

Bargaining Power

Bargaining Power in the Wine GVC

In dyadic and direct buyer–supplier relations in wine GVCs, power is exercised through bargaining over price, quality specifications, product portfolios and logistics. The importance of product specifications is paramount in the top-quality strand of the wine GVC, while price and logistics (including timing, forms of delivery and packaging) are relatively more important at the lower end of the quality range. Yet as lead firms consolidate the number of first-tier suppliers, they also demand broader product portfolios and minimum volumes for each product line – including both low-end and middle-range quality, sometimes even top-quality offerings. This means that both economies of scope and scale are important. In the 1960s and up to the 1980s (during T1), bargaining power was wielded by international traders and merchants in lower-end markets, while producers could exercise more bargaining power in higher-end markets (Ponte and Ewert, 2009). From the 1990s onwards (during T2), an increasing proportion of wine started to be sold through retailers carrying a wide portfolio of quality, rather than through specialist shops. As a result, the bargaining power of retailers significantly increased vis-à-vis international traders/merchants and wine producers (Staricco and Ponte, 2015).

Other sources of bargaining power are linked to the leveraging of a unique 'personality' of either the wine, its presentation, the winemaker, or the property behind the wine – this can include unique ways of handling sustainability issues (say, 'natural weeding' by a flock of sheep instead of chemical weeding application) or a specific story behind any of these. In this case, bargaining power arises from the properties of those making it (or marketing it), where their expertise is not necessarily based on technical competence or on tasting prowess. These aspects can also be embedded in design (a unique label, a funky name for the wine, a special bottle shape, a unique biodiversity story). In the past two decades or so (T2), environmental and social sustainability factors have also started to be required by retailers and/or offered by producers as part of the required product specifications.

In *top-quality* wines, sustainability issues are usually transmitted to consumers through information relayed on the label. For high-end and boutique producers, sustainability features can strengthen their bargaining power position vis-à-vis wine merchants and retailers, especially if they can offer innovative or unique features that are communicated through 'label stories' (Flint et al., 2016). When it comes to 'personality' and uniqueness, environmental sustainability factors can be framed as one of the main elements of positioning (e.g. wine made from grapes from a particular plot that has a biodiversity buffer next to it, or wine and grapes produced with biodynamic techniques). But in general, in the top-quality segment, third-party certifications for sustainability are not enough to make a wine unique. This actually allows producers to retain more control over 'quality', including its sustainability content, and on whether sustainability can be leveraged to their advantage.

In *mid-range-quality* wines, industry-own verification systems (e.g. the Biodiversity and Wine Initiative in South Africa)[11] and third-party certifications (such as fair trade, organic and biodynamic) prevail. Bargaining in mid-range wines is not as dependent on the endorsement by wine critics as in top-quality wines (see on demonstrative power below). Wine operators of all sizes I interviewed in South Africa argue that good scores from wine writers and publications help to leverage bargaining power vis-à-vis their buyers, as do stickers and medals awarded in international competitions, or good metrics on social media (Colman, 2008; Szolnoki et al., 2016). Producers also claim that what can help their bargaining power in this quality range is having a combination of broad geographical origin, brand, and grape variety.

Basic-quality wines are seldom sold with a sustainability label, except in some markets where state monopsony systems impose a quota for sustainable wines (as in Sweden) or where market demand for sustainability also applies to the basic wine segment as well (as in the UK). Bargaining power in basic wines is exercised through a far simpler process – retailers decide what quality is, and everyone else in the value chain follows suit. For retailers, the first and most important step is that a basic material quality is assured, including intrinsic quality and packaging; codified solutions to food safety (and sustainability in some markets); and efficient logistics. This entails the enrolment of technical expertise and skills at the level of logistics, clean winemaking (as opposed to unique or fancy) and the application of 'Smart viticulture' (inspired by the influential Australian consultant Richard Smart). Most of the South African operators I interviewed report that UK retailers communicate very specific demands on intrinsic traits and packaging to their suppliers when buying basic-quality wine: they tell them what to bottle, what kind of label and cork to use, the weight and shape of the bottle, and the recycling solutions. Specifications on intrinsic quality at this level can be objectively measured or described easily for purchasing purposes (residual sugar, colour, levels of acidity). These factors are then translated into specific winemaking techniques and further upstream into systematic viticulture practices.

In recent years, however, the package of basic quality that needs to be provided by suppliers has become even more demanding and goes well beyond the intrinsic quality of the wine. One of the main UK retailers, for example, has implemented retail-ready packaging in wine, which entails unloading from the pallet to shelf in one move.

Retailers are also moving towards screw cap and synthetic closures to minimize returns for 'corked wine'. In terms of food safety, in addition to meeting EU food safety rules, suppliers are increasingly under pressure to conform to food safety and quality management procedures through British Retailer Consortium, International Food Standard and/or ISO 22000 certifications (Ponte, 2009). In relation to logistics, UK retailers are working towards shorter lead times on promotion. As a result, UK-based agents and marketers are trying to exert more direct control over logistics. Previously, they sold wine free on board to retailers; now, some have started selling 'in-bond delivery' in the UK. This way, retailers can place a call with a very short lead time for delivery. Retailers are seeing themselves increasingly as shelf-space providers. Suppliers can log into the retailer's supply management system and monitor movements in retail space and stocks, and order replenishment themselves. These processes entail packaging and logistics expertise and knowledge in wine production and marketing.

Once basic quality is assured, price and promotional sales are the next aspects in the exercise of bargaining power. Social and environmental certifications do not play a major role in this basic-quality bracket, nor do personality, geographical origin or terroir. Wine is offered under a brand, often with the indication of a combination of varieties, but price is more important than brand recognition. External endorsements may play a role, but in-store promotion and placement are far more important. Due to increasing concentration in the retail segment of the wine GVC, buyers have been seeking to purchase from fewer traders/merchants who can deliver a wider portfolio of wines from different geographic regions and at different price points (Ponte and Ewert, 2009). Thus, wine producers who can deliver the volume necessary to enter the retailer circuit are more likely to resort to third-party certification. This places increased pressure to deliver these additional features without a premium price or with a very limited one – and increases buyers' bargaining power. Many of these producers may not be necessarily affected by sustainability demands in the basic wine segment, but are still required to deliver sustainability certifications for the mid-range part of their portfolios (Ponte, 2009).

Overall, comparing the approximately three decades before and after 1990 (T1 and T2), we can observe increasing bargaining power by retailers vis-à-vis large merchant firms in the wine GVC, but also the weakened position of producers, with the partial exception of top-quality wine producers. Sustainability management in this industry is starting to come into the picture, but is not as prominent as in the coffee and biofuels GVCs. As a result, sustainability is having a relatively minor impact on how the GVC is governed.

Bargaining Power in the Coffee GVC

Historically, bargaining power in the coffee GVC had been heavily shaped by institutional power dynamics (see below) under an international regulatory regime that lasted between 1962 and 1989 (T1). Under the International Coffee Agreement (ICA) regime, collective power relations were relatively balanced between producing and consuming countries, thus strengthening the bilateral bargaining power of suppliers, farmers and their cooperatives (Talbot, 2004). The end of the ICA led to a general weakening of bargaining power by producing countries and their producers. In the following three decades (T2), the increasing concentration in the roasting and trading functions of the coffee GVC compounded this dynamic (Daviron and Ponte, 2005).

Globally, most coffee for in-home consumption is purchased in supermarkets. The food retail sector is highly concentrated in the US, UK and Northern Europe, and plays a dominant role in food and beverage GVCs. Yet through consolidation and with massive investment in advertising their brands, coffee roasters have managed to maintain strong bargaining power in the coffee GVC even vis-à-vis retailers (Ponte, 2002b). This has happened in spite of the development of private coffee labels by supermarkets and the emergence of the specialty coffee market. In the late 1990s, the top two roasting groups combined (Nestlé and Philip Morris) controlled 49 per cent of the world market share for roasted and instant coffees. The top five groups controlled 69 per cent of the market (see Table 3.3). Nestlé dominated the soluble market, with a market share of 56 per cent (Ponte, 2002b). In the late 2010s, the coffee GVC overall is still dominated by two groups, in partially different guises: Nestlé and JAB Holdings. JAB owns Jacobs Douwe Egberts (JDE), itself the result of a 2015 merger of Mondelēz's coffee division (formerly Philip Morris) and D. E. Master Blenders 1753 (Panhuysen and Pierrot, 2014). JAB also acquired Keurig Green Mountain in 2015, which in 2014 was ranked as the third largest roaster group (Grabs, 2017: 9), and a number of specialty roasters and coffee chains (such as Peet's Coffee & Tea,

Caribou Coffee and Intelligentsia) – putting together a strong portfolio catering for a wide variety of quality and market segments.

The next group of roasters in the top rankings (Smucker's, Strauss and Tchibo, followed by Lavazza and Starbucks) together have a market share of 10 per cent, less than half of the top two groups each (see Table 3.3). In this second layer, Smucker's has been very active in M&A activity, acquiring some of the main Procter & Gamble coffee brands in 2002 and 2008, and Sara Lee's coffee and tea portfolio in 2011 (Grabs, 2017). While Nestlé is still dominant in the instant coffee market, it faces fierce competition from JAB Holdings in the fast-growing and high-margin[12] single-serve capsule market, which is dominated by Nespresso in Europe and Keuring Green Mountain (part of JAB Holdings) in the US (Grabs, 2017). Other segments, however, are led by different roasters: out-of-home specialty coffee by Starbucks, and traditional espresso coffee blends by Lavazza and Illy. In May 2018, Nestlé and Starbucks announced a marketing alliance, with Nestlé spending USD 7.15 billion for the right to market its products, including their capsules, through Starbucks in view of boosting its sagging Nespresso sales in the US.[13]

International traders have also gone through a major restructuring in the past two decades. ED&F Man has taken over Volcafé, ECOM (previously Esteve) acquired Cargill's coffee division and other trading firms, and some trading companies based in the Global South have become much more important (such as Olam). In 1998, the top five international coffee traders controlled 46 per cent of the global green coffee market, led by two large traders (Neumann and Volcafé) and followed by Cargill, Esteve and Aron (Ponte, 2002b). By 2014, this level of concentration has remained similar, with the top five controlling 48 per cent of the international green coffee market, and the top four controlling about 10 per cent each (Neumann, ED&F Man, ECOM and Olam), followed by Louis Dreyfus (Grabs, 2017). These large international traders have invested heavily in producing countries. They own processing plants and storage facilities – some also own large estates. While vertical integration into estate production is not new for Neumann, it is a relatively new expansion for Olam and ED&F Man. International traders also play an important role in managing information flows related to sustainability demands that are placed on farmers, and in implementing sustainability certifications and related projects (Grabs et al., 2016; Millard, 2017).

Despite the relative fragmentation of the roaster segment of the coffee GVC and the continuing consolidation in the international trader segment, mainstream roasters have maintained their upper hand in terms of bargaining power over other GVC actors during T2. This is also indicated by the dramatic increase in net financing terms roasters apply to international traders. JDE, for example, is reported to have increased these terms from 30 days to 120 days or longer. This means that international traders have to wait up to four months to be paid after delivering their coffee, and thus have to expand their credit lines and spend more on interest payments. This is having a cascade effect, with traders demanding longer payment terms from their own suppliers as well.[14]

The main challenge to the dominant bargaining power of roasters during T2 has been the emergence of the specialty coffee market since the late 1980s and early 1990s. This segment of the industry has been growing healthily in the past few decades, spurring a so-called 'latte revolution' (Ponte, 2002b). Both coffee bar chains and independent micro-roasters have spread dramatically, although the relative coffee content of the final consumption experience offered in these outlets is low (Daviron and Ponte, 2005; Luttinger and Dicum, 2011). The latte revolution entailed: the multiplication and increasing market value of single-origin, direct trade, high-quality and unique coffees; the multiplication of coffees bearing various kinds of sustainability certifications (Giovannucci and Ponte, 2005; Levy et al., 2016; MacGregor et al., 2017; Manning and Reinecke, 2016; Reinecke et al., 2012);[15] and a constant need to discover and bring formerly unknown coffee origins to the consumer, and/or selling the physical property of these coffees with a 'just cause', preferably with the mediation of a celebrity (Richey and Ponte, 2011).

In the specialty coffee market, especially the part that is still operated by independent, smaller-scale roasters and coffee bars, the bargaining power of roasters and coffee shops is indeed less pronounced vis-à-vis traders and farmers and their cooperatives. Some larger coffee estates and cooperatives (especially in Latin America) run sophisticated operations and have great knowledge of quality and price premia – they attend regional and international trade fairs, and may even sell their own roasted coffee. Social media platforms, Internet direct sales and direct trade relationships (Schroeder, 2015; Vicol et al., 2018) have made it easier for boutique roasters to order smaller batches of specific coffees from dedicated farms and cooperatives in producing countries. And coffee excellence competitions and specialty auctions have raised the profile and market clout of producers in this segment (Grabs, 2017).

While initially traditional roasters were slow in reacting to these changes, in the past decade they have made massive investments in recapturing at least part of the high-margin specialty market: Nestlé, for example, has developed its high-end single-serve capsule Nespresso line, coupled with the establishment of branded boutiques around the world. Starbucks, one of the architects of the latte revolution, has now grown to become the sixth largest roaster globally. It is also starting to set up micro-roasteries in some of its locations to fence off the latest vogue in the coffee retail market – bars offering coffee freshly roasted on-site.

Overall, sustainability content has become more important between T1 and T2 as major roasters now require third-party sustainability certifications for an important proportion of their purchases (see Figure 3.5 and Table 3.5). An outlier is Smucker's, a roaster mainly focused on coffee markets in the Global South, where demand for sustainability content is still limited. Some roasters have been developing their own sustainability verification systems, which allow them to obtain precious information on suppliers' cost structures as well, thus strengthening roasters' bargaining power and ability to extract value in higher-margin markets (Elder et al., 2014; Grabs, 2017; Muradian and Pelupessy, 2005). These dynamics suggest that the distinction between mainstream and specialty coffee markets is becoming less clear-cut. Thus, while specialty coffee actors had been taming some of the bargaining power of mainstream roasters, a powerful reaction by major roasting groups is under way, in view of regaining a better bargaining position.

Bargaining Power in the Biofuels GVC

With the exception of Brazil, substantial developments in the biofuels GVC can be traced to the last two decades. As indicated above, the periodization used for comparison in this GVC refers to the decade before and after 2007, when the sustainability of biofuels started to be re-conceptualized. International alliances in the private sector and an increasingly complex web of cross-regional investments have emerged in the biofuels GVC, starting tentatively during T1 and spreading dramatically during T2 – in terms of size, number and geographical spread of international joint ventures and the new involvement of global agro-food traders, oil majors, auto manufacturers and the aviation industry in biofuels (Ponte, 2014a).

The global players involved in some of these investments exert dramatic bargaining power in other GVCs, but are still relatively new to biofuels, or had previously played only a marginal role in it. Several global agro-food traders (Bunge, Noble Group, ADM and Louis Dreyfus, and to a less extent ED&F Man) have developed major interests in biofuels, while Cargill is establishing 'biofuel support services'. These processes have often led to increased vertical integration in the industry, in order to secure supply, control costs to maximize returns, and ensure processes and sources of supply of certified sustainable biofuels for the European market. This means that bargaining power is still fairly balanced among different kinds of actors in the biofuels GVC, although blenders/distributors have gained some traction by being able to demand sustainability certification in markets where regulation requires it, and by passing on the implementation costs upstream to the producers of feedstock. Blenders can leverage sustainability certification or verification to select what kinds of biofuel they source and from where (e.g. sugar cane-based ethanol from Brazil rather than corn-based ethanol from the US). Also, there are signs of producers of next-generation biofuels (e.g. derived from cellulosic feedstock or waste) increasing their bargaining power vis-à-vis blenders and distributors (and in relation to producers of first-generation biofuels) due to recent regulatory adjustments in the EU and US that provide next-generation biofuels with special quotas or mandates within overall biofuel targets (see the section on institutional power).

Bargaining Power – Key Findings

Figure 3.7 summarizes some of the key findings on how bargaining power (dyadic, direct) has evolved in the three selected GVCs between two reference periods that are specific to each value chain. This exercise is focused on a simplified representation of the two key nodes in each value chain. In *wine*, product differentiation was already present during T1, with retailers and merchants being relatively specialized in different quality segments. The bargaining power between them

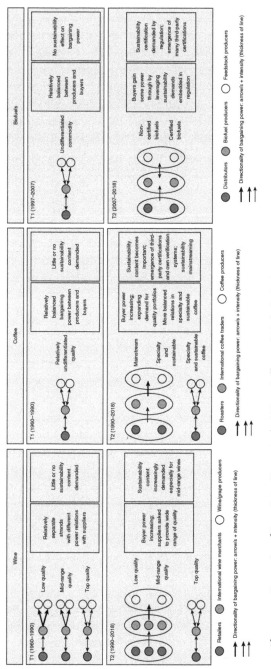

Figure 3.7 Dynamics of Bargaining Power in the Wine, Coffee and Biofuels GVCs

Source: Own analysis, based on design developed by Sturgeon in Dallas et al. (2017)

was fairly equilibrate at that time. Bargaining power was also relatively balanced between merchants and wine/grape producers in the high-quality segment – with increasing power exercised by merchants over producers as we move down the quality scale. During T2, retailers expanded their product quality portfolio demands, also competing directly with smaller wine shops. This required merchants to increase their quality portfolio range, with cascade effects as we move upstream in the GVC towards producers. This has strengthened bargaining power by retailers over merchants, and by merchants over producers, with the exception of top-quality producers. Sustainability issues have not played an important role in this evolution.

In *coffee*, relatively balanced bargaining power during T1 for a relatively undifferentiated product (due to the ICA) was followed by a process of quality portfolio widening during T2, with similar effects as observed in wine. Roasters increased their power over international traders, and the latter over producers. In the specialty coffee segment, however, power relations remained relatively more balanced, and this partially tamed the power of mainstream roasters, at least for a period of time. However, current trends suggest that roasters' bargaining power is increasing again. Retailers are not shown in the figure because their bargaining power vis-à-vis roasters has remained relatively constant – roasters are still able to hold their ground via consolidation and massive investment in advertising their brands, and in spite of the development of private coffee labels by supermarkets. As a result, supermarkets' retail margins for coffee are generally lower than for the average food portfolio (Daviron and Ponte, 2005). In some countries, such as the US, retailers sometimes sell coffee even at a loss in order to generate traffic. Retailers need to stock certain coffee brands because consumers expect them to do so. They can attract customers with relatively cheap coffee and entice them to buy other (higher-margin) items during their visit (Luttinger and Dicum, 2011; Pendergrast, 2010). Sustainability certification and verification systems are becoming increasingly important, and thus are part and parcel of the power dynamics observed in the coffee GVC.

In biofuels, product quality differentiation has occurred mainly in relation to sustainability certification, which has come into play during T2. Bargaining power in T1 was relatively balanced between distributors/blenders and biofuel producers, and between biofuel producers and feedstock farmers. During T2, the relation between blenders and biofuel producers has not changed significantly. However, biofuel blenders can now leverage sustainability certification or verification needs to select what kinds of biofuel they want to source, and in turn what kind of feedstock goes into its production, and next-generation biofuel producers are taking advantage of special treatment given to them in EU and US regulations. Although the GVC is still fragmented and bargaining power still fairly balanced, regulation provides blenders and distributors with extra leverage over biofuel and feedstock suppliers.

In all three GVCs, systemically important buyers (retailers in wine, coffee roasters, and biofuel blenders and distributors) have increased their bargaining power over their first-tier suppliers (international wine merchants, international coffee traders, and biofuel producers), which in turn have increased their bargaining power over their own suppliers (wine/grape producers, coffee producers), with the exception of biofuels, where feedstock producer associations in the EU, US and Brazil have held their ground. In wine, sustainability has not yet played a major role in shaping bargaining power. In coffee, it has become important, first addressed through third-party certification, then with roasters setting up their own verification systems, which are then implemented on the ground through international traders and their contractors/exporting branches in producing countries. In biofuels, sustainability standards are mandated by regulation but have had only a partial influence in shaping bargaining power along the GVC.

Demonstrative Power

Demonstrative Power in the Wine GVC

Both the trade literature and my own interviews with industry operators suggest that for *top-quality wines*, demonstrative power (dyadic, diffuse) has been particularly important in shaping GVC governance – through endorsement by wine writers, judges and specialist publications. The judgement of wine quality in the context of demonstrative power rests on the aesthetic approach of an endorser towards a wine. Important factors for top wines are ratings by US wine writer Robert Parker (as in his *Wine Advocate*)[16] and by other influential publications such as *Wine Spectator* and *Decanter*. When opinion is the main approach to quality, sustainability elements are not prominent. As sustainability cannot be tasted in the wine, it only features (when at all) as an additional information factor in the scoring sheet, but does not have an important weight in determining the magic score that communicates 'quality' (say, a 96-point rating in Robert Parker's 100-point scale). Demonstrative power also operates through the translation of aesthetic preferences into actual winemaking and viticulture practices that can deliver specific wine styles and profiles. Therefore, the rise and diffusion of particular aesthetics of wine also depend on actors, such as Michel Rolland and other 'flying winemakers', who can deliver portable solutions to winemakers and viticulturists around the world and act as cogs of demonstrative power (on flying winemakers, see Lagendijk, 2004).

Demonstrative power in the wine GVC was exerted by elite wine producers in some of the top regions of the 'Old World' (France, Italy, Spain, Portugal) in the decades before 1990 (T1). This was reinforced or challenged by individual journalists and professional tasters through their reviews. But the gradual ideational creation of the 'new wine consumer' (see below under constitutive power) has revolutionized the dynamics of demonstrative power in the past three decades or so (T2) (Itçaina et al., 2016). In sum, demonstrative power is strongly wielded by wine tasters/scorers (e.g. Robert Parker), marketers, and 'flying winemakers' and other consultants (e.g. viticulturists, marketers), who move from one property or country to another to help wine producers achieve whatever wine styles are fashionable at the time. These actors have shaped the new wine styles and aesthetic preferences that producers need to follow, especially in the basic- and mid-range-quality brackets. In other words, we have observed a movement from *supplier-driven* demonstrative effects to *demand-driven* demonstrative effects – which itself consolidates the shift of bargaining power towards large-scale and diversified wine buyers. Sustainability issues do not feature prominently in these dynamics.

Demonstrative Power in the Coffee GVC

During T1, mainstream roasters were focused on selling large quantities of relatively homogeneous and undifferentiated blends of mediocre to poor quality. One after another, major coffee roasters had lost their regional image and their focus on localized taste preferences a long time before. In the US, regional roasters such as Folgers,

Hills Bros. and Maxwell House became national in scope and then started being bought by food conglomerates as early as the 1920s (Luttinger and Dicum, 2011; Pendergrast, 2010). When they became part of major industrial empires, they moved away from a focus on quality and locality. They started to concentrate on consistency in price, packaging and flavour. As a result, all major roasters one after another homogenized blends, started to use cheaper coffee blends, and cut down roasting times to reduce weight loss and mask the poor quality of the beans.

During T2 (from 1989 onwards), demonstrative power started taking a very different shape with the emergence of specialty coffee and the role that Starbucks and other pioneer roasters in the US West Coast played in this process. Starbucks was founded in 1971 in Seattle, following the steps of Peet's, another quality roaster based in Berkeley. Like many other specialty operators, Starbucks spent most of the 1980s building a loyal customer base and educating consumers on the qualities of fine coffees. The breakthrough that made Starbucks a stunning success was creating a café atmosphere where customers could hang out and consume an experience at a place that was neither home nor work. This happened at the same time as other consumer products moved from mass production and marketing to being recast as more authentic, flavourful and healthy (craft beer, specialty breads, organic vegetables). By combining 'ambience' and the possibility for consumers to choose type, origin, roast, and grind, and by selling coffee 'pre-packaged with lifestyle signifiers' (Luttinger and Dicum, 2011: 153), Starbucks managed to partially de-commoditize coffee. In 1997, Starbucks was operating 2,000 outlets (mostly directly owned) in six countries. By 2017, it had over 24,000 outlets in 70 countries.[17]

Starbucks had a massive demonstrative effect in the industry by inspiring a large number of other smaller roasters and café chains. It was also one of the early movers in purchasing certified sustainable coffee (especially organic and fair trade). Later on, it developed its own sustainability criteria, following other pioneer companies such as Green Mountain Coffee Roasters and Rapunzel Pure Organics, which had already done so in the mid-1990s. In 2002, Starbucks was the first multinational company in the coffee industry to announce that it had developed a preferred supplier system for green coffee purchasing. The pilot programme was developed in collaboration with

Conservation International, and preferred suppliers were given purchase priority. The costs incurred by suppliers in transitioning to such a system was mitigated by an interim financial incentive programme (Daviron and Ponte, 2005). This incentive system, however, was terminated at the end of the pilot period. With the formal establishment of the Starbucks C.A.F.E. Practices (Coffee and Farmer Equity Practices) programme, only the qualifying criteria remained operational. The C.A.F.E. system includes 200 indicators on economic, environmental and social performance, and has a separate scorecard for smallholder producers. SCS Global Services is currently in charge of running the verification system.[18]

Until the early 2000s, traditional roasters had been slow in responding to the demonstrative power that was sweeping the specialty and sustainable coffee market. But a new phase started in 2003, when Procter & Gamble, in response to direct shareholder pressure, announced that in the following year it was going to buy at least 1 million pounds of fair trade coffee. Through a domino effect, Kraft and Rainforest Alliance then announced a multi-year arrangement that included the purchase of over 5 million pounds of certified coffee in 2004. Albert Heijn and other large European supermarket chains started requiring UTZ certification for a portion of their purchases. Since then, most of the major coffee roasters have been purchasing considerable amounts of certified sustainable coffee (see Figure 3.5 and Table 3.5) and have adopted their own sustainability standards and verification systems. They have also acquired smaller specialty roasters and café chains, and normally retain their original brand profile.

While Starbucks spurred a dramatic effect in relation to specialty and sustainable coffee, another demonstrative effect went the other way, as the company gradually adopted more mainstream corporate strategies. It acquired competing chains, opened outlets in neighbourhoods with traditional cafés to drive them out of business, and entered into joint marketing programmes with other corporate giants (e.g. PepsiCo, Barnes & Noble, United Airlines). In 2018, it concluded a major marketing and distribution agreement with Nestlé. By becoming another large corporation, by providing a homogenized retail experience with a consistent but not exceptionally good product, and by commodifying sustainability, Starbucks in many ways became the opposite of what independent coffee houses perceive themselves to be.

Demonstrative Power in the Biofuels GVC

The flurry of new investments that took place in the past decade or so (T2) in the biofuels GVC suggests an important role for demonstrative power, as corporations that compete in other industries entered the biofuel craze and mimicked cooperation, consortium and joint venture models from each other. This involved a disparate combination of actors in the automobile, aviation, biotechnology and energy industries. Some of the key initiatives that had strong demonstrative effects include: Renessen (a joint venture of Cargill and Monsanto), which is seeking to integrate animal feed and biofuel production where the feedstock can be used for both purposes (Borras et al., 2010: 577) and to develop a dedicated GM corn crop with higher oil content (White and Dasgupta, 2010: 604); a cooperation effort by Monsanto and Syngenta, which have developed GM maize varieties specifically for processing into ethanol; Cosan and Shell, which have formed a large joint venture in Brazil that is investing heavily in the country and exploring international investments as well; and British Airways and Solena Biofuels, which started producing aviation biofuels from waste, and were then followed by many other initiatives of the same kind (Henriksen and Ponte, 2018). However, and not surprisingly in a relatively young industry, many other investments and initiatives have folded (e.g. Abengoa, KiOR, SEKAB) (on the latter, see Havnevik and Haaland, 2011).

Demonstrative effects are also evident among major oil companies, which are also investing in biofuel research (Chevron, ExxonMobil and Shell have financed major university research facilities) (Smith, 2010), in ethanol production facilities and/or in integrated distribution of fuels (Shell-Cosan, Petrobras and BP). Aircraft manufacturers (Boeing, Airbus and Embraer), major global airlines (Lufthansa, Air France–KLM, British Airways and several US airlines) and the US Navy are carrying out projects for the production of 'drop-in' biofuels for aviation (Henriksen and Ponte, 2018). Developers of GM crops (Syngenta, Monsanto, DuPont, Dow, Bayer and BASF) have been working on feedstocks dedicated to biofuels through cooperation agreements with global agro-food traders. Venture capital companies are bankrolling the biotech boom in platform technologies and synthetic biology, and some of these start-ups are being bought up by oil and agrochemical giants. CGIAR and global philanthropies (the Gates Foundation) are funding major research initiatives.

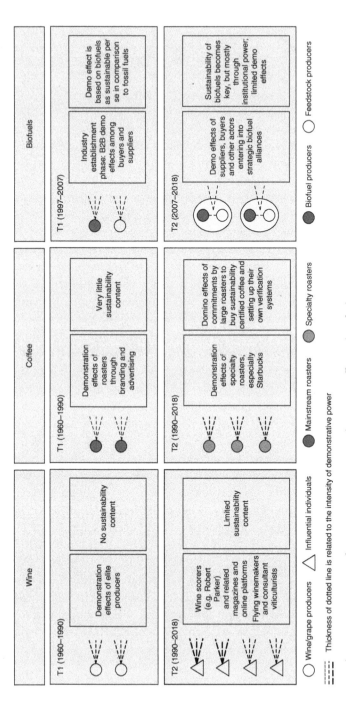

Figure 3.8 Dynamics of Demonstrative Power in the Wine, Coffee and Biofuels GVCs

Source: Own analysis, based on design developed by Sturgeon in Dallas et al. (2017)

In sum, demonstrative power is clearly at play in the biofuels GVC, but differently from wine and coffee; it has been wielded by players in several different functional positions of the value chain and has been underpinned in no small measure by government support (see below on institutional power).

Demonstrative Power – Key Findings

Figure 3.8 summarizes some of the key findings on how demonstrative power (dyadic, diffuse) has evolved in the three GVCs over time. In wine, demonstrative power has had major impacts on how quality is constituted and valued – during T1, it was wielded by elite wine producers in Old World countries; during T2, it was exercised by wine critics, publishers and 'flying winemakers'. In coffee, during T1, demonstrative power operated through the corporate strategies of major roasters, which were focused on providing a heavily advertised, homogenous and relatively low-quality branded product; during T2, specialty roasters (and especially Starbucks) imparted major demonstrative power on other operators in the GVC – this led to the multiplication of small roasters, café chains and quality offerings, and later to M&A reactions by mainstream roasters in view of recapturing market share and increasing their margins. In biofuels, during T1, the demonstrative effect had to do with new entry and/or expansion in a period of industry formation; during T2, the nature and form of demonstrative power related to strategic business alliances and joint ventures.

Sustainability factors played a very different role in the exercise of demonstrative power in these three GVCs. It had very little influence in the wine GVC in both periods. It had no role during T1 in coffee, and then a very substantial one during T2 – when roasters, one after another, first announced commitments to purchase certified sustainable coffee, and then developed their own verification systems. Sustainability was already important in the biofuels GVC during T1, when it facilitated industry expansion on the basis of an argument that biofuels were better than fossil fuels when it came to GHG emissions. It then became essential during T2, when the sustainability of biofuel production itself was questioned. This transformation, however, was led by institutional power (see below) via a wide array of regulatory measures, rather than by the demonstrative effects of GVC actors.

Institutional Power

Institutional Power in the Wine GVC

Institutional power (collective, direct) in the wine GVC during T1 (1960–1990) was most clearly exercised by the public sector through local, national and regional regulation, such as production quotas and planting registers, distillation subsidies, and production rules dictated by *appellation d'origine contrôlée* systems (Itçaina et al., 2016). Furthermore, industry associations and wine exhibitions, fairs and competitions were not only vectors of demonstrative power, but also repositories of institutional power through their role in the negotiation and (re)definition of rules and practices that may or may not become widely accepted (see below on constitutive power). Regulatory interventions and institutions have been historically important in wine-producing countries and their districts (Hira, 2013), particularly in Old World countries. They originated first in France and other Old World countries, were embedded in EU regulation, but also spread in different forms in New World countries (Giuliani et al., 2010, 2011; Hira, 2013; Ponte and Ewert, 2009). However, during T2 (1990–2018), pressure to adapt regulation to new consumption patterns and wine styles (see under constitutive power) and to recover market share from New World wines led to major regulatory adjustments in Old World producing countries, especially with the 2008 EU wine market reform. This has included a simplification of categories for geographical indications, the permission to sell 'table wines' under a brand name, the possibility to indicate grape varietals, and the abandonment of the main forms of production support (Itçaina et al., 2016).

Indications of geographical origin were central instruments of institutional power in the wine GVC during T1. The organizations that handle them seek to build a sense of (sometimes romanticized) connection to 'place', where trust is embedded in specific agro-ecological and climatic conditions, processing systems that are local and typical, specific relations to the environment, and attached to the special skills of people who grow grapes and make wine in that area. At the same time, there are vast differences in the wine-producing world on what an indication of geographical origin actually means and how it is operationalized. With the growth of wine production and exports of New World countries during T2, more generic indications of geographical origin have come to the market. These transmit information more akin to a brand than territory, and thus the expertise and knowledge enrolled in the process of selling quality to buyers are mainly those of marketing and branding. At the same time, some indications of geographic origin in Old World countries have seen a rapid increase in their jurisdictional areas in order to respond to these challenges (e.g. Chianti, Prosecco), thus somewhat diluting their content.

During T2, as mentioned in the background section on the wine GVC, a number of industry associations have also developed a variety of broad sustainability initiatives and certification systems in some wine-producing countries – thus imparting a degree of institutional power in identifying and marketing these features in their wines. Some of these initiatives are supported by public institutions (e.g. SOStain is supported by the Italian Ministry of the Environment and Development, and Sustainable Wine South Africa by the South Africa Wine and Spirit Board). Third-party environmental sustainability certifications for wine, such as organic and biodynamic, have become relatively more important in mid-quality wines, especially in markets where such demand is increasing (the UK, Northern Europe, the US). Recent survey data indicate that eco-labels on wine bottles can indeed gain consumer attention, but they are not sufficient to stimulate purchases if the wines are considered of very low or very high quality (Sogari et al., 2016a, 2016b). While sustainability certifications are too generic to leverage uniqueness in relation to a specific terroir, they fit quite well with a more generalized approach of geographical indications in mid-range quality wines, where they do not interfere with brand or grape recognition at the retail point. However, retailers often require a specific certification or verification system (such as wine made with organic grapes, or sustainability certification by the California Sustainable Winegrowing Alliance) without paying an extra premium to producers, who then have to absorb the extra costs.

In sum, most of the reforms that characterize the current period (T2) have moved institutional power *away* from benefiting producers and their associations – and in favour of marketers, merchants and retailers. Sustainability concerns have not been a major mover of these regulatory reforms.

Institutional Power in the Coffee GVC

Coffee was one of the first commodities for which control of world trade was attempted, starting in 1902 with the valorization process carried out by the Brazilian state of São Paulo. This process involved state action to raise the price of coffee, which was made possible at that time by the large share of production (between 75 and 90 per cent) of São Paulo in terms of world coffee production (Lucier, 1988: 117). Pre-World War II attempts at manipulating the world coffee market were all centred around Brazil. In the post-war period, control schemes involved other Latin American countries as well. The first International Coffee Agreement (ICA) was signed in 1962 and included most producing and consuming countries as signatories. Under the ICA regulatory system (1962–1989) (T1), a target price (or a price band) for coffee was set, and export quotas were allocated to each producer. When the indicator price calculated by the International Coffee Organization (ICO) rose over the set price, quotas were relaxed; when it fell below the set price, quotas were tightened. If an extremely high rise of coffee prices took place (as in 1975–1977), quotas were abandoned until prices fell down within the band. Although there were problems with this system, most analysts agree that it was successful in raising and stabilizing coffee prices (Bates, 1999; Daviron and Ponte, 2005; Talbot, 2004).

At the same time, the ICA system was progressively undermined by freeriding and squabbling over quotas. Other problems that affected it were the increasing volume of coffee traded with (or through) non-member importing countries (at lower prices), the continuing fragmentation of the geography of production, and the increasing heterogeneity of development models – as Brazil and Indonesia moved towards more export-oriented industrial strategies. Furthermore, quotas remained relatively stable because they were costly to negotiate. As a result, the mix of coffee supplied by producers tended to remain stable, while from the 1980s onwards consumers in the US progressively switched from soluble coffees (employing a high proportion of robusta) to ground coffees (using a higher proportion of Arabicas). The rigidity on the supply side worried roasters, who feared that competitors could get access to cheaper coffee from non-member countries. This undermined their cooperation within the ICA system. Finally, the Cold War politics of the US in relation to Latin America changed in the 1980s. The US stopped perceiving the Left in Brazil as a real threat, and the rigidity of quotas meant that the US administration could not punish its enemies in Central America (Bates, 1999). The combined result of these changes led to the failed renewal of the ICA in 1989 (Talbot, 2004).

The end of the ICA regime profoundly affected the balance of institutional power in the coffee GVC, and in turn reshaped bargaining power between individual operators during T2 to the benefit of consuming country-based actors (including their agents based in producing countries) and to the detriment of coffee farmers, local traders and producing country governments. The end of the ICA regime also meant that the bureaucracy that was needed to monitor exports and ensure compliance with quota restrictions was no longer needed. This, coupled with the general switch in economic thinking in the 1980s and 1990s away from public intervention in markets, led to the dismantling of coffee boards, institutes and other quasi-governmental bodies that regulated export sales in many countries. As a result, the capabilities of producing countries to control exports and to build up stocks weakened. At the same time, other collective actors became more important in the institutional field, especially the Specialty Coffee Association of America (SCAA), which is dominated by consuming-country GVC actors. These factors together suggest changes in institutional power that consolidated the bargaining power of buyers, and roasters in particular, vis-à-vis producers.

However, several important producing countries still support their coffee value chains through enforceable (Colombia, Costa Rica, Côte d'Ivoire) or suggested (Brazil) minimum prices for export contracts. Some countries still have strong cooperatives (Colombia, Mexico), operate export auctions (Kenya, Tanzania, Ethiopia), regulate export quality and/or require licences for exporters (Grabs, 2017). Several other support mechanisms are still being applied or have been reinstated, such as price stabilization funds, disease prevention support, producer income assistance, and programmes supporting improvement in quality and sustainability (Millard, 2017). These national-level interventions by coffee institutions and their financial backers are, at least in part, restoring some producer-led institutional power, and thus partially taming the increasing bargaining power of international traders/exporters, roasters and retailers (Grabs, 2017).

While during the ICA period sustainability issues rarely featured in institutional discussions, since the mid-1990s coffee has seen a proliferation of sustainability standards, certifications and verification systems. Coffee was actually one of the first internationally traded products where collective efforts were undertaken to develop standards on processes that address socio-economic and environmental concerns. As highlighted in the background section above, this has been accompanied by the growth of a large industry of standard developers, certification and accreditation agencies, and related service and consulting outfits, which have an embedded interest in the continuing operation of sustainability certification initiatives. The emergence of these systems suggests that institutional power, originally exerted by governments in producing and consuming countries, is now partially wielded by transnational sustainability initiatives.

Institutional Power in the Biofuels GVC

Institutional power is key in understanding the dynamics of the biofuels GVC. Since the 1990s, governments in Brazil, the US and the EU (the main biofuel-producing and -consuming countries/regions) have been heavily promoting biofuels, often under pressure from industry and agricultural lobbies. These policies have been justified in relation to climate change mitigation (especially in the EU), energy security (especially in the US) and farmer support and rural development (in Brazil, but also in the US and the EU). The allure of biofuels from a public policy perspective is that they can be framed as being able to address climate change, energy security and rural development at once, without fundamentally altering energy consumption practices (Lehrer, 2010; Mol, 2015; Schleifer, 2013; Smith, 2010; Stattman et al., 2013). Most kinds of biofuels are also seen as attractive because they can provide 'drop-in' solutions – they can be distributed through existing infrastructure (pipelines, storage facilities, fuel distribution networks) and end-use technology (internal combustion engines) (Ponte, 2014a).

From the late 1990s to around 2006/07 (T1), government interventions enacted policies that effectively forged the various national and, in the case of the EU, regional foundations of an increasingly global biofuel value chain. The EU and US set minimum mandates on the use of biofuels and provided a range of subsidies, research funding and investment facilities to farmers, processors, blenders, biotech companies and universities. Early Brazilian government support of the 1970s and 1980s had waned by the end of the century, but was revitalized in the 2000s. Agricultural lobbies (e.g. US corn farmers, German rapeseed farmers), climate change activists seeking non-fossil fuel alternatives, and government departments concerned with energy and security provided a unique combination of interests that pushed biofuel-friendly policies in a generally favourable political environment (Dauvergne and Neville, 2009, 2010). This led to a boost of investments in farming and processing in Brazil, the US and the EU, but also in large-scale land for biofuel production in Africa and South East Asia. Following decades of neglect in agricultural and rural development, governments saw large-scale investment in land by domestic and international actors as a welcome boost in infrastructure provision and foreign exchange generation (White and Dasgupta, 2010).

During T2, as criticism mounted on biofuels (see below under constitutive power), the EU enacted demands for sustainability standards for the production, trade and use of biofuels in member countries. The US also fine-tuned its subsidies and regulation to increase support for next-generation biofuels relative to first-generation biofuels. And Brazil increased its public relations effort aimed at showing that sugar cane-based ethanol production in the country has indeed a positive impact on GHG emission reductions. Thus, sustainability in the biofuels GVC has become a 'must-have' feature in main consumption markets. This is because sustainability standards play a key role in the basic definition of its tradability, and are thus a key feature of institutional power dynamics in the biofuels GVC.

In the US, the 2005 Energy Bill introduced a Renewable Fuel Standard (RFS1), which mandated the production of 7.5 billion gallons of fuel from renewable resources by 2012. This led to dramatic increases in corn acreage (to record levels) and in the number and capacity of bio-refineries (Gillon, 2010), but also to the entry of large agro-food corporations in the sector. The 2007 Energy Independence and Security Act ramped up the target to 36 billion gallons by 2022, and included for the first time binding environmental criteria (Lehrer, 2010; Renckens et al., 2017). As farm interest groups and sustainable agriculture lobbies increasingly focused on biofuels, the 2008 Farm Bill included provisions for biofuel tax credits for producers and blenders, and incentives for feedstock research and for the construction of next-generation biofuel production facilities (Lehrer, 2010). However, in the late 2000s, a backlash against biofuels from environmental and social NGOs led the Obama administration to recalibrate its targets. In parallel to this process, major private sector players (ADM, DuPont, Monsanto) established the 'Alliance for Abundant Food and Energy' to further promote biofuels within the US government in ways that decouple them from food-related concerns (Dauvergne and Neville, 2009: 1099). This slightly revised policy discourse on biofuels in the US has provided stronger ground for the development of next-generation biofuel technologies.

In 2010, a revised version of the US RFS (RFS2) came into operation, which classified renewable fuels according to different categories and set volume requirements for each. RFS2 incorporated GHG emissions from indirect land use change (ILUC) as well. For every gallon of biofuel created, a producer earns one Renewable Identification Number (RIN) that is specific to a biofuel category. Despite the general aversion of the Trump administration to renewable energy, intensive lobbying by Midwestern lawmakers and representatives of the corn industry ensured an actual slight increase of the biofuel targets for 2018.[19] In sum, the biofuel value chain in the US was essentially forged institutionally through government intervention in the 2000s (through lobbying efforts of agricultural and agro-processing industries) and has been increasingly shaped by sustainability concerns in the 2010s.

Within the EU, three main national-level initiatives exploring or seeking to regulate sustainability in the biofuel industry took place in the second half of the 2000s: the Cramer Commission (in the Netherlands, in 2005/06) (Partzsch, 2011); the Renewable Transport Fuel Obligation (in the UK, in 2007); and the sustainability ordinances (in Germany, in 2008). But the most important outputs of the policy process at the EU level were the 2009 Renewable Energy Directive (RED) (2009/28/EC) and the Fuel Quality Directive (FQD) (2009/30/EC). The RED requires 20 per cent of energy use in the EU and 10 per cent of transport fuels to come from renewable sources by 2020. It also sets sustainability requirements for the use of biofuels in the EU, including minimum GHG savings in comparison to fossil fuels and the double counting of credits for biofuels produced from waste and residues to decrease the impact on feedstock that can be used for food. The FQD entails the obligation for suppliers of fossil fuel to gradually reduce life-cycle greenhouse gas emissions by a minimum of 6 per cent by 2020.

The Commission set up an accreditation system for private certification schemes that meet its RED sustainability criteria. It also allows demonstration of compliance through national regulatory systems (and related assessment protocols) that meet the criteria set by the EU and through bilateral agreements between the EU and third countries.[20]

However, private certification schemes have been the main compliance instrument in practice so far. In June 2010, the Commission adopted a scheme for certifying sustainable biofuels under the RED. Under this scheme, in order to receive government support or count towards mandatory national renewable energy targets, all biofuels used in the EU (whether locally produced or imported) have to comply with sustainability criteria that include: land use (no conversion of land with high carbon stock or land with high biodiversity value); a minimum reduction of GHG emissions over the whole value chain (35 per cent less than gasoline);[21] and a system monitoring the whole value chain from feedstock to the pump. No social or food security aspects were included in the sustainability criteria. In July 2011, the EU recognized a first batch of seven certifications. By the end of 2017, there were 14 approved certification systems in the EU list (see Table 3.8).

Some of the RED targets were revised in 2015 under ILUC Directive 2015/1513, which capped the contribution of first-generation biofuels based on food crops. A draft of a revised RED, known as RED II, was released by the EC in late 2016 and will replace the RED in 2021. It aims at achieving a 27 per cent renewable energy share from energy consumed by the electricity, heating and cooling, and transportation sectors by 2030. As part of this overall target, RED II mandates that 6.8 per cent of transportation fuels must derive from renewable sources. It will also progressively tighten the cap on first-generation biofuels from 7 per cent of energy consumption for transport in 2021 to 3.2 per cent by 2030. These institutional interventions are strengthening the bargaining power of next-generation biofuel producers vis-à-vis those operating mainly with first-generation stocks. They have also institutionalized a more general shift in the public perception of biofuels, where first-generation biofuels are no longer deemed to be automatically 'sustainable'.

The EU-RED process has led to a veritable scramble in getting access to the captive EU market for biofuel sustainability certification. Of the certification schemes currently approved by the EU under the current RED rules, only four cover a wide variety of possible feedstocks: the Roundtable on Sustainable Biomaterials (RSB), International Sustainability and Carbon Certification (ISCC), REDcert and NTA8080. The other schemes are either feedstock-specific (or cover only a few), country-focused, or private company schemes applied to internal supply chains. Much of the biofuel sustainability certification market has

Table 3.8 Biofuel Sustainability Certification Schemes Recognized by the EU (2018)

Voluntary scheme		Scope				Demonstrates compliance with Articles:				
Name	Date commission decision	Feedstock type	Feedstock origin	Biofuel production geography	Extent of supply chain covered	17(2) GHG through	17(3) High biodiversity value	17(4) High Carbon Stock	17(5) Peatlands	18(1) mass balance
Commission Implementing Decisions in force [Status December 2017]										
International Sustainability and Carbon Certification (ISCC)	9 August 2016	Wide range of feedstocks	Global	Global	Full supply chain	Default or actual	Yes	Yes	Yes	Yes
Bonsucro EU	21 March 2017	Sugar cane	Global	Global	Full supply chain	Default or actual	Yes	Yes	Yes	Yes
Roundtable on Sustainable Biomaterials EU RED (RSB EU RED)	9 August 2016	Wide range of feedstocks	Global	Global	Full supply chain	Default or actual	Yes	Yes	Yes	Yes
RTRS EU RED	19 November 2017	Soy	Global	Global	Full supply chain	Default or actual	Yes	Yes	Yes	Yes
Biomass Biofuels voluntary scheme (2BSvs)	26 August 2016	Wide range of feedstocks	Global	Global	Full supply chain	Default or actual	Yes	Yes	Yes	Yes

Scottish Quality Farm Assured Combinable Crops Limited (SQC)	9 June 2015	All cereals and oilseeds	North Great Britain	n/a	Until the first feedstock delivery point	n/a[2]	Yes	Yes	Yes	Yes
Red Tractor Farm Assurance Combinable Crops and Sugar Beet (Red Tractor)	13 December 2017	Cereals, oilseeds, sugar beet	UK	n/a	Until the first feedstock delivery point	n/a[2]	Yes	Yes	Yes	Yes
REDcert	10 August 2017	Wide range of feedstocks	Europe	Europe	Full supply chain	Default or actual	Yes	Yes	Yes	Yes
BioGrace GHG calculation tool	30 May 2013	Wide range of feedstocks	Global	Global	Supply chain not covered	Actual[3]	No	No	No	No
HVO Renewable Diesel Scheme for Verification of Compliance with the RED sustainability criteria for biofuels	9 January 2014	All feedstocks suitable for HVO-type biodiesel	Global	Global	From the producer of HVO-type renewable diesel	Default or actual	Yes[1]	Yes[1]	Yes[1]	Yes

(continued)

Table 3.8 (*continued*)

Voluntary scheme Name	Date commission decision	Scope Feedstock type	Feedstock origin	Biofuel production geography	Extent of supply chain covered	Demonstrates compliance with Articles: 17(2) GHG through	17(3) High biodiversity value	17(4) High Carbon Stock	17(5) Peatlands	18(1) mass balance
Gafta Trade Assurance Scheme (GTAS)	3 June 2014	Wide range of feedstocks	Global	n/a	Covers chain of custody from farm gate to first processor	n/a[4]	Yes[1]	Yes[1]	Yes[1]	Yes
KZR INiG System	3 June 2014	Wide range of feedstocks	Europe	Europe	Full supply chain	Default or actual	Yes	Yes	Yes	Yes
Trade Assurance Scheme for Combinable Crops (TASCC)	17 September 2014	Combinable crops, such as cereals, oilseeds and sugar beet	UK	n/a	Covers chain of custody from farm gate to first processor	n/a[4]	Yes[1]	Yes[1]	Yes[1]	Yes
Universal Feed Assurance Scheme (UFAS)	17 September 2014	Feed ingredients and compound feeds as well as combinable crops	UK	n/a	Covers chain of custody from farm gate to first processor	n/a[4]	Yes[1]	Yes[1]	Yes[1]	Yes
Expired Commission Implementing Decisions (Status December 2017)										
Abengoa RED Bioenergy Sustainability Assurance (RBSA)	19 July 2011 (expired 10 August 2016)	Wide range of feedstocks	Global	Global	Full supply chain	Default or actual	Yes	Yes	Yes	Yes

Greenergy Brazilian Bioethanol verification programme	19 July 2011 (expired 10 August 2016)	Sugar cane	Brazil	Brazil	Full supply chain	Default only	Yes, except 17(3)(c)	Yes	Yes	Yes
Ensus Voluntary Scheme under RED for Ensus Bioethanol Production	23 April 2012 (expired 14 May 2017)	Feed wheat	EU	Ensus One plant	From origin of feedstock to the Ensus One	Actual or combination	Yes[1]	Yes	Yes	Yes
NTA 8080	31 July 2012 (expired 21 August 2017)	Wide range of feedstocks	Global	Global	Full supply chain	Default or actual	Yes, except 17(3)(c)	Yes	Yes	Yes
Roundtable on Sustainable Palm Oil RED	23 November 2012 (expired 14 December 2017)	Palm oil	Global	Global	Full supply chain	Default or actual following recognizer tool	Yes	Yes	Yes	Yes

1. The scheme relies for this on other recognized schemes.
2. Only recognized for accurate data that land use change emissions (e_l) referred to in point 1 of part C of Annex V are equal to zero, and on the appropriate geographic area referred to in point 6 of part C of Annex V (NUTS-2).
3. The scheme is a non-typical voluntary scheme that covers only assessment of greenhouse gas savings. Voluntary schemes using the tool need to ensure that it is applied appropriately, and that adequate standards of reliability, transparency and independent auditing are met.
4. The scheme ensures that all relevant information on GHG emissions is transferred from economic operators upstream the chain of custody to the economic operators downstream the chain of custody.

Source: https://ec.europa.eu/energy/sites/ener/files/documents/voluntary_schemes_overview_dec17.pdf

been captured by ISCC (Ponte, 2014b). In short, part of the strong institutional power wielded by public authority has been transferred to private certification organizations that are in charge of verifying compliance with the RED directive.

In addition to these efforts, two main international initiatives have created reference standards on how to measure sustainability in biofuels: the Global Bioenergy Partnership (GBEP) and a process under the ISO that led to the release of standard ISO 13065 in 2015. In both cases, these standards provide indicators and appropriate reporting systems, but do not set a bar for sustainability – they only define how to measure and communicate it (Renckens et al., 2017).

Institutional Power – Key Findings

Figure 3.9 summarizes some of the key findings on how institutional power (collective, direct) has evolved in the wine, coffee and biofuels GVCs between T1 and T2. Institutional power has had important effects in all three GVCs. In wine, changes in regulation, especially in the EU, have led to relative gains of buyers vis-à-vis producers, although overall public institutional support for producers remains strong. Institutional power exercised by industry associations (both producer-led and buyer-led, and of multi-stakeholder nature) remains important as well. Sustainability concerns have played a relatively small role in regulatory changes (with some exceptions, as in New Zealand), but certification systems and other sustainability initiatives are emerging. In coffee, the end of the ICA and market liberalization and deregulation in producing countries tilted the balance of institutional power strongly in favour of buyers during T2, thus reinforcing their bargaining power. Much of the institutional power that is now left is linked to multi-stakeholder initiatives and platforms that focus on sustainability. Certification and verification systems are bringing sustainable coffee into the mainstream.

Finally, the biofuel industry exists mostly because of public institutional support, which has remained strong in both periods but is now more focused on next-generation biofuels. Sustainability issues were embedded in the industry formation process during T1 on the basis of framing biofuels as more sustainable than fossil fuels. During T2, however, changes in regulation means that sustainability certification of biofuel production has become necessary in all major consuming markets. In both periods, an array of alliances and multi-stakeholder

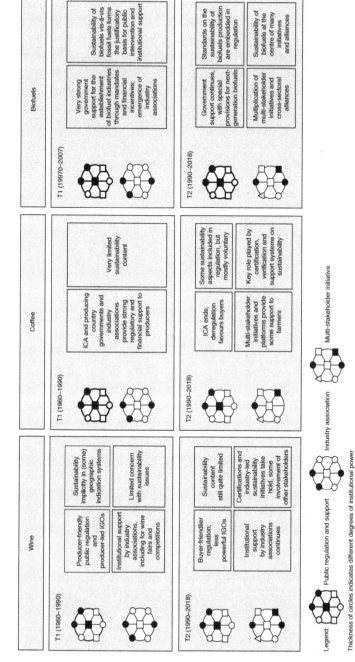

Figure 3.9 Dynamics of Institutional Power in the Wine, Coffee and Biofuels GVCs

Source: Own analysis, based on design developed by Sturgeon in Dallas et al. (2017)

Wine

T1 (1960–1990)

- Producer-friendly public regulation and producer-led IGOs
- Institutional support by industry associations, including for wine fairs and competitions
- Sustainability implicitly in (some) geographic indication systems
- Limited concern with sustainability issues

T2 (1990–2018)

- Buyer-friendlier regulation; less powerful IGOs
- Institutional support by industry associations continues
- Sustainability content still quite limited
- Certifications and industry-led sustainability initiatives take hold; some involvement of other stakeholders

Coffee

T1 (1960–1990)

- ICA and producing country governments and industry associations provide strong regulatory and financial support to producers
- Very limited sustainability content

T2 (1990–2018)

- ICA ends; deregulation favours buyers
- Multi-stakeholder initiatives and platforms provide some support to farmers
- Some sustainability aspects included in regulation, but mostly voluntary
- Key role played by certification, verification and support systems on sustainability

Biofuels

T1 (1990s–2007)

- Very strong government support for the establishment of biofuel industries through mandates and financial incentives; emergence of industry associations
- Sustainability of biofuels vis-à-vis fossil fuels forms the justificatory basis for public intervention and institutional support

T2 (1990–2018)

- Government support continues, with special provisions for next-generation biofuels
- Multiplication of multi-stakeholder initiatives and cross-sectoral alliances
- Standards on the sustainability of biofuels production are embedded in regulation
- Sustainability of biofuels at the centre of many initiatives and alliances

Legend:

Public regulation and support   Industry association   Multi-stakeholder initiative

Thickness of circles indicates different degrees of institutional power

initiatives exercised institutional power as well – but in T1 they were mostly focused on industry formation, while in T2 they are focused on sustainability issues. In biofuels, institutional power is wielded in ways that are relatively balanced between suppliers of feedstocks and producers and distributors of biofuel – this arises partly from strong lobbying efforts by industry associations of feedstock producers in the main producing countries/regions. However, there are also signs of institutional power helping to tilt bargaining power towards producers of next-generation biofuels vis-à-vis producers of first-generation biofuels.

Constitutive Power

Constitutive Power in the Wine GVC

Constitutive power (collective, diffuse) emanates from broad and informal understandings, conventions and valuations of product quality and good practices in production, manufacturing and/or business conduct at various scales – local, national, regional and/or global. Constitutive power highlights the subtler manifestations of power in GVCs. In wine, an important manifestation has been the ideational creation of the 'new wine consumer' from the 1990s onwards (T2). This was gradually developed by a group of marketing experts (supported by biochemists and economists) in some New World producing countries (the US, Australia, South Africa, Chile and Argentina), facilitated by the growing proportion of wine sales in supermarkets, and spread through social media magnification (McCoy, 2005; Szolnoki et al., 2016). The 'new consumer' is portrayed as demanding more standardized and predictable wines (including their sustainability aspects) year after year. These are wines that New World producers are better equipped to deliver, given their less regulated wine industries (Itçaina et al., 2016). This was accompanied by other transformations between T1 and T2, which operated as a key normative underpinning that led to institutional reform as well (e.g. the 2008 EU wine reform). Some of the main changes related to:

- broadly accepted preferences for wine styles or varietals (e.g. shifting preferences towards 'Parker reds', which are full-bodied wines with deep colours and high alcohol levels), and for 'noble varieties' in general (e.g. Cabernet Sauvignon, Merlot, Pinot Noir) vis-à-vis local and more 'rustic' varieties;

- understandings of novelty and tradition and their legitimacy (e.g. broader acceptance of viticultural and winemaking practices that were not allowed in traditional indications of geographic origin);
- preferred packaging and labelling (e.g. increased acceptance of screw caps and bag-in-box, even for higher-quality wines, and of less traditional designs on labels); and
- acceptable relations between geophysical properties and human intervention in winemaking (e.g. acceptance that the winemaker can 'shape' the wine rather than letting the terroir express itself; Ponte, 2009).

Changing perceptions on terroir have been particularly important. Terroir refers to the specific combination of soils and microclimate in a particular vineyard or property, and was a key feature of constitutive power during T1. Terroir places value on intimate knowledge of the land, and on long-term and repetitive fine-tuning of practices and varieties that embed land, climate and the environment into grapes and wine. These practices were long-time dominant elements of constitutive power in Old World producer countries, but were subsequently challenged by increasing wine consumption in English-speaking countries such as the UK and the US, where grape varieties, broader indications of geographic origin, and brands are more important than terroir in consumer perception. The collective effects of demonstrative power by wine tasters such as Robert Parker in the US and Jancis Robinson in the UK (and the amplification factor of social media) substantially contributed to reshaping the generally accepted norms that are at the foundation of the 'new consumer' (Itçaina et al., 2016).

Changes in constitutive power also affected the way sustainability is perceived and managed in the wine GVC. During T1, when terroir was a key element of constitutive power, sustainability was built upon the idea that a 'good wine' can only be produced from specific locations, and only after centuries of experimentation, respect for local environmental conditions and close knowledge of the land. Viticulture and winemaking skills were deemed sustainable because they 'let the land' speak – the best winemaker in this tradition was non-interventionist. This could include a 'light touch' on the environment, such as avoiding soil manipulations or not adding particular soil components, the setting aside of biodiversity corridors, and/or the use of natural pesticides instead of synthetic ones. Yet specific terroir practices can also entail clearing new land for viticulture (which generally degrades biodiversity), and some 'natural' pesticides are actually synthesized industrially and may be harmful (e.g. copper sulphate). These sustainability aspects were managed ad hoc, differed dramatically from one vineyard or winemaking facility to another, and were not generally addressed in third-party certifications. Tradition, long-term repetition and adaptation allowed viticulturists and winemakers to transfer the uniqueness of local terroir and human skills to the wine, possibly including a respectful approach to the environment. These normative roots of sustainability are still officially supported. The official definition of 'sustainable viti-viniculture' of the International Organization of Vine and Wine (OIV) includes the 'valuing of heritage, historical, cultural, ecological and aesthetic aspects'.[22] In practice, however, during T2 the idea of sustainability, in parallel with challenges to the concept of terroir, is being undermined by the growth of more codified and broadly applicable certification and verification systems used in organic grape growing and other sustainable wine initiatives.

Constitutive Power in the Coffee GVC

Key changes in constitutive power in the coffee GVC relate to the collective effects of new consumption patterns, the growing importance of single origin coffees, the proliferation of café chains and specialty shops, and increasing out-of-home consumption. As discussed above on demonstrative power, during T1 brand competition had taken the fore in corporate strategies in the US, with the product itself becoming of secondary importance (Pendergrast, 2010). This led to homogenization and mass marketing of coffee, which further increased with the gaining importance of instant coffee. By competing almost exclusively on advertising, major roasters stripped coffee of most of its charm and appeal. On the contrary, in Europe, coffee standards remained higher due to cultural factors and different patterns of consumption, even after multinationals moved into the coffee market (Luttinger and Dicum, 2011).

It is in the background of these changes that the specialty coffee industry emerged during T2 as an important player, first in the US and later in Europe. One of the characteristics of specialty coffee is that it means different things to different people. Nowadays, the term covers basically all coffees that are not traditional industrial blends, either because of their high quality and/or limited availability on the producing side, or because of flavouring, packaging and/or consumption experience. The sustainability standards embodied in third-party fair trade, organic and eco-friendly labels have been particularly successful at conveying a positive image to consumers. During T2, the general understanding of what constitutes 'proper' coffee consumption and sustainable production has changed dramatically, with more consumers now expecting to be able to choose from (and pay dearly for) hundreds of combinations of coffee variety, origin, roasting, brewing methods, flavouring, packaging, trading relation (as in 'direct trade' or 'relationship' coffees), sustainability content, and ambience of consumption. Constitutional power in the coffee GVC thus arose as a temporal accumulation of the strong demonstrative effects of early movers in specialty coffee (as indicated above), and coalesced through international fairs and conferences, often organized by the Specialty Coffee Association of America (SCAA).

International NGOs and standards developers (Rainforest Alliance, Conservation International, Oxfam) played a major role in raising the profile of sustainability issues in the industry, especially during the 'coffee crisis' (and record low international prices) of the early 2000s (Grabs, 2017; Millard, 2017). The growth in the market for sustainability certifications confirms this observation. However, in more recent years, and particularly in the past decade, sustainability has become a vector of quality management and supply chain risk minimization. This has led to a relative weakening of third-party certification and an increasing acceptance in the industry of basic guidelines (such as 4C), company-owned verification systems, and CSR-like projects in coffee-producing communities. In sum, sustainability has found an important place in the exercise of constitutive power in the coffee GVC (Solér et al., 2017), but in forms that have moved away from more genuine concerns with producers and their environment, and towards corporatized forms that are designed to ensure risk minimization and profit maximization for roasters, thus enhancing their bargaining power.

Constitutive Power in the Biofuels GVC

In the early days of the biofuel industry (T1), an unusual coalition of agricultural, environmental and military interests, together with a vibrant biofuel conference circuit, exercised constitutive power by establishing the idea that biofuels could achieve a number of collective objectives: revitalize rural areas, decrease CO_2 emissions, and ensure domestic energy independence. This perfect storm also facilitated the institutional support that further stimulated the expansion of this industry. However, increasing food prices and the related food riots of 2006/07 dramatically altered this picture in the following years (T2). Civil society groups and researchers started holding biofuel production as a major cause of increasing food prices because it takes land and water away from food production (Smith, 2010: 5). Many studies highlighted deeply problematic aspects of land investments, including shady deals, little benefit for local communities, lack of participation in decision-making at the local level, and environmental degradation (among many others, see Vermeulen and Cotula, 2010). Doubts also started to be cast on the impact of biofuel production on GHG emission reductions (Pimentel et al., 2010). Some feedstock/location combinations were found to be especially problematic in terms of GHG balance (e.g. ethanol from corn produced in the US) or for their deforestation effects (e.g. biodiesel from palm oil produced in South East Asia). A wider methodological debate also raged on how to take into account crop residues and indirect land use change in the calculation of energy balance sheets and GHG emissions (Smith, 2010). To these arguments, other analysts responded that marginal land is indeed available for biofuel production and that, with modern farm management and improved technology, it is possible to produce a meaningful proportion of fuels for transport from biological resources without affecting food supply (Rosillo-Calle and Johnson, 2010). Counterarguments to these highlighted that land is often not actually 'available' even when labelled as such, that in marginal lands yields are much lower, and that faith in technology is misplaced (Levidow and Paul, 2010).

The contours of what is generally seen as 'sustainable biofuel' have changed through these debates. Constitutional and institutional elements of power have been feeding each other in the past decade – with regulation tightening the conditions of what is considered acceptable in relation to sustainability (indicated by more support placed on next-generation biofuels), and with constitutive power dynamics playing out in the global biofuel conference circuit (Ponte, 2014b).

Constitutive Power – Key Findings

Figure 3.10 summarizes some of the key findings on how constitutive power (collective, diffuse) has evolved in the three GVCs analysed in this chapter. In the wine industry, the gradual emergence of the 'new

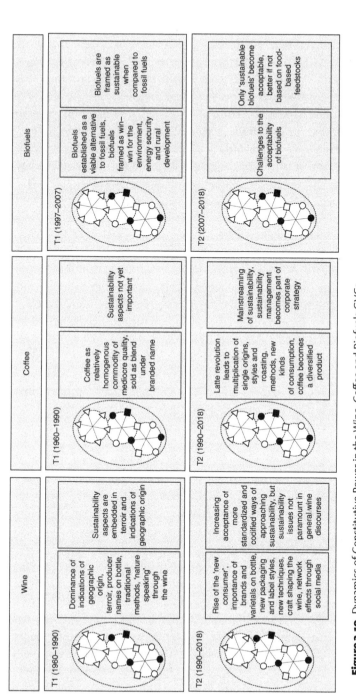

Figure 3.10 Dynamics of Constitutive Power in the Wine, Coffee and Biofuels GVCs

Source: Own analysis, based on design developed by Sturgeon in Dallas et al. (2017)

Wine

T1 (1960–1990)

Dominance of indications of geographic origin, terroir, producer names on bottle, traditional methods, 'nature speaking' through the wine

Sustainability aspects are embedded in terroir and indications of geographic origin

T2 (1990–2018)

Rise of the 'new consumer', importance of brands and varietals on bottle, new packaging and label styles, new techniques, craft shaping the wine, network effects through social media

Increasing acceptance of more standardized and codified ways of approaching sustainability, but sustainability issues not paramount in general wine discourses

---

Coffee

T1 (1960–1990)

Coffee as relatively homogenous commodity of mediocre quality, sold as blend under branded name

Sustainability aspects not yet important

T2 (1990–2018)

Latte revolution leads to multiplication of single origins, styles and roasting, methods, new kinds of consumption, coffee becomes a diversified product

Mainstreaming of sustainability, sustainability management becomes part of corporate strategy

---

Biofuels

T1 (1997–2007)

Biofuels established as a viable alternative to fossil fuels, biofuels framed as win–win for the environment, energy security and rural development

Biofuels are framed as sustainable when compared to fossil fuels

T2 (2007–2018)

Challenges to the acceptability of biofuels

Only 'sustainable biofuels' become acceptable, better if not based on food-based feedstocks

wine consumer' during T2 proceeded hand in hand with the demonstrative effects exerted by influential wine writers and flying winemakers, amplified by social media platforms. This resulted in significant changes in constitutive power related to transformations in the principles that govern acceptable ways of making wine, which in turn justified key regulatory and institutional reforms. In general, these adjustments have facilitated the consolidation of bargaining power in the hands of international merchants and retailers at the cost of wine and grape producers (and especially small producers in Old World countries). Sustainability issues have not played a significant role in these processes.

In coffee, changes in constitutive power transformed the 'definition' of coffee as a homogenous, branded commodity during T1, to a product with a number of differentiating factors, such as product form, origin, brewing system, consumption ambience and sustainability content, during T2. While mainstream roasters wielded much constitutive power in T1 (under the limits set by the regulatory framework operating at that time), in T2 constitutive power has been exercised most powerfully by specialty coffee operators and their associations, and by NGOs. Sustainable coffee is now becoming mainstream, and sustainability management is something that corporations include in their overall strategy.

In biofuels, constitutive power was an important component that resulted in institutional support during the creation phase of the GVC – on the basis of their intrinsic sustainability as an alternative to fossil fuels (during T1). It was also key in shaping institutional reform following the food crisis of 2006/07 (during T2), when not all biofuels, but only those certified or verified sustainable (and especially next-generation biofuels), maintained legitimacy. In other words, sustainability was the very foundation of changes in constitutive power.

Discussion and Next Steps

In much of the GVC literature, only bargaining power has been part of efforts to explain governance. Demonstrative power has not been explicitly considered, with the exception of some micro-level work drawing from convention theory applied to product quality (Ponte and Gibbon, 2005). Institutional power has been handled mostly under the rubric of 'institutional framework' (Gereffi, 1994; Jespersen et al., 2014; Neilson and Pritchard, 2011) – leading to criticism that these aspects are not integrally embedded in the study of GVC governance

(Coe and Yeung, 2015). Constitutive power, when considered at all, has been linked to financialization, best practice in corporate conduct, and broader societal norms (Gibbon and Ponte, 2005; Milberg and Winkler, 2013). To address these limitations, in this section I highlight the interactions between each kind of power within each GVC and show how different constellations of power can explain changes in the governance of the wine, coffee and biofuels GVCs. Both layers will be read through the lenses of sustainability.

In the wine GVC (see Figure 3.11), demonstrative power played an important part in shaking up the industry between T1 and T2 (see spark symbol in Figure 3.11). It substantially contributed to reshaping constitutive power, which in turn was instrumental in justifying changes in institutional power (see arrows in Figure 3.11). All three kinds of power undergirded changes in bargaining power directly, but demonstrative power did so both directly and indirectly through the other two. The relative shift in bargaining power to the benefit of buyers (retailers and international merchants) thus did not arise from major changes in the concentration of actors and M&A activity (as seen above, not much has changed in this regard). Rather, it emerged from major constitutive power effects related to the rise of 'the new consumer', which was itself sparked by the demonstrative effects of a relatively small group of wine tasters, winemakers, viticulturists and researchers in New World wine countries. Sustainability factors played a very minor role in these reconfigurations. These dynamics are graphically represented in Figure 3.11 in simplified form. As the narrative above attests, the whole story of changing power dynamics is far more complex and includes feedback loops and setbacks.

In the coffee GVC (see Figure 3.12), a major restructuring of bargaining power in favour of buyers (roasters and international traders) between T1 and T2 accrued from increasing industry concentration, but was also substantially reinforced by major transformations in institutional power, with the end of the ICA and deregulation in producing countries (see spark symbols in Figure 3.12). In parallel, the emergence of the specialty industry and of sustainability concerns suggests that demonstrative power (exercised by Starbucks and other specialty roasters) had cumulative effects on reshaping constitutive power, together with the increasing institutional power wielded by NGOs and multi-stakeholder sustainability initiatives.

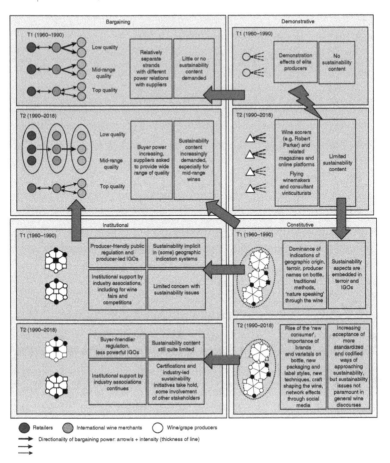

Figure 3.11 Interactions of Different Kinds of Power in the Wine GVC

Source: Own analysis, based on design developed by Sturgeon in Dallas et al. (2017)

This second dynamic, at least for a period of time, had a restraining effect on the increasingly unequal bargaining power between buyers and coffee producers. However, with mainstream roasters starting to diversify their portfolios, and with sustainability being mainstreamed in coffee markets and corporate strategies, a period of reconsolidation of bargaining power in favour of buyers is starting to re-emerge. Sustainability factors have had an important role in shaping these dynamics.

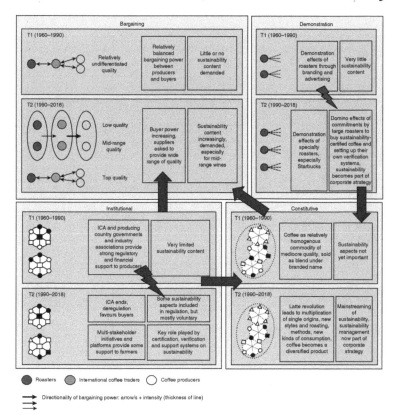

Figure 3.12 Interactions of Different Kinds of Power in the Coffee GVC
Source: Own analysis, based on design developed by Sturgeon in Dallas et al. (2017)

Finally, in the biofuels GVC (see Figure 3.13), we observe that bargaining power has remained relatively equally distributed between blenders/distributors, biofuel producers and feedstock producers. One factor is the relative fragmentation and young age of the industry. But other kinds of power dynamics have led to important changes in the way the GVC now operates. As in the coffee GVC, institutional power has played a key transformative role, first in establishing the industry, and then, together with constitutive power, in defining only 'sustainable' biofuels as acceptable (see spark symbols in Figure 3.13).

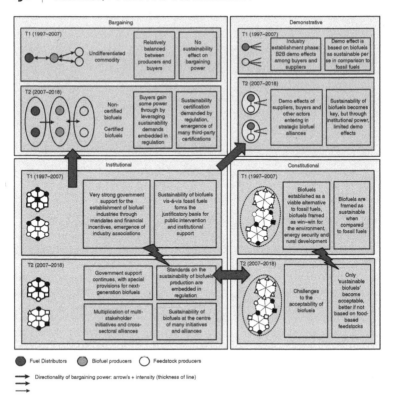

Figure 3.13 Interactions of Different Kinds of Power in the Biofuels GVC
Source: Own analysis, based on design developed by Sturgeon in Dallas et al. (2017)

Table 3.9 summarizes the implications of these power adjustments for GVC governance. Between T1 and T2, in both wine and coffee, bargaining power became more concentrated in buyers' hands. These changes in bargaining power were strengthened in both GVCs by a combination of demonstrative and institutional power (the former was more important in wine, the latter in coffee). Both GVCs moved from a multipolar configuration to a unipolar, buyer-driven one, with retailers leading the wine GVC and roasters leading the coffee GVC. The over-all level of bargaining power wielded by lead firms is higher in coffee than in wine. In coffee, counter-tendencies arose with the emergence of the specialty and sustainable coffee industry, but these are being tackled by lead firms though M&A activity, the widening of product

Table 3.9 Power, Sustainability and GVC Governance – Summary of Changes

GVC	Polarity (T1)	Changes in bargaining power (T1 to T2)	Changes in other kinds of power (T1 to T2)	Role of sustainability factors in shaping governance (T1 to T2)	Changes in GVC governance (T1 to T2)	Polarity (T2)	Lead firms (T2)	Intensity of bargaining power wielded by lead firms (T2)
Wine	Multipolar	From balanced to more buyer power	Demonstrative ++ institutional +	Small	Major disruption caused by demo power of a small group of individuals leads to changes in constitutive power and the emergence of the figure of the 'new consumer'; this in turn shapes EU institutional reform; demo and institutional power changes strengthen bargaining power of buyers, retailers in particular; GVC moves from multipolar to unipolar and buyer-driven (by retailers)	Unipolar	Retailers	Moderate
Coffee	Multipolar	From balanced to more buyer power	Institutional ++ demonstrative +	Significant	Major shock in institutional power (end of ICA) together with increasing concentration moves GVC governance from multipolar to unipolar and buyer-driven (by roasters); demo and constitutive power effects of specialty and sustainable coffee initially tames buyer-drivenness, but more recently roasters restrengthen unipolarity through M&A of specialty operators, sustainability mainstreaming and quality portfolio widening	Unipolar	Roasters	High
Biofuels	Multipolar	Remains relatively balanced	Constitutive ++ institutional +	Essential	Institutional power plays major role in industry formation; major change in constitutive power recasts legitimate biofuels as only those that are certified sustainable; no major changes in overall governance, which remains multipolar, but blenders and next-generation biofuel producers strengthen their position	Multipolar	n/a	n/a

Source: Own analysis

quality portfolios, and various forms of sustainability mainstreaming. In biofuels, bargaining power remains fairly balanced between buyers and suppliers, but constitutional and institutional power dynamics are reshaping GVC operations in important ways. Sustainability factors played an essential role in these power reconfigurations in biofuels, an important role in coffee, and little or no role in wine.

These findings are important because the GVC literature has so far examined governance mainly from the lenses of bargaining power. However, this chapter shows that important demonstrative, institutional and constitutive power dynamics may strengthen or limit the exercise of bargaining power, and thus shape GVC governance structures. It also indicates that sustainability considerations played an increasingly important role in shaping power dynamics and GVC governance, at least in two of the three GVCs examined. Furthermore, these findings have key implications on how value is created, captured and distributed along GVCs in processes of economic and environmental upgrading, which are discussed in Chapter 4. Finally, they should be at the centre of understanding how public authorities and civil society groups can orchestrate sustainability in a world of GVCs, which is the main topic of Chapter 5.

4 | VALUE CREATION AND CAPTURE THROUGH ECONOMIC AND ENVIRONMENTAL UPGRADING

The mainstreaming of sustainability management in business is providing new venues of value creation, capture and (re)distribution along global value chains (GVCs). Lead firms are leveraging sustainability for profit maximization, while suppliers build new competences or sharpen existing ones to meet these demands. The heightened information flows that are usually entailed in these processes are often used by lead firms to squeeze value out of suppliers. Suppliers may become more efficient and competitive through economic and environmental upgrading, but this value does not necessarily translate into improved profitability – as it can be captured by actors downstream in the value chain. Global buyers benefit from sustainability management through value appropriation. Consumers feel good about their 'sustainable' purchases, which come at limited or no extra cost to them. Suppliers, workers and farmers – often based in the Global South – create new value through sustainability to remain in the game, but may not be able to retain it. In the name of sustainability, a massive transfer of value is taking place from the Global South to the Global North, from producers to global buyers and consumers, and from labour to capital.

In this chapter, I examine how sustainability is leveraged in the joint processes of economic and environmental upgrading (and possibly downgrading) in GVCs. A discussion of the conceptual development of upgrading (economic and social) and the relations between GVC governance and upgrading is followed by a thematic review of emerging research on 'environmental upgrading'. The core of the empirical analysis is carried out for the same three GVCs examined in the previous chapter (wine, coffee and biofuels). In each case study, I examine economic and environmental upgrading *processes* jointly rather than separately, link it to GVC governance dynamics, and then analyse the economic and environmental *outcomes* of upgrading – for lead firms, suppliers and the natural environment. I conclude the chapter by highlighting that economic and environmental upgrading processes facilitate *green capital accumulation* by lead firms through a *sustainability-driven supplier squeeze* – while the actual impact on environmental outcomes remains limited.

Upgrading in Global Value Chains

Analytical Orientations

In GVC analysis, the general term *upgrading* has been used to highlight paths for actors to 'move up the value chain' for economic gain. There are two broad orientations within this literature. A first orientation seeks to identify the *sources* of capabilities that facilitate access to new markets. Some argue that 'horizontal' flows are key, including locational and interactive knowledge built in clusters (Giuliani et al., 2005; Morrison et al., 2008), and institutional knowledge co-generated within common business systems and national systems of innovation (Jurowetzki et al., 2018; Lundvall, 2010; Whitley, 1999). Others focus on 'vertical' relations and how knowledge and information flow within value chains between lead firms and their suppliers (Gereffi, 1999). But integrative efforts assessing which paths and aspects of upgrading originate from combinations of socio-spatial dynamics and 'learning from global buyers' are also arising (De Marchi et al., 2017; Gereffi and Lee, 2016; Murphy, 2007).

A second orientation, the one also taken in this book, is concerned with the nature of upgrading and its trajectories, often based on four kinds of economic upgrading (Humphrey and Schmitz, 2002; Schmitz, 2004, 2006): (1) *product upgrading*: moving into more sophisticated products with increased unit value; (2) *process upgrading*: achieving a more efficient transformation of inputs into outputs through the reorganization of productive activities; (3) *functional upgrading*: acquiring new functions (or abandoning old ones) that increase the skill content of activities; and (4) *inter-chain upgrading*: applying competences acquired in one function of a chain and using them in a different sector/chain.

Upgrading Trajectories

GVC scholars initially highlighted the importance of a 'high road' trajectory to upgrading (from process to product to functional upgrading), eventually leading to performing functions that have more skill and knowledge content (Gereffi, 1999). Others argue that a specific trajectory should not be an end in itself, and that attention should be paid to what conditions can improve the position of disadvantaged actors along GVCs (e.g. smallholder producers, developing country processors, women entrepreneurs) and more generally achieve a 'better deal' for developing country-based operators (Glückler and Panitz, 2016; Ponte and Ewert, 2009; Tokatli, 2012). This includes examining 'value capture trajectories' (Coe and Yeung, 2015; Neilson et al., 2018; Yeung and Coe, 2015) and the complex upgrading and downgrading trajectories that are emerging (Bernhardt and Pollak, 2016; Blažek, 2015; Cattaneo et al., 2010; Gereffi and Lee, 2016; Gibbon, 2001; Gibbon and Ponte, 2005; Hansen et al., 2014; Mitchell and Coles, 2011; Ponte et al., 2014; Tokatli, 2007, 2012 ; see also various contributions to Ponte et al., 2019).

These contributions show that 'going up the value-added ladder' is only one of the possible trajectories of economic upgrading, and that efforts to build and deepen capabilities at the same stage of the value chain are also important (Staritz et al., 2017). The source of such deepening resides not only in narrowly defined 'innovation', but also in the more general exposure to different managerial models and end markets, and in increasing sustainability management capabilities – whether demanded by retailers or strategically set by suppliers. Upgrading may also arise out of abandoning innovations to accommodate buyer demands and/or changing consumption trends, including those related to sustainability. In some cases, suppliers in developing countries may even adopt a *downgrading* strategy – to avoid losing orders in view of tightening buyer demands. Some of the upgrading trajectories highlighted in this literature, particularly in agro-food value chains, suggest that volume, economies of scale, and dynamics that would otherwise be termed downgrading in the GVC literature may coexist with more traditional upgrading paths for developing country firms (Gibbon and Ponte, 2005; Ponte and Ewert, 2009). This is especially the case when supplier firms operate in increasingly competitive environments and when retailers and branded merchandisers escalate their demands.

Recent research has explored, with increasing degrees of granularity, various trajectories and implications of upgrading – especially in relation to smaller producers and firms in developing countries and emerging economies – and suggested a number of alternative classifications and/or clarifications to the original typology of upgrading. One set of observations (Ponte and Ewert, 2009) has been that:

(1) analyses of *product upgrading* should include effects on product quality that do not necessarily lead to higher value added; conversely, there may be strategies related to the product itself (forward contracts, volume premia) that can have beneficial effects without changing anything in the nature of the product itself;

(2) *process upgrading* needs to also include improved practices that do not necessarily make processes more efficient, but that in any case can allow developing country players to improve their position in a value chain or even just maintain it in periods of restructuring; these efforts can include delivering supplies reliably and homogeneously time after time (a major challenge in agro-food products), being able to supply large volumes (thus improving economies of scale), being able to supply a variety of qualities (thus improving economies of scope), and complying with sustainability standards; and

(3) firms may be carrying out different upgrading trajectories in parallel within the same GVC, depending on context, quality sophistication of products and processes, and/or to cater to different end markets (Gibbon, 2008; Pickles et al., 2006; Ponte and Ewert, 2009; Tokatli et al., 2008); therefore, characterizing *combinations* of upgrading trajectories may be as important as establishing which one is dominant.

Other scholars have sought to further *widen* the classic typology of economic upgrading (product, process, functional, and inter-chain) by adding other forms such as:

(1) *Whole chain upgrading*, a shift of the whole GVC 'towards more demanding segments of a market' (Blažek, 2015: 855), possibly as a result of strengthening backward linkages (Morris and Staritz, 2014) and/or better horizontal coordination (Bolwig et al., 2010; Mitchell and Coles, 2011).

(2) *Strategic coupling* (and decoupling/recoupling), which occurs when local actors, supported by regional institutions and policies, interact dialectically with global actors in GVCs (Coe and Yeung, 2015; Horner, 2013; Liu, 2017; MacKinnon, 2011; Yeung, 2016), or

more narrowly when government policy paves the way for upgrading trajectories (Larsen, 2016; Ponte et al., 2014).

(3) *Reversal of power hierarchies*, when producers succeed in reshaping governance structures and manage to capture a larger share of value (Blažek, 2015; Patel-Campillo, 2011).

(4) *Relational upgrading*, when firms achieve better positionality in production networks, thus improving their 'know-who', in addition to their 'know-how' (Glückler and Panitz, 2016; Krishnan, 2017a, 2017b).

Distinctions have also been made within the category of *functional upgrading* (and downgrading). Blažek (2015), for example, distinguishes between: lower-tier suppliers moving to upper-tier positions; abandoning lower-value functions; transferring some high-value functions from buyers to their suppliers; developing new markets, products and functions (see also Morris and Staritz, 2014; Ponte and Ewert, 2009); and buying up firms to improve technological capabilities, a kind of functional upgrading that occurs through M&As (Hansen et al., 2014). In relation to functional downgrading trajectories, Blažek (2015) highlights important differences between: passive downgrading, which is buyer-induced; adaptive downgrading, where suppliers can no longer match increasingly demanding buyer specifications and decide to move to lower-value functions; and strategic downgrading, which stems from the profitability and risk calculations of suppliers themselves (see also Gibbon and Ponte, 2005).

Governance and Upgrading

Much of the discussion on the *links between governance and upgrading* has been focused on various forms of coordination along a GVC, or at least on their dominant forms at key nodes of the value chain (see Chapter 2). This literature suggests that in chains characterized by captive linkages (elsewhere also characterized as 'quasi-hierarchical'; Humphrey and Schmitz, 2004), significant product and process upgrading by 'local producers' takes place, often with an active engagement from buyers. At the same time, in captive linkages, functional upgrading is either discouraged or limited to some functions but not others (Bair and Gereffi, 2001; Gibbon, 2001, 2008; Giuliani et al., 2005; Mitchell and Coles, 2011; Schmitz, 2006; Schmitz and

Knorringa, 2000). Thus, the high road to upgrading, when followed at all, is only partial, and its rewards are either unevenly distributed or have a limited time frame (Bair and Gereffi, 2003; for an exception, see Tokatli, 2007). In chains characterized by market transactions at key nodes, functional upgrading is more likely to take place, together with the transfer of new capabilities to different value chains (Navas-Alemán, 2011; Schmitz, 2006; Tewari, 1999). The knowledge for this to happen (market, customer preferences, design), however, generally accrues in relationships with smaller buyers and/or domestic markets, and in emerging economies rather than in low-income countries. In value chains with substantial relational and modular linkages (Humphrey and Schmitz, 2004 call them 'network-based' chains), all kinds of upgrading can take place, but actors in low-income countries rarely find themselves in these chains.

Social Upgrading

Recent efforts in GVC scholarship have attempted to go beyond the discussion of economic upgrading to also examine social upgrading trajectories and the interactions between the two (Barrientos and Visser, 2013; Barrientos et al., 2010; Bernhardt and Pollak, 2016; Coe and Hess, 2013; Gereffi and Lee, 2012, 2016; Milberg and Winkler, 2013; Pegler, 2015; Rossi, 2013). The definition of social upgrading in this literature is generally drawn from the ILO 'Better Work' framework, and refers to improvements in wages, employment conditions and other social standards. In other words, social upgrading is seen as 'the process of improvement in the rights and entitlements of workers as social actors, which enhances the quality of their employment' (Barrientos et al., 2010: 324).

Gereffi and Lee (2016) highlight several possible trajectories of social upgrading: a market-driven trajectory, when demand for goods produced with higher social standards pushes producers to improve work conditions; a CSR-driven trajectory, when the same process is stimulated by private standards or codes of conduct set by global buyers/retailers (Lund-Thomsen and Lindgreen, 2014; Lund-Thomsen and Nadvi, 2010); a multi-stakeholder path, based on the cooperation of private (business, industry associations, NGOs) and sometimes public actors; a labour-centred trajectory, when workers and their labour unions assert their rights and succeed in promoting social upgrading (O'Rourke, 2006; Posthuma, 2010; Selwyn, 2013); and a public governance path driven by public regulation (Locke et al., 2013; Mayer and Gereffi, 2010). These paths coexist and interact, sometimes displacing, other times complementing, each other. This has led Gereffi and Lee (2016) to call for further research on complementary paths, how they emerge, and how they can facilitate social and economic upgrading in developing countries. This call is starting to draw attention – for example, Lund-Thomsen and Lindgreen (2018) show that the interests of buyers in the Global North, suppliers in the Global South, and workers tend to be best aligned in GVCs that are unipolar, and are least aligned where they are characterized by multipolar governance.

Milberg and Winkler (2013: 252) provide a series of proxies for economic and social upgrading and examine their interactions at both the national and GVC levels. They define four possible trajectories: high-road growth (economic and social upgrading); low-road growth (economic upgrading and social downgrading); high-road decline (economic downgrading and social upgrading); and low-road decline (economic and social downgrading). Their national-level data suggest that economic upgrading does not automatically translate in social upgrading, as pressure from lead firms on costs may lead suppliers to cut wages and other labour costs (see also Bernhardt and Pollak, 2016; Milberg and Winkler, 2011). In other words, economic upgrading is a necessary but not sufficient condition for social upgrading. These observations also hold at the level of country/GVC combinations. A study of the trajectories of economic and social upgrading in selected countries involved in four GVCs (apparel, horticulture, mobile phones and tourism) shows that social upgrading tends to occur only when accompanied by economic upgrading (Bernhardt and Milberg, 2012; Milberg and Winkler, 2011), although it is not clear which way the causality goes. These observations are confirmed by other case study research (Pegler, 2015; Riisgaard, 2011; Rossi, 2013), which shows that process upgrading is often linked to social upgrading in terms of working conditions, but rarely in terms of enabling rights. Because of the possible effects of the fallacy of composition in upgrading (see below), in situations where most suppliers upgrade to meet new or more stringent demands from buyers, they may not succeed in capturing more value; but even when they do, it does not necessary lead to social upgrading (Milberg and Winkler, 2013: 282).

A Way Forward

A great deal of attention has been paid to different typologies and trajectories of upgrading in GVCs. Yet five key upgrading issues are still in need of further conceptual development and empirical testing: (1) the scale of upgrading; (2) the distinction between upgrading as process and upgrading as outcome; (3) the fallacy of composition; (4) the relations between power, governance and upgrading; and (5) the environmental aspects of upgrading. In this book, I attempt to address these needs where possible and relevant, but far more research will be needed to further this agenda in the future.

First, existing research has been involved in discussing upgrading at three *different scales*: the firm level (as in the original formulation by Gereffi, 1999); the value chain/sectoral level (emerging from the aggregation of individual trajectories); and the national level. All three are important for better understanding economic development trajectories and possibilities, but often the scale of analysis (and thus its limitations as well) is not clearly defined. Furthermore, in many GVCs, the aggregation of individual experiences of firm-level upgrading does not necessarily lead to sectoral- and/or national-level upgrading (Coe and Yeung, 2015; Tokatli, 2012). In the empirical part of this chapter, I will approach upgrading mainly at the value chain level.

Second, much of the literature lacks clear distinctions between upgrading as a *process* (e.g. the strategies adopted and choices made by firms, industries and countries to capture more value in GVCs) and upgrading as an *outcome* (e.g. the actual achievement of better value addition, profitability or economies of scale/scope) (Bair, 2005, 2009b; Brewer, 2011). While it is important to understand the trajectories that lead to certain outcomes, the process of upgrading should not be seen as an end on its own. As a result, it is important to clarify who benefits from upgrading and in what ways. Tokatli (2012), for example, suggests analysing redistribution of competences, risks and responsibilities – such as the capacity of firms to profit and accumulate capital, and the capacity of workers to obtain higher wages and better working conditions (Selwyn, 2011; Tampe, 2016). Although supplier firms may be successful in functional upgrading, workers in these firms may be suffering from more casual forms of employment and may be subject to increased pollution. This issue has led to new research on the social and environmental aspects of upgrading, which will be explored below. Furthermore, calls have been made for long-term considerations of upgrading trajectories in order to assess possible risks, benefits and negative impacts affecting different firms, social groups and countries (Bair and Gereffi, 2001; Bair and Werner, 2011b; Brewer, 2011; Glückler and Panitz, 2016). In this chapter, I examine both upgrading as a process and the outcomes of upgrading (economic and environmental) from an evolutionary perspective.

Third, a *fallacy of composition* can affect suppliers in many GVCs, as they 'face enormous competitive pressure from other suppliers to keep costs low, keep quality consistently high, and to keep delivering to buyers on schedule or risk losing the contract' (Milberg and Winkler, 2013: 279). Firms competing for contracts often have to upgrade simply to maintain their position, let alone improve it. Early movers can draw benefits from upgrading. But if most or all firms do the same, competitive pressure will have a squeezing effect on prices. In other words, suppliers may subsequently upgrade without reaping additional benefits beyond their continued participation in a GVC. In this chapter, when relevant, I will briefly reflect on the implications of this fallacy of composition in assessing successes and failures.

Fourth, the relations between types of lead firms, the *kinds of power* they exercise in governing GVCs, and upgrading trajectories need to be researched more systematically. Ponte et al. (2014) started to work in this direction in their analysis of four seafood value chains in Asia (see also Jespersen et al., 2014). They find that suppliers are more likely to improve process, product, volume and variety at different nodes in unipolar and highly driven GVCs, rather than in multipolar GVCs with lower levels of driving. This general trend also holds in relation to changing and/or adding functions in these GVCs, but the magnitude of upgrading is far more limited for supplier country-based actors. A modified version of this approach, which incorporates power dynamics more systematically, will be used in the empirical part of this chapter to interrogate the empirical case studies of the wine, coffee and biofuels GVCs.

Fifth, while a rich literature has emerged on the relations between economic and social upgrading, work on the *environmental* aspects of upgrading from a GVC perspective is still in its infancy. In the rest of this chapter, I thus focus on the interactions and overlaps between economic and environmental upgrading. To keep the analysis feasible, I do not cover social upgrading; neither do I explore the possible combinations of all three aspects of upgrading (see Krishnan, 2017b).

The Environmental Aspects of Upgrading

The research agenda on upgrading in GVCs has recently moved from the examination of its economic and social aspects to the consideration of its environmental aspects. A common way of conceptualizing environmental upgrading in the literature is to see it as a process of improving or minimizing the environmental impact of GVC operations, including production, processing, distribution, consumption and disposal, reuse or recycling (De Marchi et al., 2013b), or more precisely as 'a process by which actors modify or alter production systems and practices that *result in positive (or reduce negative) environmental outcomes*' (Krishnan, 2017b: 117, emphasis in the original).

Environmental upgrading can result in lower costs related to optimizing the use of energy and materials, improved productivity and efficiency through organizational change, and higher prices paid for products embedding environmental qualities. It can lead to net value addition, for example through the creation, valorization and/or certification of new 'environmental qualities' embedded in products that sell at a premium. But in other instances, it can impose net costs in the short term that are not necessarily recouped in the long term. If firms are to recover these costs, they can attempt to charge higher prices, trim margins and profitability, achieve lower costs in the longer term, and/or seek economies of scale. Environmental upgrading can be limited to the improvement of processes, the use of new materials or technologies, and/or the integration of systems – but can also lead to upgraded products that embed environmental value through branding and positioning strategies, or through sustainability certification and labelling.

In this section, I review the relevant literature to highlight what we know so far about the different strategies and drivers of environmental upgrading, their economic and environmental outcomes, and the limits of a buyer-driven approach to environmental stewardship in GVCs. In the following section, I draw from these insights to go back to the wine, coffee and biofuels GVCs.

Strategies and Drivers of Environmental Upgrading

The genesis of discussions on environmental upgrading in GVCs goes back to a contribution by Jeppesen and Hansen (2004), who suggested that lead firms' engagement in environmental upgrading in GVCs can be distinguished between deep and shallow *strategies. Deep* engagement takes place when buyers provide substantial technical support and engage hands-on with their suppliers. It is more likely to be employed to drive systemic reductions in the environmental impact of the final product, when standards are not readily available and/or when the supply base does not have the capacity to comply (De Marchi et al., 2013a, 2013b). Transactions are complex and handled through trust, reputation and face-to-face meetings. Actors tend to be mutually dependent on knowledge and skills – with the lead firm usually exerting leadership on environmental knowledge and suppliers leading on technical knowledge (De Marchi et al., 2013b). Environmental problems and their solutions are considered on a case-by-case basis and do not necessarily need to fit easy-to-measure metrics. The main tools used by the lead firm are design and product specifications, which enable suppliers to improve their environmental performance even though they may have limited environmental awareness to begin with.

Shallow engagement by lead firms in environmental upgrading (Jeppesen and Hansen, 2004) tends to take place when suppliers can meet standards through established third-party certifications and/or have the capacity to comply with in-house protocols of lead firms. In shallow collaboration, buyers usually demand a certain standard (e.g. ISO 14001 or FSC certification) but do not meaningfully engage with suppliers, and provide limited or no technical or financial support (De Marchi et al., 2013a, 2013b). This strategy seems to be best suited to drive improvements that are linked to production processes and eco-efficiency. Lead firms seek to identify the main environmental impacts to be reduced, decide how to deal with them, and embed such information into standards that suppliers have to comply with (De Marchi et al., 2013b; see also Jeppesen and Hansen, 2004). These standards may affect both the supplier selection process and the relation between lead firms and existing suppliers. A milder form of shallow engagement occurs when there is some degree of hands-on involvement by buyers through monitoring and control, especially when SME suppliers are involved. In this case, buyers tend to engage with suppliers in view of complying with their own internal standards or codes of conduct, which are monitored directly through auditing, sometimes accompanied by limited technical support.

The distinction between deep and shallow engagement, however, should not be overstated – as lead firms can use different strategies within the same GVC. IKEA provides a clear example of how a lead firm may actually combine shallow and deep engagement approaches on a case-by-case basis. IKEA applies a shallow approach to environmental upgrading when third-party certifications are available and/or when suppliers already have the capacity to meet its standards (De Marchi et al., 2013b; Jeppesen and Hansen, 2004). But it also applies a deep approach when suppliers do not have the capacity to comply with its standards. For example, IKEA provided direct support and technical assistance for environmental upgrading to a number of strategic partners, both in Eastern Europe and in China and South East Asia. This was made possible because IKEA strategically reduced the number of its suppliers in the 2000s. Two of the key conditions for becoming strategic partners and category leaders are that suppliers sell 60–70 per cent of their total production to IKEA and that they implement its in-house standards on quality (QWAY) and sustainability (IWAY) (Ivarsson and Alvstam, 2010, 2011).

A second useful distinction is one between different *drivers* of environmental upgrading. *Internal* drivers refer to the factors that lead firms or suppliers leverage to meet their strategic choices (e.g. they increase efficiency or reduce energy consumption). For example, internal drivers (such as fuel savings) have been the key movers of the (limited) environmental upgrading observed in the shipping industry (Poulsen et al., 2016, 2018). Following a considerable rise in fuel costs in the early 2000s, energy efficiency measures have received increasing attention. CO_2 emissions are linearly related to fuel consumption, and up to a certain level, energy efficiency enhancement represents a win–win for business and the environment.

The *external* drivers of environmental upgrading for suppliers are normally related to new or changing regulation, pressure from civil society and/or to buyer-driven demands. In relation to regulation, Tewari and Pillai (2005), for example, observed successful environmental upgrading via regulatory intervention in the India-to-Germany leather value chain. This occurred as a result of two policy changes: new standards applied by regulators in Germany (one of the main importers of Indian leather), who banned Azo dyes and the use of pentachlorophenol; and the decision by the Indian government to institutionalize compliance with the new German regulation by banning not just the use of these chemicals, but also their production in India – thus affecting the whole leather value chain rather than only firms exporting to the German market. Further discussion of how regulation and civil society action can stimulate environmental upgrading will be carried out in Chapter 5 and the Conclusion.

In relation to buyer-driven upgrading, the case of container shipping, where the goods transported are often branded consumer goods, shows that cargo owners (often lead firms in their own GVCs) are starting to ask questions to shipping companies regarding their environmental performance. However, their efforts have only just started, and their focus has so far remained limited to various forms of emissions (carbon dioxide, sulphur oxides, nitrogen oxides and particulate matter) and fuel efficiency (Poulsen et al., 2016). Cargo owners have not (yet) developed sophisticated environmental demands – nor have they placed them at the core of negotiations regarding the procurement of shipping services. Only a few cargo owners have begun to integrate environmental performance into their shipping procurement decisions, and even fewer have included these considerations in pricing models. Limited environmental upgrading, even in the more forward-looking container segment of shipping, has been attributed to relatively balanced power relations between cargo owners and shipping companies – with the latter mainly interested, for the time being, in environmental measures that lead to cost savings (e.g. lower fuel consumption). Expectations among shipping companies and cargo owners are that environmental demands will continue to develop, strengthen and expand. Yet many barriers are still hampering environmental upgrading in this GVC. The case study of shipping also suggests that environmental upgrading is more likely to happen in GVCs characterized by unipolar governance and where lead firms are consumer-facing companies with higher reputational risks (Lister et al., 2015; Poulsen et al., 2016).

The Outcomes of Environmental Upgrading

The case study of IKEA mentioned above shows that technical support, financial assistance and advice (on sourcing materials, the organization of production, and production layout) led to improvements in the operations of over 50 per cent of its suppliers in China and South East Asia, especially in relation to the sourcing of certified wood, improved chemical storage and handling, better waste-water control, and emission reductions (Ivarsson and Alvstam, 2010, 2011). The environmental upgrading of suppliers included improvements in operational capacity, in the capacity to expand production, and in the adaptive capacity to produce under new design and environmental specifications. At the same time, innovative capacity (suppliers designing their own environmental improvements) was found to be rare. These outcomes can be linked to IKEA's unique combination of strategically focusing on building long-term relationships, its paternalistic approach both inside the firm and with suppliers, and to a strategy of avoiding complete lock-in of suppliers (Ivarsson and Alvstam, 2010, 2011). However, Ivarsson and Alvstam (2010) also show that a large share of cost savings achieved through environmental upgrading was captured by IKEA itself, even though the formal agreement was for a 50/50 share with suppliers. In other words, IKEA's paternalistic and supportive approach pays handsomely for the company, a clear example of how environmental upgrading can facilitate green capital accumulation among lead firms and a sustainability-driven supplier squeeze.

A comprehensive study of environmental upgrading trajectories in Kenyan horticulture (Krishnan, 2017b) shows positive income effects are found only when farmers perform product environmental upgrading with highly complex tasks, while other forms of environmental upgrading do not seem to pay off. Because of these limited economic returns, farmers tend to cut corners in time, and thus are likely to actually cause longer-term environmental downgrading (for similar trajectories in the Indonesian palm oil GVC, see Brandi, 2017).

As indicated earlier in this chapter, first movers can draw benefits from economic upgrading, but when most or all firms do the same, competitive pressure will not have positive outcomes on profitability for suppliers. The same situation can take place in relation to the environmental aspects of upgrading. Goger (2013), for example, examined two factories that were built under strict environmental design and operational standards to supply the British supermarket chain Marks & Spencer (M&S), and another eco-factory supplying a different buyer. These factories deliver basic standards of environmental compliance and embed an eco-friendly aesthetic (e.g. workers using green uniforms, green vegetation placed on the factory floor). Some of the common elements of these eco-factories are: green building design, LEED certification, use of solar panels and natural lighting, green power purchasing agreements, rainwater-catching infrastructure and water recycling, no waste to landfill, and energy-efficient cooling systems (Goger, 2013: 78). M&S linked its suppliers to specific environmental consultants, provided feedback on factory layouts and offered small seed funding to one of the factories – but in general the cost of investment was borne mainly by the local investors. M&S offered an exclusive buying agreement to one of the plants, but not the other. The third plant was built without a formal partnership with the buyer. While the environmental impacts in internal operations in these factories have been clearly positive (in terms of energy and water use, GHG emissions, and ratio of waste to landfill), there has been limited transmission of environmental upgrading upstream to their own suppliers, with the exception of limited purchasing of Better Cotton Initiative (BCI)-certified cotton and organic textiles.

Goger (2013) reports that no price premia are offered for garments produced in green factories in Sri Lanka, and that suppliers have come to question the business rationale of their investment in environmental upgrading. They managed to reduce costs (on energy, waste disposal, water) and improve productivity and efficiency through organizational change.[1] However, they had yet to fully recoup their initial investment at the time of Goger's fieldwork – something they had expected to have achieved by then. When suppliers became involved in this process, they were looking for additional competitive advantage in a risky and unstable industry that had already led to the consolidation of the supply base. They now argue that while buyers benefited from building their 'green image', these gains are not being adequately shared with suppliers. Khattak et al. (2015) show that the achievement of lower operational costs through environmental upgrading of garment factories in Sri Lanka has been accompanied by consistent orders, knowledge spillovers and enhanced reputation – all positive outcomes. However, environmental upgrading did not lead to higher prices from buyers and entailed extra financial costs for suppliers – meaning that supplier profitability overall did not improve. In other words, suppliers need to deliver environmental upgrading to remain in the game. Similar trajectories have been reported in the garment GVC in Turkey (Tokatli, 2012; Tokatli et al., 2008) and the sporting goods GVC in Pakistan (Khattak and Stringer, 2017). In sum, as environmental upgrading becomes more widespread, early movers are losing their competitive advantage. This suggests the working of a 'green Shumpeterian cycle' (Goger, 2013) and the fallacy of composition in environmental upgrading (Milberg and Winkler, 2013).

Global buyers claim that consumers are unwilling to pay for environmental improvements, which means that the drive to lower costs takes precedence over the profitability of suppliers. Suppliers increasingly question the business case for environmental upgrading, given that most buyers do not offer purchase commitments or other incentives. This suggests that production cost reductions provide justifications for buyers to maintain or even further reduce prices, leading to a sustainability-driven supplier squeeze. Additionally, the suppliers that can deliver environmental upgrading are those that have superior capabilities already in place. This tends to further consolidate the supply base and marginalize SMEs.

Economic and Environmental Upgrading in the Wine, Coffee and Biofuels GVCs

The literatures reviewed in the previous section provide a number of useful suggestions on how to best proceed in examining economic and environmental upgrading in the wine, coffee and biofuels GVCs. Before I move to the individual case studies, however, I clarify some of the main analytical choices that guide the empirical analysis:

(1) The original typology of upgrading (process, product, functional and inter-chain), while helpful, can be usefully repackaged to capture the nuances of different trajectories. For this reason, I employ three broad categories of upgrading and downgrading, including their environmental aspects:

    a. *improving product, processes, volume and/or variety* (in the same value chain node);

    b. *changing and/or adding functions* (up- or downstream, across several nodes); and

    c. *transferring capabilities between chains* (applying competences acquired in a chain and using them in a different sector/chain).

(2) Instead of examining the process of environmental upgrading as a separate category, I interpret the different upgrading categories delineated in point 1 through the lenses of environmental sustainability. Similar to the exercise carried out in Chapter 3 on governance, I take an evolutionary approach to trace changes in time by comparing two time periods (T1 and T2) that are specific to each GVC.

(3) I distinguish between upgrading as *process* from the economic and environmental *outcomes* of upgrading (as in Krishnan, 2017b).

I assess economic outcomes in relation to profitability, value addition and the distribution of value added along the chain, depending on what data are available for each GVC. I distinguish between the costs and benefits accruing to lead firms and those accruing to their suppliers, and I examine the environmental outcomes on a case-by-case basis – drawing on relevant research findings in this field.

(4) I reflect, when possible and relevant, on the limitations of upgrading that arise from the 'green Schumpeterian cycle' and the *fallacy of composition* – indicating that early movers in environmental upgrading may lose their competitive advantage as other actors embark on the same trajectories.

(5) I identify the connections between *governance and upgrading*, and highlight their economic and environmental outcomes. This is done through the analysis of drivers of upgrading and their limitations – in the context of changing power relations along GVCs and the different polarities of governance.

Overall, I examine upgrading to serve a wider goal, that of understanding how lead firms work through and use the environment to appropriate value (Havice and Campling, 2017), and how they create and extract intangible value from the management of environmental concerns for capital accumulation. In other words, I seek to explain how 'firm strategies are articulated with and through the environmental conditions of production' (Havice and Campling, 2017: 302), and whether and to what extent sustainability management is itself an engine for the creation and extraction of value and for the management of risk (Meckling, 2015).

In the rest of this section, I continue the analysis of the wine, coffee and biofuels GVCs started in Chapter 3 by examining: first, the intertwining of economic and environmental upgrading and downgrading trajectories; and then the relations between these and GVC governance.

Economic and Environmental Upgrading in the Wine GVC

In this section, I examine the trajectories of economic and environmental upgrading in the wine GVC, with focus on its South Africa-to-UK strand (see details in Ponte, 2007b, 2009; Ponte and Ewert, 2007, 2009). While individual firm experiences of upgrading would be a worthy objective of examination, space limitations dictate a focus on the aggregation of firm-level changes that I tracked in my primary research.

Improving Product, Process, Volume and/or Variety – Including Their Environmental Aspects

Substantial upgrading took place in the South African wine industry in the broad category of improving product, process, volume and/or variety, and environmental sustainability has been a central element in it (see Table 4.1). Throughout much of the twentieth century, the wine industry in South Africa was centred around cooperative wine cellars, which were responsible for a large proportion of total wine production. They supplied bulk wine of low quality and their farmers were dependent on cheap black labour. Although some upgrading had taken place before the end of *apartheid*, the industry has upgraded substantially since. This took place especially in the 1990s, with a less steep curve in the 2000s (Ponte and Ewert, 2007, 2009).[2]

Table 4.1 Overview of Economic and Environmental Upgrading Trajectories in the South African Wine Industry (Mid-1990s to Late 2000s)

Improving product, process, volume and/or variety

Aspect of upgrading	General trend in South African wine industry
Overall intrinsic quality	Improved
Proportion of bottled exports versus bulk exports	Increased, but then stagnated in the 2000s
Proportion of natural versus rebate/distilling wine production	More or less the same
Noble variety proportion	Increased
Top-quality wines	Number and visibility increased
Proportion of wine certified under Wine of Origin scheme	Increased
Product consistency	Improved
Economies of scale	Increased (mainly in co-ops)
Economies of scope	Improved
Managerial systems	Improved
Viticultural practices	Improved
Winemaking practices	Improved
Marketing, advertising, provision of promotional support	Improving, but still a relatively weak point
Sustainability certifications	Increasing sales of organic and biodynamic wines

Biodiversity preservation	BWI promoted conservation efforts, but current status is unclear
Environmental management	Large proportion of operators meet IPW scheme standards

Changing and/or adding functions

Location of functional upgrading/downgrading	General trend in South African wine industry
In South Africa	Cellars and producers/wholesalers moving away or reducing their enagement in grape growing
	Marketers moving away from winemaking
	Cooperatives becoming more engaged in marketing and branding through joint ventures
	Product innovation increasingly done by European/US marketers and agents
In Europe	South African producers/wholesalers and marketers divesting from own their own agencies in the UK and Europe, or entering into joint ventures
	Brand ownership by South African actors decreasing

Inter-chain capability transfer

Tourism industry	Mutually beneficial interactions and joint capability building
Environmental sustainability	Leveraged to build brand recognition and sales

Source: Own analysis, adapted and updated from Ponte (2007b) and Ponte and Ewert (2009)

As shown in Chapter 3, environmental issues have not been central in shaping governance in the wine GVC. However, they have played a more distinguished role in the upgrading trajectories of the wine value chain in South Africa. These initiatives can be distinguished in two categories. The first category includes global, codified and standardized best practices that are embedded in sustainability certifications that include environmental content, such as the BRC Global Standard-Food and/or the IFS-Food standard. The popularity of general environmental management standards, such as ISO 14001 certification, is also on the rise (in 2005, only a handful of cellars held this certification). And exports of organic or biodynamic certified wines have also grown, albeit from a small base.[3]

The second category includes industry-level initiatives in South Africa that seek to tackle specific environmental issues and/or to promote South African wine by leveraging the country's natural beauty and biodiversity, such as the Integrated Production of Wine scheme, Sustainable Wine South Africa, and the Biodiversity and Wine Initiative.[4] First, the Integrated Production of Wine (IPW) scheme is a semi-regulatory system first introduced in 1998. It provides guidelines for 'Good Agricultural Practices' for farms, 'Good Manufacturing Practices' for cellars to produce wines that are 'healthy, clean and environmentally friendly' (IPW, 2004), and biodiversity guidelines. The scheme is officially voluntary, but in practice registered IPW actors represent 98 per cent of harvested wine grapes in the country. The IPW covers production, including environmental impact studies, soil preparation and the use of recyclable packaging. New vineyards are subject to a botanical audit and conservation plan for endangered species. Some producers set aside natural areas that will remain undeveloped in perpetuity. Second, Sustainable Wine South Africa (SWSA) is a partnership between the regulatory agency (the Wine and Spirit Board – WSB), the IPW scheme, the WWF-SA Conservation Champion programme, and Wines of South Africa (WOSA). Under this umbrella, the WSB has developed a seal guaranteeing that 'the wines have been sustainably produced according to their new guidelines and consumers are able to verify this on-line by entering the unique seal numbers on the bottle'.[5]

Finally, environmental commitment is also showcased in the Biodiversity and Wine Initiative (BWI), established in 2004 with co-funding from the World Bank. The BWI seeks to avoid 'further loss of habitat in critical sites', provide a positive contribution to biodiversity conservation through setting aside natural habitat in contractual protected areas, change farming practices to enhance the suitability of vineyards as habitat for biodiversity, and use the biodiversity of the Cape Floral Kingdom as a unique selling point to differentiate 'Brand South Africa'.[6] As of 2017, the BWI had 207 members, including 19 champions. Regular members need to comply with the BWI biodiversity guidelines 'where appropriate, to the best of the company's ability', responsibly conserve a demarcated biodiversity area, and supply a 'biodiversity story' for marketing purposes.[7] Champions need to comply with more stringent standards and additional demands.

Changing and/or Adding Functions

The case study of wine in South Africa suggests two key features on upgrading via changing and/or adding functions (see Table 4.1). First, wine producers/wholesalers have shed off upstream functions linked to grape and wine production. Where complete outsourcing has not been possible, value chain operators across the board tried to move from hands-on management systems (requiring close supervision) to more hands-off systems, with the exception of top-quality wines. Most small and medium-scale wineries rely to some degree on own grape growing and always make their own wine. All marketers, by definition, do not grow grapes or make their own wine – they rely on contracted wineries (often producer cooperatives). But even the largest and historically most important producers/wholesalers have been moving away from grape growing on their own farms. Large cooperatives (or ex-cooperatives) do not have outsourcing options because their members are grape growers. As a result, they are increasingly holding stock (and facing higher risks) on behalf of other actors downstream in the value chain. This is a classic vertical specialization process, common in many GVCs, that in the wine sector entails many private cellars and producers/wholesalers moving away from, or reducing their engagement in, grape growing. Some of the most successful producers/wholesalers have largely abandoned even wine-making, thus divesting from holding fixed capital and becoming pure marketers (Ponte, 2007b, 2009).

Second, the few South African producers/wholesalers and marketers used to have their own agencies in the UK and Europe. They have now divested from them or have entered into joint ventures with Europe-based branders and marketers. Many of the most successful brands of South African wine in the UK are owned or co-owned by overseas companies. These are processes of functional *downgrading* from a point of view of South African producers – yet they have yielded positive results in terms of successfully selling their stock before the next harvest comes in (what operators call 'moving volume'). Conversely, many cooperatives and ex-cooperatives have become more engaged in direct marketing and branding through joint ventures. This is an example of functional upgrading on their part.

UK agents and marketers have also upgraded functionally. Under pressure from shorter lead times, they had to increase their control over logistics – with some importers selling to retailers with delivery executed at the warehouse in the UK instead of 'free on board' on the ship in Cape Town as in the past. Much product innovation, new packaging, and new presentations and styles are also generated by UK agents and marketers. This does not mean that upstream learning is not taking place. Up to the early 1990s, quality in South African wine was 'producer-generated', while now cellars and South African marketers are able to interpret consumer market changes and react to downstream requests much more quickly and efficiently. Overall, these functional dynamics have not been driven by sustainability issues.

Transferring Capabilities between Chains

Wine tourism is a well-developed industry in the Western Cape, with a number of organized wine routes. Cape Town is part of the Great Capitals of Wine network. A good proportion of cellars are open to the public and have tasting facilities. Many have restaurants and some have hotels on-site. Scenic beauty and many flagship properties displaying Cape Dutch architecture (and some interesting contemporary architecture as well) add flavour to the 'Cape wine experience'. A large share of the revenue accruing from wine tourism comes from food sales and accommodation – the volume of wine sales at the cellar door is not significant in absolute terms – with the exception of some flagship estates such as Vergelegen, Boschendal or some Constantia-based cellars and farms.[8] Branding and marketing capabilities are used for promoting both wine sales and broader tourism-related income. Cellar and property visits tend to improve wine sales beyond the tasting room, and visibility in retail can bring tourists to a property as well. While for the major producers/wholesalers wine sales are far more significant than wine tourism income, their flagship properties with wine tasting rooms, restaurants and/or hotels continue to be important elements of their overall brand offering. South Africa is considered a sophisticated player in the global tourism industry, and can offer great value for money – benefiting the wine industry as well (Bruwer, 2003; Ferreira and Hunter, 2017).

Power, Governance and Upgrading – Economic and Environmental Outcomes

As explained in Chapter 3, governance in the wine GVC underwent a major transformation between 1960 and 1990 (T1) and 1990 and 2018 (T2). It moved from a multipolar structure where producers, international merchants and retailers exerted limited power on each other, to an increasingly unipolar one with retailers at the helm. As explained in Chapter 3, this shift was facilitated by changes in demonstrative power, which reshaped constitutive power, and in turn institutional power. Thus, all three kinds of power undergirded a relative shift in bargaining power to the benefit of buyers (especially retailers, but also international merchants).

These transformations in the wine GVC have led to a series of new demands placed on merchants and producers in South Africa, especially in the low-end quality segment, and pressure to deliver wines at scale at different quality points. Within South Africa, in terms of governance, what emerged is a value chain where the main drivers are producers/wholesalers and marketers, although their power over other actors in the South African segment of the value chain is limited by their own need to deliver volume and quality to importers and retailers in importing countries.

Producers/wholesalers and marketers are reshaping the functional division of labour within the wine value chain in South Africa, with inventory being pushed upstream (in terms of volume and duration) all the way to cooperatives and other wine producers. At the same time, large South African producers/wholesalers have moved away from branding and marketing operations in Europe to concentrate on value chain functions within the country. Although this is a *downgrading* trajectory from a traditional GVC perspective, it has been important in terms of securing volume of purchases from other, previously competing international merchants (Ponte and Ewert, 2009). While sustainability demands from international marketers and retailers have been relatively limited so far, South African operators and regulators placed strategic importance in proactively profiling sustainability to secure elements of additional competitive advantage in a crowded global supply field. This led to a number of actions and initiatives to deliver environmental content, including most wine producers meeting the (relatively low) sustainability standards of the IPW scheme.

Moving beyond South Africa, the main international wine producers and marketers have started being involved in sustainability initiatives as well. Constellation Brands, a Fortune 500 company, has an active water policy and has been cutting GHG emissions. In 2014 and 2015, it was 'named to the CDP [Carbon Disclosure Project]

Leadership Index and ... recognized as a leader among S&P 500 companies by CDP for the depth and quality of climate change data' publicly disclosed.[9] Constellation Brands also organizes an internal annual sustainability award for the facilities that best achieve GHG, water, energy, and solid waste reductions; implements recycling/reuse programs; and has developed a 'Supplier Code of Conduct and Sustainability Guidelines'. Other top international wine merchants and producers, such as E&J Gallo, have a very similar sustainability profile. Treasury Wine Estates (Foster's Group) is a signatory to the United Nations Global Compact (UNGC), while Pernod Ricard produces an annual environmental report. The Wine Group stands out for having a much lower profile on these issues.[10] All in all, most of the international wine merchants and marketers in the wine GVC are formally committed to environmental issues as a result of sustainability mainstreaming, a potentially positive development. But this also means that they cannot leverage these aspects to distinguish themselves from their competitors. Retailers, in other words, are not making purchasing decisions on the basis of the differential sustainability profiles of their suppliers, and thus they are unlikely to pay a premium based on environmental stewardship.

A superficial reading of these trends would suggest a successful upgrading story for South Africa's wine industry: delivery of demand-driven wine styles, volume and consistency have allowed the industry to grow in the basic quality segment of the industry, while the proliferation of higher-quality wines has opened new niches. In both quality segments, South Africa has also increased its offering of certified fair trade, organic and biodynamic wines; wine producers are now able to comply with an increasingly demanding package of specifications expected as a given; this has in turn stimulated a further process of upgrading in the form of improved vineyard operations, wine cellar innovation, better managerial and environmental practices, and more systematized quality management.

However, the economic *outcomes* for South African wine producers and grape growers remain problematic, as the margins for improvement have now decreased in many areas. The extras (e.g. promotional support, certifications, sustainability) that the industry delivers to obtain or even just maintain a listing with major retailers are becoming more complex and costlier. Margins remain extremely low in the retail markets of the UK, Germany and the Netherlands, and the industry has a limited presence in the more lucrative US market (Ponte, 2007b, 2009). According to a 2005 Deloitte study[11] of all South African wineries with a revenue of less than R 25 million (approximately USD 4 million), 36 per cent were making a loss, and of those with a revenue of R 25–90 million (USD 4–14 million), 25 per cent were making a loss. The average profit in small wineries was reported at R 13 (USD 2) per 9-litre case, against R 20 (USD 3.1) in Australia. Fast-forward to 2016, and the picture has become even worse, with returns to investment dropping to less than 1 per cent. VinPro data indicate that only 13 per cent of the 3,300 producers operate at sustainable income levels, 44 per cent are operating at break-even, and 40 per cent are making a loss.[12]

The implication of these findings is that South African grape and wine producers have made substantial strides in terms of processes of economic and environmental upgrading. But this has not translated into positive *economic outcomes* in the aggregate, suggesting that suppliers are delivering more content to buyers (including marketable environmental sustainability features) but face profitability challenges. At the same time, consumers, both in South Africa and in importing countries, can enjoy a variety of wine qualities at competitive prices, including those delivering sustainability features.

Comprehensive evaluations of the *environmental outcomes* of these upgrading processes and related sustainability initiatives in South Africa are not available. However, it is probably safe to assume that there have been some positive impacts in terms of biodiversity conservation, decreasing agrochemical application (when farms convert to organic or biodynamic), and better environmental stewardship of the land and water resources. At the same time, grape growing is a monocrop cultivation method that, when applied to previously natural areas, destroys rather than enhances biodiversity (McEwan and Bek, 2009). Furthermore, biodiversity conservation provisions are fairly limited in scope (restore indigenous vegetation around tasting rooms and on the margins of vineyards) and apply to farms that have *already* cut down *fynbos* to establish vineyards planted with *vitis vinifera*, an alien species. Also, only a few operators (usually large and environmentally progressive cellars and marketers) can afford to set aside and manage large tracts of land for conservation. The average grape grower and small-scale winery have enough trouble getting by to afford using extra resources for conservation.

In sum, the case study of the wine GVC suggests that: (1) sustainability has not yet played a major role in shaping GVC governance, but is used opportunistically by lead firms for marketing, reputational enhancement and risk management purposes; (2) South African value chain actors and institutions have invested heavily in portraying the industry and individual companies as caring for the environment, and painted this portrait along with scenic and natural beauty of the winelands in this country; although the wine GVC is becoming more unipolar and driven by retailers, South African suppliers have driven environmental sustainability proactively in view of highlighting the unique features that can provide some form of competitive advantage; and (3) major economic and environmental upgrading processes in the South African wine value chain took place, but did not lead to positive economic outcomes for most domestic players, and to environmental outcomes that are likely to have been limited. Collectively, these lessons suggest a combined process of capital accumulation by lead firms coupled with a process of supplier squeeze – but one where the environmental sustainability component is not (yet) a major feature.

Economic and Environmental Upgrading in the Coffee GVC

Coffee is particularly interesting in the context of the discussions carried out in this book because almost all its production takes place in the Global South, while a large proportion of consumption takes place in the Global North. Notable exceptions are Ethiopia and Brazil, which have substantial domestic consumption markets. By examining how economic and environmental upgrading unfolds along the coffee GVC, this case study can provide important insights in view of identifying where value is produced and where it is captured, and of assessing whether upgrading has actually led to substantial environmental outcomes.

Improving Product, Process, Volume and/or Variety – Including Their Environmental Aspects

In response to the growth of the specialty market, coffee processors, producers and their cooperatives have had to improve the range of product qualities they supply to the specialty and sustainable coffee markets. The coffee GVC in some ways is becoming more similar to that of wine, with a multiplication of unique offerings and the increasing importance of economies of scope as well as scale. In time, with the mainstreaming of sustainable coffee and the entrance of mainstream roasters and traders into the specialty market, economies of scope have become indispensable for most producer countries. This demand dynamic has led to a wide differentiation of supply – in some cases going all the way to the production level (especially in large estates and more sophisticated cooperatives, mostly in Latin America). In other cases, intermediaries (traders and exporters in producing countries) operate this differentiation by selecting and isolating certain origins with special characteristics – this way, they create value that is not necessarily transmitted upstream to producers, and thus does not translate into direct quality-related incentives (Ponte, 2002a).

Differently from wine, sustainability features, which were originally stimulated by NGO activism and specialty coffee operators, have now become a central part of the demands placed by roasters, which are then transmitted by international traders to domestic coffee operators and farmers in producing countries (Grabs, 2019; Millard, 2017). In Chapter 3, I specified the assemblage that emerged to provide sustainability certification or verification options to coffee farmers and traders to deliver these demands. Coffee producers around the world used to supply a relatively homogenous product at volume, with their rewards propped up by the ICA system. They now deliver coffee of many different quality specifications, accompanied by a variety of sustainability certifications and geographical indications (Neilson et al., 2018) at different volumes (including micro-shipments), and sometimes through direct trade relations (Vicol et al., 2018). In other words, there has been a clear improvement in upgrading related to 'product, process, volume and/or variety' in coffee value chains in producing countries, with important sustainability components.

Changing and/or Adding Functions

Changes in functional division of labour have been relatively limited in coffee-producing countries. Functional upgrading in terms of moving into roasting coffee for export is constrained by the shorter shelf life of roasted coffee in comparison to green coffee, and the general preference by mainstream roasters for blending various origins. However, some origin roasting for export is starting to happen for small-batch production at the very top of the specialty coffee market, especially in Latin America. Internationally, traders have had to take over some of the functions that roasters have willingly shed, as detailed in Chapter 3. Demands from specialty and sustainability coffee buyers have also led international traders to vertically integrate into some estate coffee production (Grabs, 2017).

Transferring Capabilities between Chains

Inter-chain capability transfer has been limited at the production level, as advanced knowledge acquired in specialty and sustainable coffee production cannot easily be transferred to other export crops (and vice versa) that are grown in similar agro-ecological conditions. Exceptions to this are some projects helping producers diversify into high-end cocoa, and some fair trade coffee cooperatives that can also supply other products (e.g. coffee and sugar cane in Costa Rica).[13]

Power, Governance and Upgrading – Economic and Environmental Outcomes

Like in the case study of wine, the coffee GVC has moved from a multipolar governance configuration in 1960–1990 (T1) to a unipolar and buyer-driven one in 1990–2018 (T2), with roasters as lead firms exerting a level of power even more pronounced than the one leveraged by retailers in the wine GVC. This restructuring took place through major changes in bargaining power in favour of buyers – arising from increasing industry concentration but also reinforced by major transformations in institutional power with the end of the ICA and deregulation in producing countries. Counter-tendencies have appeared with the emergence of the specialty and sustainable coffee industry, with Starbucks and other specialty roasters wielding key demonstrative power, and with multi-stakeholder sustainability initiatives exercising significant institutional power. These dynamics have had a moderation effect on the unequal bargaining power between coffee buyers and producers, but this is now changing again as mainstream roasters reassert their presence in the specialty and sustainable coffee market. In the following discussion, I will argue that, in terms of economic outcomes, upgrading into specialty and sustainability coffees has paid handsomely for roasters, but not so much for producers, and that the environmental outcomes arising from these upgrading trajectories have been limited.

In relation to *economic outcomes*, as shown in Chapter 3, there is a strong relation between the market share controlled by the top roasters and the proportion of sustainable coffee they procure (see Figure 3.5 and Table 3.5). Existing research also clearly shows that the distribution of value added has progressively moved to the detriment of producers and to the benefit of consumer country-based operators. This trend applies both to mainstream coffee and to specialty/sustainable coffee. Talbot (1997: 65), for example, estimates that in the 1970s, an average of 20 per cent of total value generated by roast and ground coffee sales globally was retained by producers, while the average proportion retained in consuming countries was almost 53 per cent. In the 1980s, producers still controlled almost 20 per cent of total value, but after the collapse of the ICA their share dropped to 13 per cent in the mid-1990s. This represents a substantial transfer of resources from producing to consuming countries, irrespective of price levels (Fitter and Kaplinsky, 2001a, 2001b).

Contributions that assess the distribution of value along specific coffee value chains, rather than in the aggregate, show results that are fairly similar to those emerging in Pelupessy (1999) and Talbot (1997). My own research shows that the process of 'squeezing' farmers (in terms of proportion of the retail price paid at the farm gate) started in the 1990s and progressed further in the early 2000s. For example, farm-gate prices in the value chain for robusta (a key ingredient in lower-end espresso blends) from Uganda and Tanzania to Italy represented between 5 and 7 per cent of the equivalent retail price in the early 2000s (Daviron and Ponte, 2005; Ponte, 2002b). As one moves up the quality ladder and/or includes organic certification, farmers received even *less* proportionally (between 4 and 5 per cent). Work on 'direct trade' relationships shows that the distribution of value in these coffee value chains is no different from that of mainstream coffees (Borrella et al., 2015).

Other analyses have examined the transmission mechanisms and size of possible price premia arising from sustainability certification. Minten et al. (2018b) show that only less than one-third of the quality premium paid for certified coffee is transmitted to farmers in Ethiopia, with a very marginal impact on incomes (see also Minten et al., 2018a). Wilson and Wilson (2014) indicate that certified coffee, once controlled for different levels of quality, does not attract higher prices at the Cup of Excellence auctions hosted by the Association for Coffee Excellence. What these observations suggest is that farmers do not gain from upgrading in terms of the proportion of the retail price that they receive, which has dropped dramatically. They may indeed receive a higher price for higher quality, but they are unable to exert a more equal distribution of value along the coffee GVC – and thus potentially obtain a much higher proportion of the final price.

Much of the literature on coffee also shows that indications of geographic origin (Neilson et al., 2018) and sustainability certification focused on environmental issues do not translate to improvements in farmers' income and livelihoods (Akoyi and Maertens, 2017; Chiputwa et al., 2015; Jena et al., 2017). Some exceptions to this picture are organic certification (Bolwig et al., 2009) and sustainability standards that are embedded in quality-based schemes, such as Nespresso AAA. The latter tend to pay higher prices for coffee, but their exacting standards make it possible only for a few better-endowed farmers to become suppliers, and only for a small part of their harvest (Alvarez et al., 2010). Because these schemes are company-specific, farmers meeting these standards can often only sell to one buyer and are vulnerable to changes in sourcing decisions (Grabs, 2017). At the other end of the quality scale, entry-level standards, such as those embedded in 4C, are having very limited impacts on farmers' livelihoods (Kuit et al., 2010).

Recent research on 'direct trade' shows that these schemes maximize the achievement of roasters' goals – procuring coffee of the desired quality (MacGregor et al., 2017) – and that they tend to benefit local elites (Vicol et al., 2018). The use of the term direct trade has spread rapidly since its coinage by Intelligentsia, a Chicago-based specialty roaster – now owned by JAB Holdings, the world's largest roasting group. Direct trade was originally used by smaller high-end roasters to indicate that they bought coffee directly from producers. They often communicated this system in their marketing strategy, and in a few cases, as in Nordic markets, they also offered a certification (MacGregor et al., 2017; Schroeder, 2015). However, it is now being leveraged by larger players as well, including by retailers such as Target. Roasters apply direct trade as a strategic tool to identify and secure coffees of exceptional quality, tailor the trade relationship to differences in supplier capabilities, communicate product value to consumers, and manage volatility in the global coffee market (Schroeder, 2015).

At the same time, sustainability certifications have been instrumentalized by roasters and international traders for supply chain and risk management purposes (Grabs, 2017; Muradian and Pelupessy, 2005). It has become common for producer country-based operators (traders and cooperatives) to carry the cost of audits and certifications, which negatively impacts the final price paid to producers (Grabs et al., 2016). International traders complain that decreasing premia are making it difficult to maintain their sustainability outreach activities, which are needed to maintain certification, let alone pay a premium to farmers (COSA, 2013; Grabs, 2017). At the same time, sustainability systems are proving useful to international traders and roasters because they provide assurance, traceability and plausible deniability of wrongdoing (Grabs, 2017: 21). Overall, farmers can gain economically from sustainability certifications and specialty coffee through improved management or productivity. But in order to remain in the game, they need to deliver environmental sustainability even when the financial gains arising from it are limited or non-existent.

In relation to the impact of upgrading on *environmental outcomes*, impact studies have found a positive link between sustainability certification or verification systems and improved environmental conduct among coffee farmers (see Blackman and Naranjo, 2012; Ibanez and Blackman, 2016; Nguyen and Sarker, 2018; Rueda et al., 2015; Solér et al., 2017; Takahashi and Todo, 2013). Similarly, a COSA study finds that the 'environmental practices and conditions found on farms that participate in sustainability initiatives tend to be somewhat better than those on conventional farms. They are more likely to use soil and water conservation measures such as soil cover, contour planting and terracing, drainage channels, and soil ridges around plants' (COSA, 2013: 4).

The available research on *in-house* sustainability verification systems suggests that coffee farmers included in these schemes achieve better environmental performance (Giuliani et al., 2017),[14] especially when they sell coffee through a cooperative and in contexts where the institutional framework in the producing country is weak. Cooperatives seem to 'encourage upgrading through social monitoring or enhanced coordination ... which eventually allows farmers to adopt more environmentally sustainable practices' (Giuliani et al., 2017: 308; see also Luna and Wilson, 2015; Wollni and Zeller, 2007). However, the environmental index used in Giuliani et al. (2017) is heavily skewed towards management systems and registries for water, energy and agrochemicals; efficiency improvements, especially in water and electricity; and recycling activities (accounting for one-quarter of the total score). Many other environmental variables (such as shade cover, soil cover, wind breaks and erosion prevention) are not included. Therefore, it provides a heavily 'eco-efficiency' version of 'environmental performance'.[15] Also, the COSA study mentioned above finds that when sustainability certification pushes for both productivity and environmental improvements, this usually translates into the intensification of production on existing land, and thus to lower on-farm biodiversity. The best biodiversity outcomes in coffee tend to be seen on rustic agroforestry farms, which have much lower yields.[16] Overall, COSA could 'only see modest differences between those participating in initiatives and control groups' (COSA, 2013: 5).

In sum, and in line with what has been argued so far in this book, we do observe modest environmental outcomes at the farm level of the coffee GVC, but in general sustainability certification and verification systems are being used by mainstream roasters and international traders as a marketing and reputation management tool (Solér et al., 2017). This means that the value produced by farmers through better environmental management is captured by roasters and enjoyed (mostly for free) by consumers. Roasters also leverage these systems to create trust with consumers, and at the same time supply certified coffee at almost parity price with regular coffee, thus delivering the possibility of conscious consumption that requires no extra effort (Richey and Ponte, 2011). As concluded earlier for wine, in coffee we also find a GVC that has become unipolar and highly driven, and where substantial upgrading processes have led to a very specific 'contested value regime' (Levy et al., 2016) – one characterized by green capital accumulation by lead firms and a sustainability-driven supplier squeeze.

Economic and Environmental Upgrading in the Biofuels GVC

The biofuels case study provides an extreme example of how economic and environmental upgrading can be inextricably linked. Also, given that this GVC is still characterized by a multipolar governance structure, it provides a needed comparative element vis-à-vis the unipolar coffee and wine GVCs. As we have seen in Chapter 3, the biofuels industry has expanded dramatically in the past two decades. First, it framed itself as being environmentally friendly per se (during T1, 1997–2007) by claiming that GHG emissions from biofuels are lower than for fossil fuels. Then, following the food crisis of 2006/07 (T2), by ramping up environmental upgrading efforts to make sure that only sustainable biofuels are supplied to key consumption markets.

Improving Product, Process, Volume and/or Variety – Including Their Environmental Aspects

The biofuels GVC has experienced dramatic upgrading processes. With the exception of sugar cane-based ethanol in Brazil, very limited large-scale production had taken place before 2000. Although first-generation biofuels have been around for decades, volumes and variety of feedstocks have grown dramatically only since the turn of the century. Suppliers can now deliver ethanol and biodiesel with different specifications at large volume and from a variety of feedstocks, such as corn (from the US), soya (from Argentina), rapeseed (from the EU) and palm oil (from Indonesia and Malaysia). Virtually all biofuels consumed in the EU and the US have to meet one or another form of sustainability certification or verification. New production and processing systems are also emerging that transform cellulosic material, other oils (e.g. from seaweed) and municipal waste into biofuel. Efficiency and new processes have pushed production costs down to the point of almost parity for some feedstock, process and location combinations – at least when fossil fuel prices are relatively high. Demand for aviation biofuels is also increasing, as the aviation industry seeks to find solutions to the environmental challenges it faces (Henriksen and Ponte, 2018). In short, the biofuels GVC has been characterized by a rapid development of new products in the past two decades by improved efficiency in processing, and by a large increase in volume and variety of offering (Ponte, 2014a). All in all, the biofuels GVC has witnessed major upgrading in product, process, volume and variety, with their environmental content playing a central role.

Changing and/or Adding Functions

New functional divisions of labour have developed along the biofuels GVC, especially during T2. In Brazil, for example, partial vertical integration and strategic alliances have taken place between millers/processors and international traders, and between millers/processors and refiners/fuel distributors. For example, Cosan and Shell have formed a USD 12 billion joint venture to produce and commercialize bioethanol and electricity from sugar cane and distribute a variety of fuels through a combined distribution and retail network in Brazil. Other international trading houses, sugar producers and agrochemical companies have also started investments in the sector. Part of the motivation towards vertical integration is to ensure supply, minimize costs and maximize returns, and part is to control processes and sources of supply of certified sustainable biofuels for the European market. This complex jostling of actors changing, dropping or adding functions is taking place mostly in processing and fuel distribution, with feedstock suppliers by and large remaining focused on production (Ponte, 2014a).

Inter-Chain Capability Transfer

Inter-chain capability transfer (both inwards and outwards) is very prominent in the biofuels GVC. Part of the reason is that many actors were and still are not exclusively engaged in biofuels – for example, feedstock producers can use the same crops, different crops or crop varieties to switch between biofuel and food production. Global players that are new to the industry or that previously played only a marginal role have entered the fray (such as Bunge, Noble Group, ADM, Louis Dreyfus, Cargill and ED&F Man). Major oil companies are also financing biofuel research, ethanol production facilities and/or integrated distribution of fuels (Smith, 2010). Aircraft manufacturers and major global airlines are cooperating to stimulate the production of 'drop-in' biofuels for aviation (Henriksen and Ponte, 2018). And developers of GM crops (such as Syngenta, Monsanto, DuPont, Dow, Bayer and BASF) are working on feedstocks dedicated to biofuels, also through cooperation agreements with global agro-food traders. Some instances of inter-chain capability transfer (as well as changes in the functional division of labour) are also linked to the emergence of more critical views of biofuels as a tool for climate change mitigation and the development of sustainability certifications during T2, as evidenced by the emerging multisectoral alliances and joint ventures, and the blending of different capabilities from disparate sectors.

Power, Governance and Upgrading – Economic and Environmental Outcomes

As argued in Chapter 3, governance in the biofuels GVC has remained multipolar, with important roles played by governments (and industry players through lobby groups), international NGOs and sustainability standard makers, and by an emerging group of global players that operate at different functional positions along the biofuel value chain and that are lead firms in other GVCs. These include providers of inputs and technology (global agrochemical and biotech companies), producers and international traders of feedstocks and biofuels, fuel producers and distributors, and developers of end-use technology (aircraft and engine manufacturers, auto manufacturers). This relatively balanced distribution of bargaining power in both T1 and T2 has been shaped in no small degree by institutional power – first in the establishment phase of the industry, and then, together with constitutive power, in redefining sustainable biofuels. In T2, however, actors operating in next-generation biofuels have gained stronger bargaining power, while those operating in first-generation biofuels have lost some. This relatively balanced situation, and the fact that the industry is at an early stage of development, left space open for a variety of economic-cum-environmental upgrading possibilities for all sorts of actors. Sustainability has played a key role in GVC governance in the sense that market access to the EU and the US (and an increasing number of other countries) is linked to meeting regulatory standards or certifications. Sustainability operates strongly as a barrier to entry, but at the same time is a key driver of environmental upgrading.

What does this mean in terms of economic and environmental outcomes for various players in the biofuels GVC? In a GVC at this stage of development, it is difficult to clearly assess trends in *economic outcomes*. It is reasonable to expect that at least some of the costs entailed in sustainability demands that are linked to the production of first-generation biofuels are transferred to producers, but to a lesser extent than in other agricultural and agro-industrial GVCs given that the biofuels GVCs is multipolar. At the same time, next-generation producers and processors are building their business models to leverage their superior environmental performance. Comparisons of profitability and/ or value-added distribution in such a complex and young GVC are not yet available. There have been some highly controversial busts, such as the bankruptcy in 2015 of the giant biofuel producer Abengoa Bioenergy. But these hiccups have occurred in various functions and niches of the biofuel industry, and thus are unlikely to be an indication of a more general sustainability-driven supplier squeeze exerted by buyers (e.g. fuel distributors). We do observe a process of green capital accumulation in the GVC, but in markedly different ways than in wine and coffee. In the latter two, green capital accumulation can be ascribed to value capture by lead firms, while in biofuels profitability and capital accumulation have emerged through claims on the sustainability of biofuels per se, and thus have been intimately woven with creating, restoring and maintaining legitimacy through environmental upgrading.

The main *environmental outcomes* of biofuel production are related to differential GHG emission reductions in comparison to fossil fuels, and the effects of feedstock production on biodiversity and forest conservation, soil quality, and water use. Increasing feedstock production for biofuels often leads to heightened pressure on natural resource use, not only when new land is cleared but also when intensification occurs to increase yields (Smith, 2010). A particularly problematic situation has emerged in relation to deforestation coming from palm oil expansion in Indonesia (McCarthy, 2012). Many other instances have also been reported on feedstock production leading to the destruction or damage of high-biodiversity areas, soil degradation, and contamination or depletion of water resources (Borras et al., 2010; Dauvergne and Neville, 2009; Mol, 2007; Rosillo-Calle and Johnson, 2010; Smith, 2010).

On GHG emissions, by regulatory demand, biofuels used in the EU have to meet the criteria set in the RED. As discussed in Chapter 3, both the EU and the US set up binding environmental criteria on biofuel production and distribution (Lehrer, 2010; Renckens et al., 2017). Collectively, this regulatory apparatus is now providing much stronger incentives to deliver biofuels yielding better GHG abatement, especially when compared to the previous free-for-all approach – when any feedstock, process and location combination was framed as positive for the environment. However, we cannot assume that these regulatory measures have led to actual GHG emission reductions globally. A vibrant scientific debate is taking place on the net effects of biofuel production and use, including those coming from indirect land use change – which takes place when feedstock production is based on diverting land use originally used for food and feed. On the one hand, Searchinger et al. (2015) show that ethanol produced from US corn and EU wheat does not actually lead to lower GHG emissions, unless it is accompanied by lower food consumption. And even when this is the case, GHG emission reductions remain relatively small. Negative impacts have been estimated for soybean-based biodiesel production in Argentina (Panichelli et al., 2009). On the other hand, studies on ethanol from Brazilian sugar cane indicate that it clearly yields substantial emission reductions in comparison to fossil fuels (Filoso et al., 2015; Wang et al., 2012). Other feedstock/technology combinations sit somewhere in between US corn and Brazilian sugar cane, with an unclear overall impact on global GHG emissions. Next-generation biofuels have much better emission abatement profiles, but are currently much more expensive to produce, and available volumes are still limited.

In sum, the case study of biofuel suggests that in a context of a GVC that is not (yet) dominated by a specific powerful group of lead firms, all sorts of trajectories of economic and environmental upgrading are taking place, including inter-chain upgrading. It also shows that when sustainability is deeply embedded in the *raison d'être* of a GVC, and when it receives appropriate regulatory support, it can lead to positive economic outcomes for a wide range of actors operating at different functions along the value chain. Because of the low consumer visibility of biofuels (for the most part, it is blended in regular gasoline mixes with little or no consumer-facing information), consumer agency has been very limited in shaping or framing sustainability demands. Both biofuel blending and sustainability certification have been led by regulatory processes, setting the biofuels GVC apart from coffee and wine. Yet the actual environmental outcomes of these upgrading processes are at the best mixed, with some benefits arising from GHG emission reductions for some feedstock, process and location combinations, accompanied by problematic impacts on deforestation, biodiversity, soil quality and water use – let alone the commonly reported negative impacts on food security and processes of land-grabbing.

Discussion and Next Steps

The analysis of the wine, coffee and biofuels GVCs suggests that the drivers of upgrading in unipolar GVCs (wine and coffee) have been their lead firms, with international traders acting as implementing agents, while in the multipolar GVC (biofuels), a major role was played by regulators. The results summarized in Table 4.2 show that suppliers have undergone impressive upgrading trajectories and yet have achieved limited economic gains. Suppliers are offering more content, including sustainability features, often to simply keep participating in GVCs – as buyers place increasing demands on them. This often leads to lower margins for suppliers unless productivity gains can more than compensate for higher costs. When suppliers do manage to receive higher prices, it is usually in the context of much larger gains that buyers obtain in the same GVC. In other words, green capital accumulation by lead firms goes hand in hand with a sustainability-driven supplier squeeze. The value created by producers through economic-cum-environmental upgrading is mostly captured by buyers. At the same time, consumers can enjoy a wide variety of special and/or 'sustainable' products that deliver a feel-good factor. In specialty markets,

Table 4.2 Summary of Upgrading Trajectories and Outcomes in the Wine, Coffee and Biofuels GVCs

		Upgrading trajectories				Economic outcomes			Environmental outcomes
		Improving product, process, volume and variety	Changing, adding and/or dropping functions	Inter-chain capability transfer	Drivers of upgrading	For lead firms	For suppliers	For consumers	
Wine	General	Substantial improvements	Many wine producers moving out of grape growing, exporters dropping downstream functions in importing countries	Observed between wine and tourism sectors in South Africa	Retailers and international wine merchants	Positive	Supplier squeeze	Positive: availability of larger variety of quality wines at competitive prices	Unclear, but likely to be limited
	Sustainability elements	Limited pressure from buyers, proactive sustainability management within South Africa	None	Limited	Wine producers	Positive: wider portfolio of wines and delivery of sustainability at no extra cost	Proactive delivery of sustainability elements by producers does not improve their profitability	One of the elements of differentiation, but not a key one	

						Supplier squeeze	
Coffee	General	Substantial improvements	Limited within producing countries, international traders incorporating functions downstream and (to some extent) upstream	Limited	Roasters and international coffee traders	Positive	Positive: availability of larger variety of quality coffees	Limited
	Sustainability elements	Strong demand by retailers and roasters as part of sustainability mainstreaming and product differentiation	Important, due to traceability and risk minimization, especially in private, corporate verification systems	No influence	Originally NGOs and specialty roasters, later mainstream roasters and international traders	Important element of green capital accumulation	Key element in the delivery of a feel-good factor to consumers	Substantial factor in supplier squeeze

(continued)

Table 4.2 (continued)

		Upgrading trajectories				Economic outcomes		Environmental outcomes
Biofuels	General	Substantial improvements	Substantial and ongoing changes as the GVC is still at early stages of development	Substantial and ongoing	Regulatory agencies	Varied picture, but generally positive for many different actors in the GVC	Little visibility to consumers, as biofuels are mostly blended with fossil fuels	GHG emission reductions: impacts vary according to feedstock/location combinations, unclear overall impact, other environmental impacts generally negative
	Sustainability elements	Key element, set in regulation	Key element, especially in relation to incentives for next-generation biofuel production	Key element, especially in relation to incentives for next-generation biofuel production	Regulatory agencies	Essential: sustainability elements embedded in the new definition of biofuels in main consumption markets	Limited consumer knowledge	

Source: Own analysis

this is accompanied by a consumer price premium, which is unequally distributed along the GVC; in mainstream markets, consumer prices tend to remain the same, thus leading to pressure on margins upstream along the chain all the way to producers. This observation is especially relevant in the case of unipolar and highly driven GVCs (coffee and, to some extent, wine), while multipolar GVCs such as biofuels offer a more variegated situation.

These trends are not limited to the wine, coffee and biofuels GVCs. The review of experiences of environmental upgrading summarized earlier in this chapter confirms that the environmental aspects of upgrading are more likely to be stimulated in GVCs characterized by unipolar governance, and where the lead firms are consumer-facing companies with reputational risks. In shipping, a bipolar GVC, environmental upgrading remains limited in absence of regulatory efforts that could facilitate it (as happened in biofuels). In labour-intensive manufacturing, which are often unipolar, environmental upgrading is stimulated mostly by lead firms, but we also see trajectories taking place through mentoring processes in niche markets.

The distribution of *economic outcomes* between lead firms and suppliers arising from upgrading indicate a disproportional capture of sustainability value by buyers to the expense of suppliers in all unipolar GVCs. In bipolar and multipolar GVCs, such as biofuels and shipping, however, the distribution of value added is more balanced among various kinds of operators. Overall, the impact of upgrading on *environmental outcomes* has been limited, especially in comparison with the upgrading efforts entailed. Existing research specifically focused on the environmental outcomes of sustainability certifications in agro-food industries confirms this general picture. A review of over 2,600 peer-reviewed impact studies of sustainability certification (in the banana, cocoa, coffee, oil palm and tea sectors) on social and environmental conditions of production identified only a subset of 24 cases that 'rigorously analysed differences between treatment (certified households) and control groups (uncertified households) for a wide range of response variables' (DeFries et al., 2017: 1). This study found that certification could be associated with positive outcomes (social and/or environmental) for 34 per cent of response variables, with no significant difference for 58 per cent of variables, and negative outcomes for 8 per cent of variables. This suggests that sustainability certifications can have a positive impact, but they are usually narrow and happen only under certain conditions. This is not surprising, and it would be naïve to expect blanket positive results across different contexts and in relation to a variety of environmental (and social) issues. However, it does signal that the success of sustainability certification is related to market expansion rather than actual environmental outcomes.

Overall, we observe a multiplication and expansion of *markets* for sustainable products and services – and the standard development, certification, auditing, accreditation and consulting industry that goes with it (Lernoud et al., 2016), rather than the achievement of sustainability in production and processing along GVCs (Ponte, 2012). So far, this has led to many efforts to better include suppliers in 'sustainable GVCs' through value chain interventions (DeFries et al., 2017; Humphrey and Navas-Alemán, 2010; Neilson and Shonk, 2014; Taglioni and Winkler, 2016), but much less so in ensuring that certifications, standards and other sustainability initiatives actually lead to improved environmental outcomes. This may be changing, as the ISEAL Alliance (an association of sustainability standards developers) now requires its core members to comply with its 'Impacts Code of Good Practice', which may increase pressure on the main sustainability certification initiatives to show that they actually make a difference. For the time being, lead firms are still placing 'blame' on upstream actors for the negative environmental repercussions of GVC activities. In other words, they limit their risk and generate capital accumulation by solving the environmental problems that they contributed to create (Havice and Campling, 2017).

These findings dispel the long-held view, until quite recently, that managing sustainability issues may hurt the economic performance of lead firms. The case study evidence provided in this book shows that sustainability management often actually facilitates green capital accumulation for lead firms in GVCs, which partly arises from a sustainability-driven squeeze of those suppliers that embark in economic-cum-environmental upgrading. In the next chapter, I discuss what public sector institutions and international organizations can do to make sure that sustainability management and upgrading deliver not only the bottom line for lead firms, but also a more equal distribution of economic benefits along GVCs and tangible benefits for the environment.

5 | ORCHESTRATING SUSTAINABILITY

Business conduct alone will not be sufficient to address the sustainability challenges that societies are facing around the globe. Governments and international organizations have an essential role to play in ensuring common rules of engagement for business, and in raising the bar of environmental sustainability. Regulation, at the local, national, regional and global levels, is one of these tools – but needs to be complemented by other directive and facilitative instruments. It also needs to be designed to reflect the realities and everyday practices that take place in global value chains, not because they need to be accepted as they are, but because they need to be reshaped. Not all challenges of sustainability are created by GVC operators, of course, but the conduit for addressing many of these challenges goes through value chains (Milberg and Winkler, 2013: 281).

In this chapter, I examine the possible mechanisms and strategies that nation states and international organizations (IOs)[1] can use to shape (local and global) environmental outcomes for the public good (Abbott et al., 2015, 2017; Graham and Thompson, 2015; Hale and Roger, 2014; Keohane and Victor, 2011). I assess to what extent orchestration can facilitate not only processes of upgrading in GVCs, but also improved environmental outcomes. While in Chapter 3 I analyzed how institutional power has shaped governance in selected GVCs over time, in this chapter I take a normative approach and highlight how orchestration can be carried out to shape desired outcomes. This will involve drawing from existing knowledge to identify possible factors that can facilitate successful orchestration, and then assess whether these factors apply in the case studies of the wine, coffee and biofuels GVCs. This analysis will be embedded in broader academic and policy discussions on environmental governance and policy, and especially in relation to transnational sustainability governance. In the conclusion chapter, I will discuss to what extent these options – together with civil society pressure, media exposure, activism and protest – are likely to achieve meaningful change given how contemporary 'green capitalism' operates.

Transnational Governance of Sustainability

A major area of interest in the field of transnational governance has been establishing cooperation, conflict and coexistence of private and public authority (Bartley, 2007; Bernstein and Cashore, 2007; Büthe and Mattli, 2011; Cashore et al., 2004; Gulbrandsen, 2010, 2014; Pattberg, 2007), as indicated in Chapter 2. The complex, layered and fragmented governance architectures that characterize the environmental field have resulted in a 'governance deficit' (Biermann et al., 2009; Haas, 2004; Zelli and Van Asselt, 2013), which public authorities and international organizations need to address by acting as 'entrepreneurs to facilitate collaboration with non-state actors within their spheres of expertise' (Andonova, 2010: 26). A now extensive literature has shown that public sector capacity still has a crucial role in facilitating the emergence, implementation and enforcement of private regulation, and that successful public support is more likely to happen when norms, objectives and interests overlap between the public and private spheres (Auld, 2014; Foley, 2013; Gale and Haward, 2011; Gulbrandsen, 2014; Verbruggen, 2013). But we know a lot less about what combinations of soft and hard, direct and indirect instruments work in what circumstances.

The current fragmentation of governance architectures in the sustainability field means that governments and international organizations need to steer a wide variety of actors and employ a combination of mechanisms to succeed in addressing environmental challenges. One way of conceiving the actual and potential role of public authority in this field is through the figures of the 'green state' (Death, 2016a), the 'green entrepreneurial state' (Mazzucato, 2015a, 2015b) and 'green industrial policy' (Pegels, 2014; Rodrik, 2014; Whitfield et al., 2015). In all these variations, the state carries out industrial policy targeted to stimulate the green economy, through subsidies, research, infrastructure and financing, including lending targeted towards 'the most innovative, risky and uncertain parts of the "green economy"' (Mazzucato, 2015b: 134). The green state is willing and able to take on risk and uncertainty, as 'most of the radical, revolutionary innovations that have fuelled the dynamics of capitalism ... trace the most courageous, early and capital intensive "entrepreneurial" investments back to the State' (Mazzucato, 2015b: 134). State investment banks in this context direct lending to areas where private banks and venture capital do not enter or fear. These supply-side policies and the indirect creation of incentives are as important as demand-side policies, such as sustainability standards, carbon taxes and GHG reduction targets. While nudging might be helpful on the demand side (Sunstein, 2014), a strong push is also needed on the supply side to minimize uncertainty.

The concept of 'orchestration' provides a helpful public authority angle to the process of sustainability governance. It is also an intuitive heuristic device – as the conductor of an orchestra seeks to make musicians work towards a common goal, public authorities seek to combine different kinds of instruments for the public good. Orchestration entails paying critical attention 'not only to who is involved in transnational governance, but also to the ways in which [public] transnational networks deploy different sources of authority and mechanisms of steering in order to govern' (Andonova et al., 2009: 57). It goes beyond the established distinctions between self-regulation, co-regulation and hierarchy to highlight the combinations that may be successful in pushing forward a public environmental agenda in transnational governance (Gunningham, 2002; Gunningham et al., 1998; Sinclair, 1997).

Abbott and Snidal (2009b) distinguish two broad sets of mechanisms under the concept of orchestration: 'directive' and 'facilitative' (see also Schleifer, 2013). On the one hand, they see directive orchestration as relying on the authority of the state and seeking to incorporate private initiatives into its regulatory framework (through mandating principles, transparency, and codes of conduct). On the other hand, they conceive of facilitative orchestration as relying on softer instruments, such as the provision of material and ideational support (financial support, technical support, endorsement) used to kick-start new initiatives and/or to further shape and support them. Similarly, Hale and Roger (2014: 60–61) see orchestration as 'a process whereby states or intergovernmental organizations initiate, guide, broaden, and strengthen transnational governance by non-state and/or sub-state actors', and distinguish between 'initiating' orchestration, where states or IOs are active in forging a new initiative, and 'shaping' orchestration, where they lend support to already existing initiatives.

More recently, Abbott et al. (2015: 4) have taken a narrower view of orchestration as occurring when an 'international organization enlists and supports intermediary actors to address target actors in pursuit of … governance goals'. Orchestration from this perspective is a specific form of governance characterized by soft instruments and indirect influence on target actors, in what they call the 'O-I-T model' (orchestrator-intermediary-target) (Abbott et al., 2015) or 'R-I-T model' (regulator-intermediary-target) (Abbott et al., 2017). In these approaches, intermediation and orchestration are used synonymously to identify a specific form of governance that is distinguished from three other forms: (1) hierarchy, the more traditional form where a governor applies hard regulatory tools directly to its targets; (2) delegation, where the governor uses hard regulatory tools but delegates the regulatory function to another party, and thus has indirect influence (Green, 2013, 2017b); and (3) collaboration, where the governor utilizes soft tools, such as ideational or material incentives, and collaborates directly with the targets of regulation (Cutler et al., 1999).

In Abbott et al.'s (2015) model, intermediation is indirect because orchestrators enlist an intermediary institution between them and the targets of regulation, and is soft because it uses facilitative instruments. Abbott et al. (2015) also propose a series of hypotheses to explore when intermediation is more likely to work: low orchestrator capabilities in the focal domain; intermediary availability; low orchestrator focus (other actors are also operating in the governance domain); and an organizational structure that facilitates entrepreneurship. To these, they add two hypotheses that apply specifically to international organizations: there is divergence of goals among member states; and there is weak oversight of member states in the focal domain (Abbott et al., 2015: 20–30). These conditions, with the exception of organizational culture, are based on rational choice and institutionalist considerations.

In the following discussion, I return to Abbott and Snidal's (2009a) earlier and broader conceptualization of orchestration as an approach where a public authority applies a combination of different instruments – direct and indirect, soft and hard (Henriksen and Ponte, 2018; Schleifer, 2013), thus acting as a kind of green entrepreneurial state (Mazzucato, 2015b). I do so in recognition that public governors often use a combination of mechanisms in attempting to achieve policy goals, and that outcome effectiveness is linked to different combinations of these mechanisms in the context of industry or issue specificity, rather than the superiority of one governance form or institutional setting over another.

In the approach used in this chapter, intermediation is indeed an important governance tool, but does not equate with orchestration. In other words, orchestrators may combine hard regulatory tools with softer instruments, such as mandates or subsidies, sometimes with the threat of future or stronger regulation. Orchestrators, when using soft instruments, may also act both directly and through intermediaries. Furthermore, they can use other hybrid mechanisms, such as placing their representatives in regulatory intermediaries – an approach that is neither pure intermediation (the orchestrator populates the intermediary) nor collaboration (the orchestrator does not regulate directly). Orchestrators can also employ different tools at different times.

The Enabling Factors of Public Orchestration

Lister et al. (2015) proposed four possible enabling factors of orchestration (rather than intermediation per se) in successfully addressing sustainability issues along GVCs: *combinatory efforts, high issue visibility, interest alignment* and *low levels of regulatory uncertainty*.

For *combinatory efforts*, I refer to the descriptive classification of orchestration instruments developed in Abbott and Snidal's (2009b) earlier work. In my application of this classification, I distinguish between: (1) directive orchestration instruments, including international and national regulation, the 'threat of regulation', also known in the literature as the 'gorilla in the closet' or 'shadow of hierarchy' factor (Bäckstrand, 2008; Verbruggen, 2013), the incorporation of private standards, codes of conduct or transparency measures in public regulation, the provision of direct subsidies and the setting of mandates, and public procurement and other direct forms of financial support and investment; and (2) facilitative orchestration instruments, where public authorities either facilitate, indirectly influence, network, and/or participate with other stakeholders in key initiatives or groups – such as industry associations, multi-stakeholder initiatives, and industry conferences. I suggest that we can expect more successful orchestration when public authorities employ a *combination* of substantial directive *and* facilitative instruments.

On *issue visibility*, we can expect more potential for orchestration if the product, industry and/or related set of environmental issues are visible to the general public, and particularly to consumers (Dauvergne and Lister, 2013). This can occur because the environmental issue itself is obviously visible (e.g. accumulating trash on urban streets, dark exhaust coming from ships) or because it is rendered so through consumer labels, public campaigns or social media exposure. Therefore, orchestration is more likely to succeed in GVCs that handle consumer-facing and branded products and/or in those that have been targeted by social movements, the media or regulation. When the environmental issue is not clearly visible to key stakeholders, orchestration efforts can include instruments that can enhance visibility.

On *interest alignment*, we can expect better orchestration possibilities if there is substantial overlap between public and private interests (Schleifer, 2013; Verbruggen, 2013). Because different value chain nodes are regulated by different authorities, there may be different kinds of (mis)alignments between private and public sector interests in different GVC nodes. While it is rare for interests to be aligned at all nodes, alignment at key nodes can provide a strong entry point for orchestrators to attempt to stimulate the transmission of environmental improvements along the whole GVC. An additional complication is that alignment between public and private sector interests may differ in different groups of countries (e.g. coffee-producing countries in the Global South and coffee-consuming countries in the Global North). In any case, interest alignment is not static, and it can be targeted as an objective of orchestration.

The nature of GVCs makes orchestration difficult because the regulation of environmental concerns is functionally fragmented and geographically multilayered, and because it is often overlapping with multiple and diverse voluntary sustainability initiatives (Alter and Meunier, 2009; Biermann et al., 2009; Fransen, 2012; Haas, 2004; Zelli and Van Asselt, 2013). *Regulatory uncertainty*, however, can make it even more difficult to orchestrate successfully. Private actors are less prone to invest in environmental upgrading when the operational framework allowing them to recoup related costs is unstable. Regulatory uncertainty is more likely to affect orchestration when it applies to key GVC nodes, making it more challenging for an orchestrator at any node to promote transmission mechanisms upstream and/or downstream. However, regulatory uncertainty can be addressed by interventions such as: regulatory cooling-off periods (during which time rules cannot be changed); open processes of regulatory reform (e.g. setting clear and credible time frames and discussing possible changes with all major stakeholders); regional protocols and mutual recognition processes for sustainability standards and certifications; alignment of different national and regional regulations; and the promotion of common standard systems that employ modular extras for specific issues and/or different levels of compliance (as in scoring, star or traffic light systems).

In the rest of this chapter, I proceed in two steps. In the *first step*, I examine how these four factors (combinatory efforts, issue visibility, interest alignment and regulatory uncertainty) are shaping public orchestration for sustainability in two capital-intensive GVCs (aviation and maritime shipping). To maintain a feasible focus, I apply this approach to one specific environmental issue – that of greenhouse gas (GHG) emissions. Transport is a perfect exemplifying case of the complexities of orchestration. It is a truly global industry, and thus subject to multiple and overlapping jurisdictions, and has a systemically important impact – accounting for 13 per cent of global CO_2 emissions. While total CO_2 emissions in the EU-27 declined by 15 per cent between 1990 and 2009, emissions from transport actually increased by 29 per cent. Within transport, aviation and maritime shipping represent two extreme cases. Aviation has the highest CO_2 emissions per weight-passenger/km; shipping has the lowest. Aviation is at the forefront of innovation in alternative fuels, while shipping has only recently started to explore ways of minimizing its environmental impact. Comparing these two industries is also particularly useful because they are similar in many other respects: (1) both are capital-intensive; (2) both are of major importance in greasing the cogs of the global economy; (3) both are systemically important polluters – accounting for 2–3 per cent of global GHG emissions each, with business-as-usual scenarios indicating significant future increases; (4) their assets (aircraft and ships) are mobile, making orchestration particularly difficult; and (5) both are bipolar in their GVC governance structures – in shipping, the two groups of lead firms are cargo owners and shipping companies (Lister et al., 2015), while in aviation they are airlines and aircraft manufacturers (Henriksen and Ponte, 2018). In the *second step*, I filter the empirical evidence provided in Chapters 3 and 4 on the wine, coffee and biofuels GVCs through the lenses of orchestration, and examine whether different governance structures (unipolar in coffee and wine, multipolar in biofuels) affect orchestration dynamics and possibilities.

Public Orchestration in the Aviation GVC

The aviation industry provides a critical case study to understand orchestration. Within the transport sector, it has the highest CO_2 emissions per unit/weight transported, and is projected to have a faster growth rate than any other mode of transport.[2] It has experienced constant growth over the last three decades and continues to do so, spurred by low-cost airlines and growth in emerging markets (Gossling and Upham, 2009). Air travel emits 650 million tons of CO_2 per year[3] and is responsible for approximately 2 per cent of annual anthropogenic CO_2 emissions or 10 per cent of total emissions from transport, with estimates suggesting that it could rise to 3 per cent of global emissions by 2030 and to 5 per cent by 2050.[4] Longer flights and more passengers have entailed a rapid growth of total passenger-kilometres (pkm) travelled, from 28 billion pkm in 1950 to 5.4 trillion pkm in 2012. By 2012, aviation was moving almost 3 billion people, a growth rate of almost 5 per cent over the previous year and up from 960 million passengers in 1986 and 31 million in 1950.[5] Improved aircraft and engine design and materials, as well as improved air control and airport operations, have decreased the unit rate of emissions, but these actions are not enough to curb the predicted future increase of emissions.[6] Design changes have doubled the efficiency of commercial aircraft since 1960, but progress has been slower from the late 1980s to the early 2000s due to lower fuel prices and a tripling in the average age of aircraft (Gossling and Upham, 2009).[7]

Aviation is under normative pressure to address its growth of GHG emissions, but needs to do so in a global, comprehensive manner – given that it operates at extremely low margins (Gossling and Upham, 2009). Yet the international organization that regulates the industry (the International Civil Aviation Organization – ICAO) has historically failed to seriously tackle the environmental impacts of its operators. The other international agreement that could have regulated GHG emissions (the Paris Agreement) failed to include aviation in its remit. Therefore, a combination of normative pressure and regulatory failure at the global level entails that national and regional governments have taken up the mantle of orchestrators.

A period of higher oil prices in 2010–2014 provided stronger economic incentives to improve efficiency efforts, given that fuel costs account for about one-third of airline operating costs on average (Gossling and Upham, 2009). As a result, the industry is now focused on regulating and supporting the development of aviation biofuels. In the short period of a little over a decade, we have witnessed the emergence of an aviation biofuel industry – from the development of production pathways, to demonstration-scale operations and commercial-scale production facilities (Henriksen and Ponte, 2018). The American Society for Testing and Materials (ASTM), a voluntary standards developer, has designed and approved specifications for various biofuels; over 20 major airlines have pledged to use biofuels with lower carbon impact than regular jet fuel; and more than 10 commercial airlines have been using a blend including biofuels for an increasing number of scheduled flights.[8] According to *Biofuels Digest*,[9] as of February 2018, about 100,000 flights have been carried out with a blend of aviation biofuels since the inaugural flight by Virgin Airlines in February 2008 – still a very small proportion, but increasing rapidly.

Combinatory Efforts

Public orchestration for sustainability has been relatively successful in aviation because the relevant government agencies in the EU and the US have enacted a green entrepreneurial state model (Mazzucato, 2015b) by leveraging a *combination* of directive and facilitative measures to create feasible incentives – backed up by regulation or credible regulatory threats.

Directive Orchestration Instruments

Several directive orchestration instruments in the aviation GVC have focused on regulating and supporting the development of biofuels. For the time being, the price of biofuel remains higher than for regular jet fuel, although the gap was closing previous to the 2014–2017 drop in international oil prices. The aviation industry runs on very small margins, and individual airlines cannot afford to pay extra for biofuels unless all airlines do. This means that aviation biofuels not only need subsidies and/or a system of taxes on fossil fuels for carbon emissions, but also a global governance framework setting up a level playing field. They need investment incentives and the creation of a volume of demand that is not currently present at market prices (Henriksen and Ponte, 2018).

At the intergovernmental level, several directive tools are relevant to CO_2 emissions. Domestic flights were included in CO_2 emission calculations of the Kyoto Protocol, and remain so in the Paris Agreement of 2015. However, international flights have been kept out of both the Kyoto Protocol and the Paris Agreement. The ICAO is supposed to regulate the environmental impact of aviation at the international level, but has done little until very recently. In February 2016, the ICAO agreed on a global standard for CO_2 emissions for aircraft to be applied, but only from 2020 onwards and only to new aircraft. In October 2016, it finally agreed on a global market-based measure (MBM) for emissions – the Carbon Offsetting and Reduction Scheme for International Aviation (CORSIA).[10] The scheme will be voluntary from 2021 to 2026 and mandatory thereafter. Offsets are expected to apply to around 80 per cent of emissions, but only in relation to 2020 levels.

At the regional and national levels, notable has been the EU's attempt in 2012 to extend its Emissions Trading Scheme (ETS) to international flights arriving in the EU. However, the EU subsequently delayed its application due to opposition from the US and China in particular. Now that CORSIA has been enacted, the EU may actually change its approach, although this is too early to say. Importantly, in the EU ETS biofuels would count for zero emissions. The European Commission has taken a number of other directive orchestration initiatives that have a direct bearing on the development and use of biofuels in aviation. As explained in the analysis of institutional power in Chapter 3, the Renewable Energy Directive (2009/28/EC)[11] on the promotion of the use of energy from renewable sources established mandatory targets to be achieved, some of which also apply to biofuels used in aviation (including international flights) when sold in a member state. Therefore, aviation biofuels qualify for incentives by the member states when they comply with the established sustainability criteria (Ponte, 2014a, 2014b). To avoid the controversies that have plagued first-generation biofuels produced from feedstock that could be used for food and feed, the industry is focusing on the development of next-generation aviation biofuels that are based on improved and new transformation processes of cellulosic material and other waste, and/or on the development of algae feedstock.

In the US, governmental agencies and the military have been of special importance in supporting the development of aviation biofuels. The Environmental Protection Agency (EPA) sets annual quotas of biofuel to be blended into fossil fuels. Fuel operators are obliged to meet certain quotas and are required to submit a certain amount of Renewable Identification Numbers (RINs). This provides opportunities for developing an aviation biofuel market, as these fuel pathways are now eligible for crediting and generating RINs in accordance with the US Renewable Fuel Standard (RFS) regulation.

Important investment has been provided by the US Department of Defense, the Department of Agriculture (USDA), the Department of Energy (DoE) and the Federal Aviation Authority (FAA). The US military has promoted the testing and certification of biofuels, has secured the allocation of USD 510 million on co-financing production facilities (together with the USDA and the DoE), and has started purchasing aviation biofuels for use in its aircraft. The justifications for directive orchestration are multifaceted in the US: from 'creating opportunity for rural America', including the production of feedstock from a variety of sources and bioprocessing opportunities in small towns;[12] to improving energy security by decreasing oil imports and increasing oil price stability; and securing the long-term reliability of fuel supply to the military, diversifying fuel sources and increasing operational flexibility.

Of particular interest is the special role that the US Navy has played in this realm. In 2009, the Secretary of the Navy announced that it sought to reduce its consumption of energy, decrease its reliance on foreign sources of oil, and significantly increase its use of alternative energy – in view of improving its combat capability and increasing energy security. One of the five energy goals of this strategy was to demonstrate and then deploy a 'Great Green Fleet' that would include ships and aircraft using alternative sources of energy.[13] The navy demonstration conducted during the 2012 Rim of the Pacific (RIMPAC) exercise, the world's largest international maritime exercise, was a key step in the direction of the navy's goal to use a 50 per cent biofuel blend in its ships and aircraft by 2016. Although biofuels are still more expensive than regular military jet fuel, the navy counts on having cost-competitive aviation biofuel for its aircraft within a few years. Therefore, when the 'Great Green Fleet' programme was threatened in the US Senate and House Armed Services Committee in

May 2012, Congress reversed that decision on the basis of a national security argument in view of increasing war-fighting capability. This was the result of a unique coalition of military-industrial, environmental and agricultural interests.[14] The RIMPAC exercise was repeated in 2016, signalling the actual deployment of the 'Great Green Fleet'.[15] However, the future of this operation has been uncertain since the start of the Trump administration in 2017.

Facilitative Orchestration Instruments

Public orchestrators provided important facilitative support to a variety of actors, interests and multi-stakeholder initiatives in the aviation industry. The exception to this trend has been the ICAO, which has used very few facilitative orchestration instruments. In relation to negotiations leading to the development of CORSIA, it carried out two Global Aviation Dialogues (GLADs) in 2015 and 2016 to facilitate information sharing and exchange of ideas. In relation to biofuels, I could only identify two initiatives: (1) in 2010, it passed a resolution (A37–19) 'encouraging' member states and industry to actively participate in further work on sustainable alternative fuels for aviation as part of the basket of measures to limit carbon emissions from international aviation; and (2) in June 2012, it created the Aviation and Sustainable Alternative Fuels Expert Group to develop recommendations in view of further facilitating the global development and deployment of sustainable alternative fuels for aviation.

While the ICAO was taking tentative and modest steps, the most important industry association, the International Air Transport Association (IATA), in 2010 decided to commit to carbon-neutral growth by 2020 and reduce carbon emissions by 50 per cent by 2050. The IATA represents 240 airlines in over 115 countries, carrying 84 per cent of the world's air traffic.[16] The IATA took this step to provide a vision and aspirational goals that could allow its members to keep growing while improving their environmental impact and maintaining their licence to operate in the eyes of the political system and civil society – as many industry actors perceived that they could soon be taxed for CO_2 emissions or be asked to purchase emission trading certificates. The IATA signalled that it would seek these reductions mainly through the adoption of biofuels, first in small quantities, but with the goal of eventually flying most aircrafts on 50/50 blends of regular jet fuel and biofuel.

In absence of ICAO activity in this realm, and given the proactive IATA stance, it was the US and the EU that took initiative as public orchestrators, engaging with: *industry associations*, such as the IATA itself, but also with Airlines for America and the Advanced Biofuels Association; the *biofuel conference circuit*, in particular the annual Advanced Biofuels Leadership Conference (ABLC) in the US, and the World Bio Markets conference in the EU – both of which usually include special sessions on aviation biofuels; and a series of *multi-stakeholder initiatives* (MSIs) on sustainable aviation. Regulators used their social networks and conference fora to facilitate the uptake of sustainable biofuels in markets that are out of their jurisdiction (e.g. for fuel used in international flights) (Henriksen and Ponte, 2018).

In the US, the most prominent MSI has been the Commercial Aviation Alternative Fuels Initiative (CAAFI), but the Midwest Aviation Sustainable Biofuel Initiative (MASBI) and Sustainable Aviation Biofuels Northwest (SAFN) have also played important roles. In the EU, regional/national initiatives of this kind are present in Germany (Aireg), France (GiFAS/IFP Energies Nouvelles), the Netherlands (SkyNRG), Spain (Bioqueroseno) and the Nordic region (NISA).[17] These initiatives have benefited from political and sometimes material support by individual governments and the EU. Government agencies (sometimes through these very MSIs) have been key players in forging bilateral/multilateral alliances on aviation biofuels, and government support has included the funding of several research centres focused on biofuels for aviation, both in the US and in the EU.[18] In more recent times, airport authorities have also come into the fray, in view of providing common infrastructure for the supply of aviation biofuels for all airlines using their facilities. Oslo was the first airport to do so in 2016, joined by Bergen in 2017 (they are both managed by Norway's state-run airport operator, Avinor), while Seattle-Tacoma, Helsinki and others are planning to follow suit.

As we have seen above, in the US, various government departments and agencies played a decisive and direct role, but they have also played a more indirect role – without resorting to pure intermediation. The Federal Aviation Authority (FAA), for example, was pivotal in forming CAAFI back in 2006 and then in helping its consolidation. At that time, the FAA acted as convenor and called upon key relevant stakeholders to provide responses to three concerns affecting the development of aviation biofuels: supply security, affordability and price stability, and environmental impact. As a result, the Aerospace Industries Association, Airlines for America and the FAA formally established CAAFI, bringing together key players from the private sector, government and (later on) civil society. These three organizations (together with the Airports Council International/North America) are the current sponsors of CAAFI, which counts approximately 300 stakeholders. CAAFI's main aim is to exchange information and coordinate stakeholder efforts in alternative aviation fuels, and its main activities centre on technical workshops, industry conference participation and other outreach activities, lobbying, and communication with the news media.[19]

In the EU, several policy documents have provided ideational support to the aviation biofuel industry. In 2011, the EC adopted the White Paper 'The Transport 2050 Roadmap to a Single European Transport Area',[20] which included 40 specific initiatives aimed at reducing Europe's dependence on imported oil and at cutting carbon emissions in transport by 60 per cent by 2050. The report 'Flightpath 2050: Europe's Vision for Aviation',[21] also published in 2011, presented a long-term vision for European aviation, suggested further improving the energy efficiency of aircraft and operations, and highlighted the need to produce liquid biofuels. A road map developed to support the achievement of Flightpath's goals and challenges called for increasing the share of biofuel use in aviation from 2 per cent in 2020 to at least 40 per cent by 2050 – as set out in the Transport White Paper. Finally, the 2013 'European Alternative Fuels Strategy'[22] provided political strategies and specific actions towards decarbonizing transport without impacting on economic growth, a typical 'green capitalism' statement. It addressed for the first time the potential of new aviation fuels and highlighted the need for financing instruments and market incentives to support the construction of production plants for aviation biofuels.

Other Enabling Factors

The evidence presented in the previous section suggests that public orchestration for GHG abatement was relatively successful because it was based on a *combination* of directive and facilitative measures. However, three other facilitating factors also contributed to moving the aviation industry in the right direction: (1) high *issue visibility*, as the industry is consumer-facing and has a widespread reputation for being a high CO_2 emitter; (2) an *alignment of interests* between regulators in the EU and US and the main industry association (IATA) and regional associations; and (3) a relatively high level of *regulatory uncertainty*, as sustainability issues have *not* been regulated either by national aviation authorities or by the Commissioner for Transport at the EU level. Yet the general perception in the aviation GVC has been that it is likely to be subject to regulation of emissions, either through carbon taxation or a cap-and-trade system. Until recently, however, it was not clear what shape regulation of emissions for international flights would take, and how it would be implemented. Therefore, aviation at the time of analysis was facing a relatively high level of regulatory uncertainty along the whole GVC. This uncertainty has now somewhat decreased with the coming into force of CORSIA under the ICAO, although doubts remain on its actual implementation by member states.

Looking Ahead

Despite vibrant orchestration efforts by the EU and the US, the weak role played by the ICAO until recently has translated into generally weak regulatory muscle, modest reduction targets, and long implementation time frames in the aviation GVC. Paradoxically, the legitimating effect of existing orchestration efforts may have actually been instrumental in keeping the industry outside the Paris Agreement regulatory framework. The justification for staying out of Paris was based on the existence of a dedicated intergovernmental organization (ICAO) that could regulate emission abatements, a similar argument used by the shipping industry in relation to its own intergovernmental organization (see below). The ICAO has finally stepped up its efforts by finalizing its CORSIA emission monitoring system, but needs to ensure its proper application, ramp up targets and shorten implementation schedules. The ICAO should also apply combinatory efforts to orchestration, including the use of various facilitative instruments. It should support and possibly coordinate the various MSIs on sustainable aviation and encourage and stimulate the development of common infrastructure for aviation biofuel supply at many more airports than at present. Large battery-operated aircraft for commercial aviation are decades away from being technically and financially feasible, and thus sustainable aviation biofuels can provide an important stopgap contribution to partially taming GHG emissions in a fast-growing industry. These measures all together would constitute important interim steps, but are unlikely to yield a much-needed major reduction in emissions, which would need much more radical and systemic interventions (see the Conclusion).

Public Orchestration in the Maritime Shipping GVC

Maritime shipping is the transmission belt of global production, trade and consumption, as it carries 90 per cent of international trade volume by weight.[23] Compared to other transport modes, sea transport carries a relatively 'green image' because ships emit less CO_2 per ton-mile than rail, truck or air transport. Given its scale and rapid growth, however, the maritime sector has become a major contributor to global GHG emissions,[24] and yet has remained largely unaccountable until recently, with sustainability considerations seriously lagging behind other industries. This is puzzling, considering that maritime shipping has its own dedicated international organization (the International Maritime Organization – IMO) that could be expected to catalyse efforts for environmental improvements (Lister et al., 2015).

While technical analyses of sustainable shipping are emerging, questions about effective governance have just started to be addressed in existing research, which has covered ship recycling, energy efficiency, ballast water management, and emissions of CO_2, particulate matter, sulphur oxides (SOx) and nitrogen oxides (NOx). The literature in this field suggests that shipping standards seem to have gravitated towards a 'regulatory middle' (DeSombre, 2006), and that state-centric, hierarchical governance frameworks have failed to effectively regulate environmental and social issues (Roe, 2012). Regulatory fragmentation on environmental issues is reported to be increasing (Hackmann, 2012) – due to the weak regulatory efforts by the IMO (Van Leeuwen, 2010). In the rest of this section, I proceed in the same manner as I did in the analysis of the aviation GVC. I first examine what combinatory efforts of orchestration, if any, have been employed in the shipping industry, then I return briefly to the other three facilitating factors of orchestration (issue visibility, interest alignment and regulatory uncertainty).

Combinatory Efforts

The IMO has played a weak role as an environmental orchestrator in the shipping industry. Its directive instruments have been fairly weak and incomplete until very recently, and it has been largely unable or unwilling to enact facilitative instruments. Orchestration via facilitative measures by national and regional regulatory agencies has been haphazard and piecemeal, rather than being part of a clear strategy. The multiplication of green rating schemes in shipping has taken place largely without government facilitation (Lister et al., 2015). Some other low-hanging fruits of orchestration have not yet been used, such as enrolling classification societies as environmental auditors – since they have been audited ships for other purposes for over three centuries. Therefore, orchestration in the shipping industry has been carried out with a very limited *combinatory* approach.

Directive Orchestration Instruments

Directive instruments to regulate maritime shipping pollution and biodiversity damage have evolved slowly since the 1990s. With the exception of oil spills, regulatory development has stalled with respect to all of the major issue areas, including CO_2 and other emissions. Created in 1948, the IMO has a mandate to promote maritime safety, security and environmental protection to 'create a regulatory framework for the shipping industry that is fair and effective, universally adopted and universally implemented'.[25] As such, it has authority over several important international conventions, including the 1973 International Convention for the Prevention of Pollution from Ships (MARPOL) and subsequent amendments and annexes, which has been tasked with environmental protection, including the possible regulation of CO_2 emissions (Lister et al., 2015).

Global climate change mitigation started being discussed as a key issue in shipping circles only from the late 1990s onwards. During the period 2007–2012, shipping accounted for an average of 2.8 per cent of annual global CO_2 emissions.[26] Due to the highly mobile and transnational nature of the sector, allocation of maritime emissions to a specific nation has proven difficult. The regulation of emissions in this sector was left out of the Kyoto Protocol in 1997 and placed with the IMO. Since then, the IMO has discussed various market-based measures (MBMs), such as an emissions trading scheme or a bunker levy, to cut emissions (Lister et al., 2015). Shipping was left out from the Paris Agreement of 2015 as well, with the IMO again tasked with regulating CO_2 emissions.

The first regulation adopted by the IMO to mitigate global climate change entered into force in 2013 and consists of two technical measures: (1) the Energy Efficiency Design Index (EEDI), which is a minimum design requirement for energy efficiency for all new ships; and (2) the Ship Energy Efficiency Management Plan (SEEMP), a mandatory document for existing and new ships that specifies operational initiatives to enhance energy efficiency. The SEEMP requirements are vaguely specified, and in the coming decades the EEDI and SEEMP are expected to only slow down growth in emissions, which are expected to rise in absolute terms due to a forecasted global growth in demand for shipping services (Lister et al., 2015). In April 2018, the IMO finally adopted a strategy for the reduction of CO_2 emissions for international shipping, with a target of at least 50 per cent reduction by 2050 (compared to 2008), while also seeking efforts towards phasing out CO_2 emissions completely.[27]

Given the IMO's delayed action and weak leadership, national and regional regulatory initiatives have attempted to fill the void. For example, the European Commission has pursued a mandatory scheme for monitoring, reporting and verification of CO_2 emissions (MRV) for ships calling at European ports.[28] The MRV scheme entered into force in 2018, thus adding a regional layer to IMO regulation. Both the EU and the IMO schemes require shipping companies to monitor and report their CO_2 emissions, but the EU scheme is more comprehensive and transparent, provides disaggregated data, and requires external verification. The IMO scheme is verified by the flag state and only provides aggregate and anonymized data. The EU has started a process of consultation in view of possibly revising its MRV scheme to be aligned with the IMO system of CO_2 emission monitoring,[29] reporting and verification. This could water down the EU regulatory framework on shipping emissions.

Facilitative Orchestration Instruments

Facilitative instruments of orchestration in shipping have not been deployed as much as in the case of aviation. The lack of coherent international regulation for CO_2 emissions until very recently spurred a wave of voluntary governance mechanisms, but mostly with very limited support or guidance from regulators (Lister, 2015). With perceptions in the industry of growing regulatory pressure but uncertain implementation, shipping industry operators started engaging in multi-stakeholder initiatives on 'green shipping' and in the development and adoption of voluntary standards, such as the Clean Cargo Working Group (CCWG), the Sustainable Shipping Initiative (SSI), the Clean Shipping Index

(CSI), the Environmental Ship Index (ESI), the Triple-E Initiative, and RightShip (see details in Lister et al., 2015: 191).

The CCWG was formed in 2003 by Business for Social Responsibility, a consultancy group. The CCWG includes cargo owners and shipping companies as members, and aims at improving the transparency and environmental performance of container ships and shipping companies through standardized measures and what they identify as best practices. The SSI sees itself as more of a lighthouse, providing a vision and future direction for sustainable shipping efforts. The SSI was established by the Forum for the Future, and includes the participation of the WWF as well as cargo owners (e.g. Unilever) and shipping companies. While the CCWG is setting private standards, the SSI aims to influence policymakers and to inspire the IMO and other regulators to advance greener shipping practices. The SSI has developed an online tool and published a report to help sort through the many green shipping rating schemes that have emerged in recent years. These schemes are only starting to influence environmental protection in shipping. In a world fleet counting more than 47,000 commercial vessels, they cover only a small share – as of 2014, the SSI listed 2,000 vessels and the CCWG 2,300 vessels.[30] Also, different schemes target different segments of the shipping industry (e.g. the CCWG is focused on container shipping only, RightShip on tankers) and the scope of environmental problems addressed in the rating schemes differ, as do definitions and data reporting methodologies.

Given the limited role of the IMO in orchestrating sustainability in shipping so far, research efforts are focusing on whether and how *port authorities* could play an important orchestration role as well (Gibbs et al., 2014; Poulsen et al., 2018; Verhoeven, 2010). Port authorities perform four key functions: as landlords (providing land and infrastructure); as regulators (setting tariffs, environmental standards for tenants and other port users, and engaging in spatial planning); as operators (having their own fleets of harbour craft and equipment to provide safe fairways); and as community managers (bringing together a variety of port stakeholders to improve collaboration and port performance) (Poulsen et al., 2018; Verhoeven, 2010).

Ports deploy relatively immobile assets and bind together various GVC operations. Because of their localized nature, ports are increasingly subject to pressure from residents and stakeholders in adjacent communities and have a material interest in maintaining their social licence to operate. Several port authorities have launched voluntary emission abatement initiatives (Poulsen et al., 2018), and in 2008 a consortium of 55 ports established the World Ports Climate Initiative (WPCI) (Fenton, 2017). As Poulsen et al. (2018) show, port authorities have been more successful in improving efficiency and introducing low-emission technologies in their own operations. They have also been relatively successful as landlords and regulators – rising environmental standards for tenants, trucks and trains through a combination of regulation and incentives. These tools, however, have had a limited impact on environmental upgrading in maritime transport and in GVCs more generally, as they do not affect the operation of ocean-going ships, which are the main emitters. Port competition also restrains the effectiveness of these tools.

Other Enabling Factors

In relation to *issue visibility*, the CO_2 emission impacts of shipping have generally had a low public profile, contributing to relative inaction. Low visibility is a consequence of the business-to-business nature of shipping and its relative distance from consumers. Cargo carried on dry bulk ships, and to a large extent on tankers,[31] undergoes several transformations in manufacturing plants before it reaches consumers. Containerized cargo, however, is more directly visible to consumers, and companies owning consumer brands have recently started to ask for information and tentatively place explicit environmental demands on container shipping companies. However, the relative weight of emissions arising from shipping in the life cycle of products is low, which makes it a low priority for retailers and branded merchandisers. While SOx and NOx emissions are clearly visible to the residents of areas close to ports, CO_2 emissions are not. Overall, limited visibility weakens the political will to orchestrate.

Shipping is a mature and highly competitive global industry characterized by poor cooperation between the public and private sectors. It exhibits a low level of *interest alignment* at all nodes of the GVC, as the interests of governments and industry tend to diverge when it comes to environmental protection. For a long time, shipowner associations worked explicitly to block or minimize international regulatory measures on the environmental footprint of shipping and threatened to move their registration to 'flag of convenience' states. Shippers have also been lukewarm in relation to the voluntary sustainability initiatives that have emerged in recent years. However, this situation is shifting as cargo owners and a small segment of the shipping industry are moving towards a more proactive stance on environmental improvements, especially in jurisdictions (such as Denmark) where some shipping companies are seeking to leverage their superior environmental performance to push for higher standards to be applied to everyone (Poulsen et al., 2016). This may ease some of the future constraints to orchestration.

In terms of *regulatory uncertainty*, although the IMO has the authority to provide global regulatory cohesion, shipping is characterized by a high level of policy uncertainty along the whole GVC. This has limited environmental progress and spurred the rise of voluntary initiatives with their own associated challenges. Considerable uncertainty is also related to the ratification of the IMO's environmental instruments and their implementation into national regulation. Shipowners argue that this uncertainty also deters their investments in environmental protection. As regional rules have been developed to compensate for IMO inaction, regulatory unevenness across jurisdictions makes international ship operations costlier and more complicated. Furthermore, national enforcement levels vary. Weak enforcement in some jurisdictions can penalize shipping companies that invest in environmental improvements.

Looking Ahead

The global shipping sector has lagged behind in attempts to reduce its GHG emissions despite the long, well-established presence of a dedicated intergovernmental organization, the IMO. Procedural delays in IMO rule-making, stalled national ratification and implementation, strong industry pushback, and weak enforcement have all contributed to this situation. The unique structural features of this industry are also dampening some of the regulatory advances that are taking place. The flag of convenience system, for example, means that some countries (such as Panama, Liberia and the Marshall Islands) operate open register systems, allowing shipowners to register vessels even though they are not nationals or residents in these jurisdictions. These countries usually have weaker labour and/or environmental regulation (DeSombre, 2006). Failures also arise from low issue visibility, poor interest alignment, and high, but possibly improving, regulatory uncertainty.

This situation highlights the need for a serious strategic reconsideration within the IMO in relation to how it could orchestrate through both directive as well as facilitative instruments. As a priority, the IMO needs to directly address the uncertainty and growing impatience concerning slipping regulatory deadlines, redouble its efforts to fold the other regional regulatory initiatives back under its global mantle, and gradually increase its reference standards. Regarding green ship rating programmes, at a minimum the IMO needs to indirectly observe and track these initiatives to ensure they align as much as possible in their ultimate objectives. It should also consider granting consultative status to the NGO-led green shipping initiatives in order to spur a greater alignment of new initiatives. Currently, NGOs such as Greenpeace and the WWF enjoy consultative status at the IMO, but other important initiatives, such as the CCWG and SSI, do not. The IMO could also attempt to better understand and leverage the many lessons and experiences that the existing green rating programmes have gathered over the last decade or so. It could promote the usage of independent audits of these rating data sets to improve their quality. This could be carried out successfully by intermediaries, such as the classification societies. Ultimately, to improve global shipping performance, the IMO will need to oversee, leverage and enable voluntary efforts to complement national and international regulation (Poulsen et al., 2016).

Port authorities and port alliances can also contribute to orchestration. Front-runner ports have achieved significant local air quality improvements in the last decade, even as cargo volumes have generally increased. However, port environmental measures have only limited leverage on ships while at sea. Stricter regulation by the IMO or regional bodies can facilitate better visibility, and thus help ports to be more effective as promoters of environmental improvement. Port alliances should also start forging cooperation with the selected cargo owners that are at the forefront of environmental upgrading in GVCs (see Chapter 4; Poulsen et al., 2018).

The shipping industry is at an important juncture. Ship overcapacity has led to major drops in prices at the time of research (the Shanghai Containerized Freight Index dropped by 73 per cent between 2012 and 2016).[32] The historical perception of shipping as a cleaner transport mode is making way to the view that shipping is increasing its emissions rapidly and needs to tackle them. New ship designs, operational systems and technologies are improving its unit-level environmental performance, but not enough to stem future aggregate emissions increases. The IMO has a duty to step up its orchestration leverage, not only by ramping up the implementation and levels of ambition of its new GHG strategy, but also by employing key facilitative instruments – including support for the environmental initiatives that port alliances are building.

Aviation and Shipping Compared

The case studies of aviation and maritime shipping examined in the previous two sections show that national and regional governments, as well as (air)port authorities, can potentially take the mantle of orchestration when the relevant international organizations fail to do so. Both the ICAO and IMO did not use facilitative orchestration instruments, a failure that is explained by several factors in Abbott et al.'s (2015) model of orchestration for international organizations. This model predicts that the IO will resort to orchestration when: it has low capabilities in the focal domain; there is a readily available intermediary; the IO has high focus in the environmental field; it has an organizational structure that facilitates entrepreneurship; there is high divergence of goals among member states; and there is weak oversight of member states in the focal domain. The scoring exercise for aviation and shipping summarized in Table 5.1 shows that for both the ICAO and IMO, all factors score in ways that would make it difficult for the relevant IO to orchestrate sustainability.

However, Abbott et al.'s (2015) model is unable to account for why and how other public orchestrators (the EU, US, other national governments) may or may not take up the mantle of orchestration *in the absence* of effective action by IOs. In order to explain this, I revert to the four explanatory factors proposed earlier in this chapter: combinatory efforts, issue visibility, interest alignment, and regulatory uncertainty. Table 5.2 shows the scoring results of these four factors. In the aviation industry, orchestrators (the EU and US) have used combinatory efforts (both directive and facilitative orchestration instruments); CO_2 emissions have high visibility; there has been good alignment between US/EU regulators and industry; and regulatory uncertainty has been high. In the shipping industry, these factors score exactly the opposite, with the exception of regulatory uncertainty. Even though the EU has made important moves with its MRV regulation, it has not carried out substantial facilitative instruments, so it is lacking in combinatory efforts; CO_2 emissions are not very visible because the shipping industry is not consumer-facing and emissions from this form of transport are a small proportion of the total emissions entailed in the life cycle of a product; industry actors and governments have been at loggerheads on environmental issues; and regulatory uncertainty has been high. These factors can help explain why the orchestration of sustainability has failed to emerge so far in shipping, even at the national and regional levels. In sum, at least three of these four enabling factors (combinatory efforts, issue visibility and interest alignment) can explain the divergent orchestration dynamics at the national/regional levels in the aviation and shipping industries.

The main limitation of the analysis carried out so far is that it cannot account for whether and how GVC governance, and the power dynamics that underpin them, could also help explain different trajectories of orchestration – as the two GVCs have the same governance form, both are bipolar. In the next section, I take three steps to address this: (1) I go back to the wine, coffee and biofuels GVCs and examine whether the four enabling factors of orchestration developed in this chapter can help explain different environmental upgrading trajectories (see Chapter 4); (2) I draw from the analysis of power dynamics in these three GVCs (see Chapter 3) to show how tackling different kinds of power constellations requires different combinations of orchestration instruments; and (3) I bring together the cumulative insights of

Table 5.1 Expected and Actual Outcomes of Orchestration by International Organization in the Aviation and Shipping GVCs

	Aviation	Shipping	Predicted combinations	
Potential IO orchestrator of sustainability	ICAO	IMO	—	
Regulatory capability	High	High	Low	High
Intermediary availability	Low	Low	High	Low
Focality	Low	Low	High	Low
Entrepreneurship	Low	Low	High	Low
Divergence of goals among members	High	High	High	Low
Oversight of states in their domain	High	High	Low	High
Actual orchestration by IO	*Low*	*Low*	*High*	*Low*

Source: Application of Abbott et al.'s (2015) model of IO orchestration

Table 5.2 Expected and Actual Outcomes of Orchestration by National/Regional Authorities in the Aviation and Shipping GVCs

	Aviation	Shipping	Predicted combinations	
Orchestrators of sustainability	*National governments, EU*	*National governments, EU*	—	
Combinatory efforts	High	Low	High	Low
Issue visibility	High	Low	High	Low
Interest alignment	High	Low	High	Low
Regulatory uncertainty	High*	High*	Low	High
Actual orchestration	*High*	*Low*	*High*	*Low*

* Scoring at the time of research. Recent regulatory measures in both industries can potentially change this situation, but substantial uncertainty remains on implementation processes and (in the case of shipping) with overlaps with regional regulatory regimes.

Source: Own analysis, adapted from Lister et al. (2015)

all five GVCs (wine, coffee, biofuels, aviation and shipping) to provide some overall observations on how to design orchestration that is most effective in different GVC governance situations.

Power, Governance and Orchestration in the Wine, Coffee and Biofuels GVCs

Enabling Orchestration Factors

In the wine, coffee and biofuels GVCs, the relevant international organizations have had very limited or no orchestration activity related to sustainability issues. The International Organization of Vine and Wine (OIV) has published resolutions on sustainable vitiviniculture[33] and recommendations on accounting protocols for GHG emissions – but has no regulatory powers over its members.[34] The International Coffee Organization (ICO) used to have important regulatory powers through its production quota system, but these were dismantled in 1989. The 2007 International Coffee Agreement included as one of its objectives 'to encourage Members to develop a sustainable coffee sector in economic, social and environmental terms'.[35] But, in general, the ICO has had a very minor role in supporting the proliferation of coffee sustainability initiatives and platforms. The International Renewable Energy Agency (IRENA) has no direct regulatory powers either. It supports transitions

Table 5.3 Expected and Actual Outcomes of Orchestration by National/ Regional Authorities in the Wine, Coffee and Biofuels GVCs

	Wine	Coffee	Biofuels	Predicted combinations	
Orchestrators of sustainability	*National governments, EU*	*National governments*	*National governments, EU*	—	
Combinatory efforts	Low	Medium	High	High	Low
Issue visibility	Low	Medium	High	High	Low
Interest alignment	High	Medium	Medium	High	Low
Regulatory uncertainty	Low	Low	Medium	Low	High
Actual orchestration	*Low*	*Medium*	*High*	*High*	*Low*

Source: Own analysis

to sustainable energy and serves as a platform for international cooperation and knowledge, but covers a wide array of renewables and has had a limited role in the development of sustainability standards and protocols for biofuels.[36] Therefore, in the analysis below, I focus on national and regional orchestrators. Table 5.3 summarizes how the four enabling factors of orchestration apply to the case studies of wine, coffee and biofuels, and whether they can help explain the degree of orchestration efforts observed (see details in Chapters 3 and 4).

Combinatory Efforts

In the wine GVC, combinatory efforts of sustainability orchestration that include both directive and facilitative instruments have been fairly limited, with the exception of some initiatives carried out in New Zealand and California. Therefore, the combinatory efforts are scored low in Table 5.3. In coffee, there has been more noticeable orchestration activity, not only by producing countries locally supporting coffee sustainability initiatives, but also by consuming country governments facilitating various MSIs and providing technical assistance for their implementation. Some producing countries have also applied directive instruments – for example, the trade of certified coffee is handled separately than for regular coffee in Tanzania, where it can be exempted from going through the export auction. However, by and large, orchestrators have focused on facilitative efforts, and thus the combinatory efforts are scored medium. In biofuels, national and regional governments have employed major directive *and* facilitative instruments, thus achieving a high score on combinatory efforts.

Issue Visibility

In wine, label-based communication of sustainability issues is starting to happen, especially in New World producing countries, but sustainability issues still lack the appeal they have in coffee and the urgency they manifest in biofuels. Thus, issue visibility is deemed to be low. Sustainability of coffee production has been quite visible through direct communication to consumers via labels and stories told on packaging and via NGO campaigns, especially following the coffee crisis of the early 2000s. But social issues have been more prominent than environmental issues; therefore, issue visibility is scored as medium. In biofuels, the food price hikes of the mid-2000s provided a major platform that boosted the political visibility of sustainability in biofuel production – even though biofuels are less directly visible to the consumer – thus scoring high.

Interest Alignment

In wine, alignment between private and public interest from the perspective of an individual orchestrating country/region is high. In Old World producing countries, both regulators and GVC actors still broadly frame sustainability issues in terms of tradition, place and terroir – and implicitly embed them in indications of geographical origin – although this is changing. In New World countries, public and private actors use sustainability more strategically in marketing, and embed it in labels, certifications and stories communicated on the bottle label. Thus, there is a relatively high level of interest alignment within each group of countries, which justifies the high score, but also some divergence among different groups of countries.

In coffee, private and public interests related to sustainability tend to align within consuming countries, which have been the main movers and shakers of sustainability. In producing countries, however, many farmer cooperatives and local traders perceive sustainability protocols as impositions (see Chapter 4). At the same time, producing country governments have been more than happy to receive or direct development funding locally and host a myriad of projects on coffee sustainability. Overall, this contrast suggests a medium level of interest alignment between public and private actors.

In biofuels, there has been a high alignment of private and public interests in relation to orchestration of sustainability within key countries. The Malaysian and Indonesian public sectors, for example, have been at the forefront of initiatives attempting to recast palm oil (also used for biodiesel production) from a more sustainable angle and developed their own sustainability certification systems. The Brazilian government has leveraged the relative superiority of sugar cane-based ethanol in terms of GHG emission abatement to portray its industry as more sustainable than in other countries. At the same time, in several key producing countries, different biofuel feedstocks also compete with each other, leading to misalignment between the intent of orchestrators and different segments of the feedstock industry. This split is especially evident between first-generation and next-generation biofuels. Therefore, interest alignment in biofuels is scored as medium.

Regulatory Uncertainty

In wine and coffee, in the absence of major regulatory efforts by international organizations and governments on sustainability, and low expectations that this situation will change in the future, there is very little regulatory uncertainty (scored low in both GVCs). In biofuels, regulatory uncertainty has decreased substantially following the EU RED directive and the implementation of the RFS in the US. However, some uncertainty remains in relation to specific aspects of sustainability, the implementation of new rules embedded in RED II, and the size and kinds of regulatory support for first-generation biofuels vis-à-vis next-generation biofuels in the near future. This kind of uncertainty affects most nodes in the GVC. Thus, the level of regulatory uncertainty in biofuels can be characterized as medium.

Table 5.3 also scores the actual level of orchestration activity in relation to the degree of importance of sustainability factors in underpinning institutional power (see Chapters 3 and 4): low in wine; medium in coffee; and high in biofuels. Linking the enabling factors to the actual level of orchestration in these three GVCs paints a more variegated picture than in aviation and shipping: combinatory efforts and high issue visibility are confirmed as key factors; variations in interest alignment seem to matter, but only in two cases out of three (biofuels and coffee); and regulatory uncertainty does not seem to explain variation in orchestration efforts. For this reason, in the following discussion, I will focus on the three factors that seem to have more explanatory potential overall: combinatory efforts, issue visibility and interest alignment.

GVC Governance, Power and Orchestration

In this section, I draw from the analysis of power, governance and upgrading in the wine, coffee and biofuels GVCs carried out in Chapters 3 and 4 (see Tables 3.9 and 4.2 for relevant information) to examine how national/regional governments could combine a variety of orchestration instruments in different GVCs – depending on their governance structures and the power dynamics that underpin them. So far in this chapter, we have learned that successful orchestration is more likely to happen when a combination of directive and facilitative instruments is used, when sustainability issues have high visibility, and (to some extent) when there is interest alignment between private and public actors at key nodes of the GVC. In order to develop a portfolio of strategic choices that public actors can use to successfully orchestrate sustainability in different GVCs, I address three questions in the following discussion: (1) How can orchestrators choose what kinds of directive and facilitative instruments to use, and with what balance? (2) How can they enhance issue visibility? (3) How can they better align private and public sector interests?

Orchestrating Sustainability in the Wine GVC

In relation to the wine GVC, Chapter 3 highlighted that bargaining power moved from a balanced situation in 1960–1990 (T1) to increased buyer power in the hands of retailers in 1990–2018 (T2), and that GVC governance went from a multipolar system to a unipolar system (see Table 5.4). Demonstrative and (to less extent) institutional power dynamics played a major role in undergirding changes in bargaining power, and thus in shaping GVC governance. Demonstrative power was wielded by a relatively small group of individuals in New World wine countries, who managed to introduce new wine styles and viticulture systems on the back of ideational work that constructed the figure of the 'new consumer'. These changes in turn shaped institutional reform in the EU and ended up strengthening the bargaining power of buyers, retailers in particular. Sustainability

Table 5.4 Overview of Orchestration Options in the Wine, Coffee and Biofuels GVCs

	Wine	Coffee	Biofuels
Changes in GVC governance from T1 to T2	From multipolar to unipolar	From multipolar to unipolar	Remained multipolar
Key kinds of power that interacted with bargaining power	Demonstrative, institutional	Institutional, demonstrative	Constitutive, institutional
Key public orchestrators of sustainability	National governments, EU	National governments	National governments, EU
GVC pressure points for orchestration	Retailers, wine tasters, wine journalists, magazines and online platforms, flying winemakers and viticulturists	Mainstream roasters, specialty coffee actors	Multiple
Current level of orchestration effort	Low	Medium	High
Change needed in *combinatory* efforts	From low to high	From medium to high	Only marginal improvements needed
Possible directive instruments	Require, develop and/ or support standards and certifications of sustainability for wine production, trade and export	*Consuming countries*: public procurement, rising the low bar set by 4C, require sustainability certification for coffee to be imported; *producing countries*: require a minimum sustainability standard for export, charge a sustainability export tax	Calling for minimum standards on the quality of governance in private certification systems that are recognized by the EU

Possible facilitative instruments	Facilitate platforms to include sustainability issues in wine scoring, promote sustainability in vocational training and other education	Further support producers, cooperatives and exporters seeking voluntary certifications, embed sustainability in national branding efforts	Assess impact of sustainability certifications on actual outcomes, further support the scaling up of next-generation biofuels
Change needed in *issue visibility*	From low to high	From medium to high	Only marginal improvements needed
Approaches to improve issue visibility	Shape demonstrative power via engagement with wine tasters and reviewers, wine journalists, magazines and online platforms, and flying winemakers and viticulturists; cooperate with – and exert regulatory pressure on – retailers	Shape demonstrative power by engaging with (smaller) specialty coffee roasters to include, for example, carbon sequestration as part of sustainability and/or minimum farmer prices for meeting specific environmental standards; facilitate initiatives in producing countries that seek to frame sustainability as part of geographic origin and/or national branding	Shape constitutive power to strengthen the framing of sustainability in biofuel production, for example by facilitating a better incorporation of indirect land use change (ILUC) in calculations of GHG emission abatements
Change needed in *interest alignment*	None	From medium to high	From medium to high
Approaches to improve interest alignment	Not a priority	Producing countries: charging a mandatory sustainability export tax at the export level to be returned to farmers meeting these standards	Long-term transition measures to facilitate a smooth transition away from first-generation biofuels in order to better align the interests of different groups within the private sector, as this also improves the alignment of private and public interests

issues played little or no role in these transformations, and orchestration efforts in this realm have been relatively limited. Given the weak regulatory role of the OIV, the role of orchestration for sustainability can be best played by the EU, national and (US) state governments.

By cross-examining GVC governance and power dynamics on one side, and the three enabling orchestration factors on the other, three main conclusions arise. First, to improve sustainability orchestration in the wine GVC, orchestrators should employ their institutional power to better execute *combinatory efforts* that include directive and facilitative instruments. Orchestrators could more directly stimulate environmental upgrading through regulation, as they have successfully done in other realms of production. For example, they could require, develop and/or support standards and certifications on the sustainability of wine production, trade and export. The EU and national governments have historically engaged in a variety of facilitative efforts as well, but not so much on sustainability. They could, for example, fund and/or support platforms seeking to include sustainability issues in wine scoring, and/or facilitate the systematic inclusion of sustainability issues in vocational training and other educational offerings. Second, the analysis of power and governance in the wine GVC suggests that orchestrators are unlikely to be able to improve *issue visibility* without engaging with the type of actors who have already transformed the wine industry through demonstrative and then constitutional power: wine tasters and reviewers, wine journalists, magazines and online platforms, and flying winemakers and viticulturists. Given the current unipolar governance structure of this GVC, cooperation with – and regulatory pressure on – retailers is also essential. Third, *interest alignment* is already high in this GVC, and thus efforts in this direction should not be a priority.

Orchestrating Sustainability in the Coffee GVC

In the coffee GVC, governance moved from multipolar in 1960–1990 (T1) to unipolar in 1990–2018 (T2), with bargaining power increasing dramatically in the hands of coffee roasters. This transition took place through a major change in institutional power with the end of the ICA system. A more recent period of upheaval emanated from the demonstrative power of sustainability and specialty coffee industry actors, which led to a relative dampening of bargaining power by mainstream roasters until recently. This process, however, is now being reversed as mainstream roasters acquire smaller, specialty roasters, and as some specialty roasters have grown to become more mainstream in their operations and procurement systems. Sustainability issues have been an important component of these power dynamics. As seen in Chapter 4, this has led to major environmental upgrading trajectories among suppliers, which were supported in important ways by the interventions of governments in both producing and consuming countries.

Given that the ICO regulatory role is unlikely to be restored, it is public authorities at the national level in producing and consuming countries that could play a sustainability orchestration role by exerting their institutional power. Further improvements can be stimulated in combinatory efforts, issue visibility and interest alignment (which all scored medium; see Table 5.3). In relation to *combinatory efforts*, both consuming and producing countries can further ramp up many of the facilitative efforts they are already carrying out to support producers, cooperatives and exporters that are seeking voluntary certifications. Producing countries could also include sustainability consideration in national branding efforts, and consuming countries could lobby to raise the low level of sustainability standards currently embedded in the 4C programme. In terms of directive efforts, producing countries could set a minimum sustainability standard for export, charge a sustainability export tax at times of high international prices, and/or include sustainability standards in indications of geographic origin. Consuming countries could more forcefully enact demands for sustainable coffee certification for public procurement (e.g. in schools and hospitals) and/or require sustainability standards to clear imports – as the WTO has been relatively lenient in accepting the protection of the environment and health as legitimate policy objectives.

Improving environmental *issue visibility* in the coffee GVC is a more complex challenge. Coffee stories, labels and certifications are already dotting the packaging landscape that speaks directly to consumers. However, in Chapter 3, I showed that the demonstrative power of specialty and sustainable coffee operators was key in partially limiting the bargaining power of mainstream roasters during T2. Orchestrators could reinvigorate demonstrative (and eventually constitutive) power in alliance with (smaller) specialty coffee roasters in view of including, for example, climate change and carbon sequestration as part of sustainability. They could also promote efforts to pay a minimum price at the farmer level for coffee that meets certain environmental criteria. Initiatives in producing countries that seek to frame sustainability as part of geographic origin and/or national branding can act in this direction as well. Finally, in relation to *interest alignment*, orchestrators could charge a mandatory sustainability export tax to be returned to farmers. This would provide more direct sustainability incentives at the farm level, as well as better align public and private interests in producing countries – given that many producers perceive sustainability as an imposition placed by buyers and abetted by their own governments.

Orchestrating Sustainability in the Biofuels GVC

In the biofuels GVC, we did not observe major changes in the multipolar nature of governance between T1 and T2 (1997–2007 and 2007–2018). However, important changes took place in the overlap of different kinds of power, which has key implications for orchestration strategies. Institutional power played a major role in the industry formation period, and bargaining power remained fairly equally distributed among multiple groups of firms in different functional positions. It was a major shift in constitutive power, following the food price crisis of 2006/07, that recast biofuels as acceptable only when they are certified or verified as sustainable. Orchestrators, such as the EU and the US, have already carried out important *combinatory efforts* to seek improvements in sustainability, including substantial directive and facilitative measures. However, there is still margin for improvement. For instance, private certification systems that are recognized by the EU to meet its RED directive vary widely, thus calling for minimum standards on governance processes, and the impact of sustainability certification needs to be assessed in view of actual outcomes on the ground. Given that changes in constitutive power dynamics led to a main reshuffling of regulatory instruments between T1 and T2, the same could be leveraged to improve *issue visibility*. Orchestrators could, for example, promote a more open debate and consideration of indirect land use change (ILUC) in the calculations of GHG emissions abatement in biofuel production. ILUC so far has not been satisfactorily incorporated into EU sustainability standards.

Finally, orchestration measures that are strengthening the position of next-generation feedstock and biofuel producers vis-à-vis first-generation operators should include long-term transition measures to facilitate a smooth transition away from first-generation biofuels, thus improving the overall *interest alignment* between the public sector and different segments of the private sector. Incidentally, a long-term strategy of this kind could also help minimize regulatory uncertainty on sustainability regulation, which is a substantial issue in the biofuels GVC.

Discussion and Next Steps

Much of the existing debate on sustainability governance has been focused on international agreement formation, best institutional design, and the plethora of transnational experiments and entrepreneurial governance initiatives that have been taking place at different geographic levels by different combinations of public and private actors. There is increasing agreement in this field that the current fragmentation of governance architectures entails the need for public authorities to act as orchestrators in the interest of a green entrepreneurial state – by combining indirect tools and soft power with direct regulatory tools, regulatory threats and/or finance and incentives. However, so far, much less attention has been paid to the effectiveness of these actions in the context of the everyday practices of lead firms and other actors in global value chains, even though this system of economic organization has become a dominant feature of the global economy in the past few decades.

In this chapter, I examined to what extent public sector organizations at the national, regional and international levels have used different combinations of mechanisms and strategies to address various environmental concerns in different GVCs, and with what results. I proposed four possible enabling factors that can help orchestration to succeed in addressing sustainability issues along GVCs: combinatory efforts, including both directive and facilitative instruments; high issue visibility; interest alignment between public and private actors; and low levels of regulatory uncertainty. The case studies of aviation and maritime shipping provided important lessons on why international organizations, even when explicitly tasked with tackling environmental issues, have failed to deliver meaningful results. This stemmed not only from the inherent difficulties of international agreement formation and implementation, but also from the inability or unwillingness of these international organizations to use facilitative instruments. On a more positive note, the comparison of aviation and shipping also showed that, in absence of actions by international organizations, key nation states and regional groups can step up and provide important orchestration functions. Combinatory efforts, issue visibility and interest alignment have been key in explaining why national and regional orchestration for sustainability took place in aviation but not in shipping. These factors were also confirmed as important by the analysis of orchestration in the wine, coffee and biofuels GVCs, where international organizations currently have very weak or no regulatory powers. While in the previous chapter we found that environmental upgrading (led by GVC actors) is most likely to take place in unipolar GVCs, this chapter suggests that orchestration (led by public authorities), all other factors equal, tends to be more successful in multipolar GVCs such as biofuels, and bipolar GVCs such as aviation, rather than in unipolar ones.

Improving the chances of successful orchestration thus involves appropriate combinations of directive and facilitative instruments, ways of enhancing issue visibility and tools to better align private and public sector interests, possibly also across jurisdictions. However, these choices and strategies are issue- and GVC-specific and cannot stem from a general model of sustainability orchestration. They have to be informed by the specific power and governance dynamics that characterize relevant GVCs. This entails targeting appropriate leverage points along a GVC with the right instruments, depending on the balance of bargaining power among different actors on whether this balance is (or has been) underpinned or challenged by various overlaps of demonstrative, institutional and constitutional power.

In the Conclusion, I will apply the lessons learned so far to further explore the potential and limitations of consumer, civil society and media pressure in supporting orchestration for sustainability, in the context of how lead firms seek green capital accumulation and practice a sustainability-driven supplier squeeze. I will also discuss the broader structural constraints placed by green capitalism more generally to propose some suggestions on how to facilitate 'just sustainabilities' in a world of global value chains.

CONCLUSION

Green Capital, Brown Environments

What if we used our size and resources to make this country and this earth an even better place for all of us: customers, Associates, our children, and generations unborn? What if the very things that many people criticize us for – our size and reach – became a trusted friend?

Excerpt from 'Leadership in the 21st Century',
speech by Lee Scott, then CEO of Walmart,
Bentonville, Arkansas, 24 October 2005,
cited in Humes, 2011: 102

Whenever we engage in consumption or production patterns which take more than we need, we are engaging in violence.

Vandana Shiva, *Earth Democracy:
Justice, Sustainability, and Peace*, 2016: 102

Sustainability management has become a key element of contemporary capitalism, in addition to cost, flexibility and speed (Coe and Yeung, 2015). The practices that corporations enact to address sustainability issues are also (re)shaping the existing spatial, organizational and technological fixes that are needed to ensure continuous capital accumulation. Geographically, production is moving to locations that can meet basic sustainability specifications in large volumes and at low cost. Organizationally, multi-stakeholder initiatives on sustainability are playing a key role in redefining the minimum accepted standards for products. Labour conditions among suppliers are under pressure from the need to meet increasing environmental demands from lead firms. And the need to verify compliance has led to the adoption of new technologies of measurement, verification and trust (Busch, 2011; Fouilleux and Loconto, 2017; Freidberg, 2013, 2014).

The 'business case' for sustainability has been, by and large, solved – lead firms in global value chains (GVCs) not only extract sustainability value from their suppliers, but can also benefit from internal cost savings, supplier squeezing, reputation enhancements and improved market capitalization. As the value of goods increasingly depends more on their intangible properties (including those related to the environment) than on their functional or economic value, sustainability management becomes a central function of corporate strategy – and thus filters through organization, marketing, operations and logistics. Lead firms are leveraging sustainability to extract more information from suppliers, strengthen power relations to their advantage, and find new venues of value creation and capture.

In other words, lead firms use sustainability to appropriate surplus value from other GVC actors (Quentin and Campling, 2018; Starosta, 2010). This sustainability-driven supplier squeeze is yet another manifestation of a larger process of value extraction from suppliers that has been observed in many GVCs (Milberg and Winkler, 2013), which can lead to the adverse incorporation of suppliers (Gibbon and Ponte, 2005; Phillips, 2011) and to immiserizing growth (Kaplinsky, 2005). In sum, sustainability management is at work for *green capital*, but does not address *brown environments*. It is also creating new spatial inequalities within countries, across countries and regions, along GVCs (between producers, processors, traders, retailers), and among different groups of actors (small- versus large-scale operators).

In this book, I have argued that powerful lead firms in GVCs have moved beyond questioning the 'business case' for sustainability. They are creating and extracting new value from addressing environmental concerns, both inside their corporate boundaries and along their value chains. They benefit from sustainability management in terms of profitability without major negative consequences on their market valuation, thus enacting *green capital accumulation*. They also demand more information from their suppliers, including that on environmental practices and impacts, in order to push the profitability of their suppliers to the limit, thus capturing value through a *sustainability-driven supplier squeeze*. The power of lead firms in GVCs not only arises from their superior bargaining position, which can include specific environmental demands for suppliers, but also from specific institutional dynamics (e.g. regulations that provide green incentives) and from being able to take advantage of more diffuse norms and conventions on sustainability, either in dyadic or collective settings. Becoming and remaining a lead firm thus means strengthening their bargaining power through specific combinations of institutional, demonstrative and constitutional power – including the components that arise from sustainability management.

The Ruses of Green Capitalism, Sustainable Development and 'Shopping for Good'

In the past two decades or so, 'green capitalism', 'green growth', the 'green economy' and the 'circular economy' have become popular constructs in view of addressing climate change and other pressing environmental crises (popular books include Esty and Winston, 2009; Friedman, 2009; Lovins et al., 2007; McDonough and Braungart, 2010; Schwab, 2017). Essentially, these concepts have been employed to argue that capitalism can be leveraged to solve the pressing environmental issues that arise from its very logic. We are told that new business models, innovation and technological progress can save the environment and still facilitate capital accumulation and everlasting growth in production and consumption. In other words, we are led to believe that green capitalism contains the seed of salvation.

Robotics, artificial intelligence, 3D printing, geo-engineering, new biomaterials, the blockchain revolution, and a whole new set of business, production and consumption models (the sharing economy, service contracts instead of ownerships, peer-to-peer exchange, crowdsourcing, digital platforms, and 'Industry 4.0' more generally) are variously mentioned as solutions that can ensure a more sustainable future (Husain, 2017; McAfee and Brynjolfsson, 2017; Schwab, 2018; Tapscott and Tapscott, 2016). Of course, some of these technologies and models have the potential to address pressing environmental challenges – but almost always address the manifestations rather than the roots of problems and focus on individual models and technologies without exploring the systemic and structural elements in which they are embedded.

From the perspective of green capitalism, tackling ever-increasing production and consumption is not a priority. The focus is on how technology and new business models can improve the efficiency of resource use, instead of decreasing the aggregate impact on the Earth and its biosphere. Efficiency in resource use should indeed improve as income in the Global South increases (Stern, 2004), but this is likely to be more than compensated for by the aggregate scale effect of higher growth. Furthermore, more efficient extraction and use of natural resources often leads to lower prices (witness the shale revolution in oil extraction), and this can prolong and even increase fossil fuel consumption and the extraction rate of natural resources – what is known as the 'Jevons effect'.[1] And while in the Global North economies may be 'dematerializing', GVC analysis shows that the use of energy and materials is actually moving to production facilities in the Global South rather than decreasing overall (Dale et al., 2016).

In other words, while green capital accumulation strategies that optimize resource consumption are helping to lower the relative energy and material intensity of production, they do not address the overall ecological limits to growth because they are based on a logic of continuous expansion (Higgs, 2014; Kovel, 2007; Newell and Paterson, 2010). Technological and organizational fixes, such as cutting energy costs, improving packaging materials, minimizing transport distances, and building green brands' credentials, can improve *unit-level* efficiency, and indeed can have important positive impacts on resource and energy use. But this does not necessarily lead to *overall* reductions when production and consumption continue to rise. Furthermore, lead firms in GVCs are placing new environmental demands on their suppliers, which comes with requests for more information on supplier cost structures and operations. In supplier jurisdictions where regulatory monitoring is poor or difficult, this can lead to pro forma compliance with buyer demands and certifications, while further limiting the actual impact on environmental sustainability. When profit margins decrease for suppliers (negatively affecting their economic sustainability), these demands can also have negative rebounding effects on social sustainability – for example, driving suppliers to cut labour costs or worsen work conditions to recoup the extra environmental costs.

As competitive advantage becomes denationalized and increasingly shaped by GVC and sustainability dynamics, we observe new winners and losers within and across nations (Baldwin, 2016; Milanovic, 2016). The emergence of a global plutocracy is deleterious for the orchestration of sustainability and for environmental regulation more generally, because global plutocrats can insulate themselves from the consequences of climate change and environmental degradation. As contemporary capitalism creates new winners (the 'global middle class', mostly located in China and other emerging Asian countries) and new losers (the lower middle class in the Global North and the very poor in the Global South) (Milanovic, 2016), the orchestration of sustainability needs to pay particular attention to the specific consequences for these groups.

Therefore, discussions on sustainability need to be discussions of power relations, inequality, and social, environmental and climate justice. Yet in its current manifestation, 'sustainable development' (including much of the UN Sustainable Development Goals construction) has been stripped of its justice elements and has become 'all but synonymous with "sustained economic growth"' (Dale et al., 2016). It has embedded unfettered and apolitical technological optimism and sustainability consumerism. Sustainability concerns, such as wildlife conservation, have become commodities to be sold and bought like any other, and have been transformed into 'spectacle' for the enjoyment of the wealthy (Brockington, 2002; Brockington et al., 2012; Büscher et al., 2014; Igoe, 2017). Green capitalism goes hand in hand with 'green grabbing' and 'blue grabbing' (Benjaminsen and Bryceson, 2012; Fairhead et al., 2012; Hill, 2017) that are contemporary instances of accumulation by dispossession (Harvey, 2004) operated through the exploitation of land and water resources. As capitalism metamorphoses into green capitalism, it comes along with its financial imperatives, its (im)moralities and its values (Asiyanbi, 2018; Bracking, 2012; Dempsey, 2016; Ouma et al., 2018; Sullivan, 2013). 'Unjust sustainabilities' are part and parcel of green capitalism – dematerialization of production in one country based on increased material extraction in others; land grabbing under the pretext of conservation; the creation of 'green jobs' that are precarious, informal and/or exploitative; and lead firms capturing sustainability value from their suppliers.

Many of the findings of this book confirm that properly handling sustainability issues from a green capitalism angle can indeed pay handsomely for lead firms in GVCs; often this value is extracted at the cost of suppliers in the Global South; and the benefits for nature are either not evident or far from enough. As long as environmental impacts are considered externalities, rather than being priced or taxed, business will continue operating within an economic system that places disincentives on long-term sustainability. Even the most innovative business models, such as service leasing instead of ownership of durable goods, and technological innovation, such as advances in photovoltaics, will only allow us to take one step forward while we take two steps back by scaling up production and consumption.

'Shopping for good' is also a key element of green capitalism. It is alluring and simple – we can save the world just by being better consumers without requiring sacrifice, such as consuming less (Richey and Ponte, 2011). Voting with our wallets is an easy substitute to exercising our citizens' rights and powers. Green consumer culture is essentially a culture *of* consumption, where the values of society are organized through and derive from consumption. It is a culture portraying freedom of choice and consumer sovereignty, a culture of needs that are in principle unlimited and insatiable, and a culture of prioritizing the satisfaction of these needs over the limitations of our environment (Slater, 1997). The myriad of labels and certifications appended on 'green' products facilitate a grab-and-go approach to saving humanity-cum-nature.

Sustainability certifications and labels are important ways of delivering feel-good content. But green consumer culture is neither just a consumption of signs, nor is it just a reflection of an existing social order (Slater, 1997). It is a site of contestation and struggle over social, cultural and *environmental* arrangements that underpin the mobilization of material resources. This book provides a necessary examination of how the procurement of the objects of consumption is regulated, and by whom, and what specific productive arrangements, technologies, environmental processes and labour relations underpin the provision of goods (Fine, 2002).

GVC lead firms, and especially retailers, apply heavy forms of 'editing' of what gets offered to consumers and how. While this was traditionally a one-way road from branded merchandisers and retailers to consumers via advertising, advances in big data analytics and point-of-sale information mean that consumption patterns can finely shape procurement choices. However, procurement officers of major retailers still have enormous power in shaping consumption trends. Walmart, for example, became the largest seller of organic produce in the US not because consumers were clamouring for organics in its stores, but because organics are more profitable. This has led to increased consumption of organic food, but also to the consolidation of organic farms and a move from an agro-ecological, diverse approach to a monoculture, input-substitution approach (Guthman, 2014). Walmart, since the mid-2000s, has embarked on a broad sustainability drive to save energy and optimize packaging, transport and logistics – not because these fit with its corporate philosophy of low prices, but because its executives, influenced by 'sustainability consultants', came to see that there was profit to be made in environmental improvements (Humes, 2011). Yet as Walmart improves its unit-level energy and material consumption, it continues expanding, thus increasing its overall environmental footprint. By focusing on unit-level improvements, Walmart moves attention away from the inherent unsustainability of big box retailing – and of green capitalism more generally. These processes suggest the dominance of trajectories of value capture (Coe and Yeung, 2015), rather than those of shared value (Porter and Kramer, 2011).

When we reach beyond the duality of humanity and the environment and see human organizations as environment-making processes and projects, we also realize that green capitalism is based on a holistic relation between capital, power and nature (Moore, 2015, 2016). In green capitalism, consumers can get access to products that are perceived to be better for the environment and/or healthier for themselves. Lead firms accumulate capital. Suppliers struggle to remain profitable under the pressure of lower margins and increasing environmental demands. The unit-level environmental impact of production, processing, trade and retail improves. But constantly growing consumption, both in the Global North and in the Global South, means that in the aggregate, environmental sustainability suffers. In other words, green capital accumulation goes hand in hand with brown environments.

Public Orchestration and Activism for Sustainability

In this book, I have shown how lead firms use sustainability management for green capital accumulation. I have documented that many suppliers in the Global South have undergone impressive economic-cum-environmental upgrading trajectories, but also that they have been subjected to a sustainability-driven supplier squeeze by lead firms, and that upgrading has led to limited or no impact on actual environmental outcomes. The power of lead firms is based on their bargaining position, but is also supported by other forms of power – institutional, demonstrative and constitutional. Therefore, the specific power and governance dynamics that characterize individual value chains, and the role sustainability issues play in them, can provide important and fine-tuned pointers for orchestrators and social movements alike on how to address this situation. This kind of analysis can suggest what leverage points can be used and with what instruments, or how various actions applying demonstrative, institutional and/or constitutional power can be used to undermine unequal bargaining positions. I have also shown that orchestration for sustainability is more likely to happen when a combination of directive and facilitative instruments is used by public authorities, when sustainability issues are highly visible, and when private and public actor interests are made to align at key nodes of the GVC. While environmental upgrading by GVC actors is most successful in unipolar chains, for public orchestration the opposite applies – it is most effective when power is more equally distributed, as in multipolar GVCs.

I am not arguing that orchestrators should return to top-down regulation alone in view of changing the inherent disincentives embedded in green capitalism. Regulation is essential, but the scale and complexity of the problems at hand require governments and international organizations to use a combination of tools, direct and facilitative, in view of enhancing the visibility of the environmental issues that are more hidden, and of providing incentives and infrastructure to align private and public interests. This requires an understanding of how GVCs are governed and by whom – and the power dynamics that facilitate these processes. Orchestrators need to act not only through their institutional power, but also by shaping constitutive power through ideational change and demonstrative power through collaboration with key influential actors in view of taming the bargaining power of lead firms.

This discussion is important as the winners of green capital accumulation tend to be lead firms in the Global North and their financial backers, and sometimes emerging lead firms in the Global South; consumers who can discharge their environmental duty by consuming green, instead of reducing consumption; and market-friendly international NGOs and sustainability initiatives, which are playing a major facilitating role in greasing the wheels of green capitalism. The losers tend to be suppliers in the Global South, especially small-scale enterprises and smallholder farmers; labour everywhere; more radical activist networks and social movements in search of long-term solutions to sustainability challenges; and international organizations and the public sector more generally. Public authorities have witnessed a weakened legitimacy of environmental regulation and the erosion of tax bases from which to tap resources for stimulating environmentally sound practices.

Given this situation, changes in business conduct and new technologies will not be sufficient to address the current sustainability challenges. Public authority, the green entrepreneurial state (Mazzucato, 2015b) and civil society have essential roles to play in raising the bar of environmental sustainability, but their strategies and approaches need to be informed by how business operates in the global economy and how powerful firms govern GVCs – not because green capitalism needs to be accepted as it is, but because we need to know how it works in order to reform it, or go beyond it. In this process, social movements and civil society groups can make a difference through their transnational advocacy networks (Della Porta and Mattoni, 1999; Garwood, 2011; Keck and Sikkink, 1998). Existing research suggests that social movements tend to exert more leverage when they select and target well-known brands and retailers (Bloomfield, 2014; Conroy, 2007; Newell, 2008; O'Rourke, 2005), when they forge alliances with a key corporation in a GVC, and when their demands are specific and visible. They are more likely to make a difference when the costs for corporations of meeting social movement demands are low or the potential reputational loss is high (Bloomfield, 2017a, 2017b; Dauvergne and Lister, 2013), when they socialize senior executives through multi-stakeholder networks (Van der Ven, 2014), and when they see potential to gain competitive advantage through brand reputation enhancements (Richey and Ponte, 2011).

Public institutions, political cultures and industry structures are important factors in shaping whether activists can make a difference and how (Bair and Palpacuer, 2012, 2015; Levy, 2008; Schurman, 2004). As corporations increasingly adopt global standards on labour and the environment, activist groups encounter constraints and face reconfigurations as these standards become embedded in local political and governance dynamics (Bartley, 2003, 2018). Corporations tend to appease demands in the short term, while continuing to extract value from suppliers, work to weaken regulation, and focus narrowly on specific practices in a dialogue with civil society that promotes first movers as 'sustainability leaders' (Dauvergne, 2017: 139). While social media can be a powerful and low-cost instrument of activism (Milan, 2013), it can also produce confusing and ever-changing messages and be affected by hackers and corporate defenders posing as campaigners (Dauvergne, 2017). And when activist campaigns are indeed successful in influencing corporate behaviour (Bloomfield, 2017a; den Hond and de Bakker, 2007; Sasser et al., 2006), this does not necessarily translate in positive impacts on the environment (Dauvergne, 2017). Activists also find it difficult to transmit their demands unless they become part of multi-stakeholder initiatives (Bloomfield, 2017b;

Locke et al., 2009). Yet when they are embedded in MSIs, they are asked to seek compromises rather than establish a hierarchy of options (Cashore and Bernstein, 2018). Finally, activist campaigns tend to focus on branded companies and products, thus failing to draw attention to the environmentally destructive practices in the production or extraction of goods that are not clearly and directly consumer-facing, such as fertilizer, coal, or cement production, and shipping and transport more generally.

Since business is leveraging sustainability mainly for its own purposes, governments and international organizations need to find ways of better orchestrating a variety of sustainability initiatives if they actually wish to achieve environmental protection. Social movements and civil society organizations also need to find ways of advocating change that is cognizant of GVC dynamics. Both public authorities and civil society groups need to be aware of the major limitations of what business can achieve through self-regulation and multi-stakeholder cooperation. Therefore, orchestrators need to adopt strategies that include knowledge of how GVCs operate, where the pressure points within GVCs are most likely to stimulate positive change, and where wealth is stored – including measures to fight tax havens and minimize corporate tax avoidance.

Through tax optimization strategies and offshore finance, the same corporations that officially champion sustainability place taxable income effectively out of the reach of governments (Seabrooke and Wigan, 2017), depriving them of essential resources needed for addressing social and environmental concerns. Fewer public resources then make it even more pressing for governments to enter into partnerships with industry associations, corporations and NGOs. This in turn further increases the legitimacy of business-oriented solutions to sustainability and limits the space for more radical action or regulation, such as decreasing consumption, limiting growth and/or applying carbon taxation. When lead firms do not meet their sustainability targets, failure is aptly embedded in discourses of continuous improvement, thus minimizing the possible immediate negative repercussions on their reputation. Governments are accused of not being able to effectively regulate sustainability, while corporations are framed as an important part of the solution because they have massive resources at their disposal, including those that were supposed to be taxed more effectively.

A future agenda for research should thus involve analysing global value chains in combination with 'global wealth chains' (Seabrooke and Wigan, 2014, 2017). This effort entails tracking where value is added in material production along the value chain, and where it is captured and redistributed elsewhere in the chain. It includes examining how multinational corporations manipulate the distribution of functions along value chains to tax value in jurisdictions where taxation rates are lowest, and whether this in turn puts pressure on other jurisdictions to lower their tax burden on capital and increase it on labour, with regressive results (Quentin and Campling, 2018). As capital leverages nature to produce more capital, research can provide important insights on how the circulation of finance 'in and through nature' (Ouma et al., 2018) abets green capitalism.

Towards 'Just Sustainabilities'

In this book, I have shown that even the most appropriate orchestration measures can only partially tackle global sustainability challenges. While incremental change is needed, it is not sufficient without a systemic rethinking of the relations between capitalism and nature. This conclusion arises from the empirical results of decades of research, including those presented in this book. Human activity is having major impact on the earth and its biosphere, to the point that geologists have now defined a new era – the *Anthropocene* – to reflect this phenomenon (Crutzen and Stoermer, 2000: 82). Some scholars have argued that this is period started in the late eighteenth century with a marked increase in fossil fuel use and has accelerated dramatically since the middle of the nineteenth century, when human action started to overshadow nature's work in influencing the ecology of the Earth (McNeill and Engelke, 2016; Steffen et al., 2007). Global sustainability crises, such as climate change, the acidification of oceans, and the 'sixth great extinction' of planetary life (Leakey, 1996) characterize this period of great turbulence in the relation between humanity and nature. Other scholars question the focus on humanity as an undifferentiated whole in the term Anthropocene and propose a different concept to explain the same result: *Capitalocene*, 'the era of capitalism as a world-ecology of power, capital and nature' (Moore, 2016: 6). This term shifts focus away from the putative duality of human–nature relations, with its neo-Malthusian connotations, and towards capitalism as a way of organizing nature (Haraway, 2015; Moore, 2015, 2016). As Moore (2016: 82) argues, 'the Anthropocene makes for an easy story: Easy, because it does not challenge the naturalized inequalities, alienation, and violence inscribed in modernity's strategic relations of power and production'.

From a Capitalocene perspective, major changes in the world-ecology started taking place already in the mid-fifteenth century – with a progressive transition from control of land as a way to appropriate surplus value, to control of land as a way of increasing labour productivity for commodity production (Moore, 2015, 2016). In other words, it is not enough to simply examine what capitalism does to nature and how humanity can solve global sustainability challenges through innovation in technology and business models. We need to conceptualize power, value and nature as thinkable only in relation to each other (Havice and Campling, 2017; Parenti, 2016), and seek to understand how capitalism is 'putting the whole of nature to work for capital' (Moore, 2016: 86). This book, by documenting the organic intertwining of sustainability management in GVCs at the service of capital accumulation, provides a contribution in this direction.

Sustainability management as operated by lead firms in GVCs is built on the foundation provided by green capitalism, with sustainability coalitions and approaches combining in ways that promote and maintain a liberal economic order (Bernstein, 2012). Dauvergne (2016) draws our attention in particular to what he calls the 'environmentalism of the rich' – an approach to sustainability assuming that individuals can still consume as much as they wish, that corporate responsibility and self-regulation hold great promise, and that the resulting gains are meaningful for global sustainability. These processes are abetted by NGOs, which are increasingly building partnerships with business instead of pushing for radical change; by individuals, who are placing priority on small lifestyle changes; by consumers, who are buying products offered through cause-related marketing (Richey and Ponte, 2011); and by governments, which continue to promote economic growth as a top priority.

Overall, the idea of 'sustainable development' in the context of green capitalism will not be achieved unless we rethink the current organization of the global economy, reform the economic and political institutions that govern it, and devise new forms of governance and collective action (Newell, 2012). As long as sustainability is used mainly as a marketing and strategic tool, a means of capital and wealth accumulation, and is subservient to economic growth – efficiency gains will continue to be reinvested in further expanding production and consumption and to be transformed in wealth for the global plutocracy, ultimately exacerbating the global sustainability crisis (Dauvergne, 2016; Newell, 2012).

This vicious cycle needs to be broken. Sustainability has become a commodity to be traded, bought, sold and managed like all others. Business has turned the sustainability challenge into an asset, at least in the short term. Those who argue that the main role of business is to make profit will not be surprised by this turn of events. But because environmental outcomes do not necessarily improve as a result of sustainability initiatives, we cannot rely on changes in business conduct alone to address pressing sustainability concerns. Business representatives seem to be asking for more regulation and a level playing field. At the same time, business keeps up lobbying efforts to *resist* further regulation.

Given that capitalism, rather than humanity per se, is the root cause of the global sustainability crisis, reformist tweaks can only go so far (Kovel, 2007). 'Political and corporate leaders, and some in the environmental establishment, are putting aside what works in exchange for what poses the least challenge to established power structures' (Rogers, 2013: 180). But alternative ideas, models and practices to the contemporary form of green capitalism are emerging. Some approaches suggest a focus on the planetary boundaries within which humanity operates (Rockström et al., 2009b; Steffen et al., 2015). Others propose a 'prosperity without growth' (Jackson, 2009) and even 'de-growth' (D'Alisa et al., 2014). More radical options show possible paths towards 'eco-socialism' (Kovel, 2007). A myriad of examples are available on how these alternative models of the economy can work and where they are working – especially when coupled with community involvement, union and social activism, decentralization, cooperative forms of organization, and radical and democratic ecological experimentation (Dale et al., 2016; Rogers, 2013). Yet these are still fringe movements and pale in comparison to the damage inflicted by capitalism, even under its green mantle.

Ideationally, current discussions of 'just sustainabilities' have important insights to offer. Enacting systemic and radical alternatives requires creating new imaginaries and nurturing sustainability cultures (Gibson-Graham, 2006; Parr, 2012). The idea of just sustainabilities is based on 'the need to ensure a better quality of life for all, now and into the future, in a just and equitable manner, whilst living within the limits of supporting ecosystems' (Agyeman et al., 2003: 5). It is framed in the plural to reflect the multiplicity of alternatives that can be tuned to different realities and follow different paths – in rural or urban areas, in the Global North and the Global South, with more social democratic or libertarian notes, and under cooperative or municipal forms of ownership.

A path towards just sustainabilities means addressing inequality – since it drives competitive consumption and leads to lower levels of trust in societies, which makes public action more difficult (Wilkinson et al., 2010); it entails focusing on improving quality of life and well-being, rather than growth; it demands a community economy and increased public consumption (Gibson-Graham, 2006; Gibson-Graham et al., 2013); it involves meeting the needs of both current and future generations and at the same time reimagining these needs; it demands a paradigm of sufficiency, rather than maximization of consumption; it recognizes that overconsumption and environmental degradation affect the right to enjoy a decent quality of life (Agyeman, 2013); and it requires a different kind of green entrepreneurial state that caters to these needs.

An approach towards 'just sustainabilities' necessitates building a social foundation for an inclusive and stable economic system that operates within our environmental planetary boundaries (as exemplified in the 'Oxfam Doughnut'; see Raworth, 2012). It demands business to behave responsibly, within its organizational boundaries and along GVCs, to maintain its social licence to operate (Agyeman, 2013; Gunningham et al., 2003). Although GVCs account in one form or another for a large majority of international trade, they hardly feature in existing critiques of green capitalism. The modest contribution of this book to these ideas and alternatives has been to highlight the hurdles, structural constraints and redistributions that are involved in a world of global value chains.

Paying attention to what we buy and how it was produced remains important, but we cannot buy our way into a sustainable future. The imperatives of growth and consumption are part of the problem and cannot be the solution. Although the ideas for reform and incremental change highlighted in this book are important, we also need radical social and economic transformation, we need to subvert and reinvent the current system, and we need to create new spaces for alternatives. This is why understanding the power dynamics underpinning governance of GVCs is so important, as it indicates the pressure points that public orchestrators and civil society can use to leverage not only reform, but also radical change. This knowledge can expose the Achilles heel of green capitalism and stack the quivers of government and civil society with the arrows necessary for 'just sustainabilities' to be achieved.[2]

NOTES

Chapter 3: Sustainability, Power and Governance in the Wine, Coffee and Biofuels Global Value Chains

1 Source: www.oiv.int/en/databases-and-statistics/statistics

2 Source: www.oiv.int/en/databases-and-statistics/statistics

3 Source: www.sustainablewinegrowing.org

4 Source: www.forbes.com/sites/thomaspellechia/2017/02/01/the-u-s-wine-industry-focuses-on-a-sustainable-future/#73c10c6d51e2

5 Source: www.sostain.it

6 Source: www.ico.org/trade_statistics.asp?section=Statistics

7 Source: www.ers.usda.gov/amber-waves/2016/may/investigating-retail-price-premiums-for-organic-foods/

8 Source: www.conservation.org/publications/Documents/Coffee_Sustainability_Catalogue_2016_FULL_with_appendices.pdf

9 Source: www.eia.gov

10 Source: http://globalrfa.org/biofuels-map

11 See www.wwf.org.za/?1681/Biodiversity--Wine-Initiative

12 In 2015, Nestlé had operating margins of 25 per cent in the single-serve segment, and Keurig of almost 39 per cent. By comparison, Nestlé had a 21 per cent margin in other coffee formats (Grabs, 2017: 10).

13 Source: www.bloomberg.com/news/articles/2018-05-07/nestle-enters-7-2-billion-global-coffee-alliance-with-starbucks

14 Source: Luc Cohen, 'Exclusive: Keurig deal gives coffee traders jitters about payments', Reuters, December 9, 2015.

15 See also http://agritrade.cta.int/Agriculture/Commodities/Coffee/Executive-Brief-Update-2013-Coffee-sector

16 Previously fully owned by Robert Parker, since 2012 *The Wine Advocate* has been controlled by a group of Singaporean investors. Parker is no longer the editor-in-chief, but still plays a key role in tasting. He is now supported by a team of other tasters.

17 Source: www.starbucks.com/business/international-stores

18 Source: www.scsglobalservices.com/starbucks-cafe-practices

19 Source: www.reuters.com/article/us-usa-biofuels/u-s-epa-ups-biofuel-targets-slightly-draws-scorn-from-refiners-idUSKBN1DU1SA

20 So far, no bilateral agreement has been concluded, and only one national scheme (Austria's) has been put in place.

21 The RED stipulated that from 2017, GHG emission reductions will have to be at least 50 per cent for existing production and 60 per cent for new installations.

22 Source: OIV RESOLUTION CST 1/2004, as in Sogari et al. (2016b: 58–59).

Chapter 4: Value Creation and Capture through Economic and Environmental Upgrading

1 Something similar is taking place in coffee as well. The time lag between starting a certification process and actually supplying certified products contributes to information asymmetry because of the uncertainty regarding future demand and price premia for certified products. In case of oversupply, however, producers who obtained certification have already made upfront investments and are reluctant to drop the certified market, even if it does not provide significant financial advantages (see Grabs, 2019).

2 Source: www.sawis.co.za

3 Source: www.sawis.co.za

4 There are also a number of initiatives seeking to address social issues, which are particularly important in South African due to the history of apartheid and labour exploitation. Among these, the most important are various Black Economic Empowerment initiatives and legislation (see Bek et al., 2007; Du Toit et al., 2008).

5 Source: www.wosa.co.za/Sustainability/Environmentally-Sustainable/Intro/

6 Source: *Wineland*, Cape Town, January 2005.

7 Source: *Wineland*, Stellenbosch, May 2007.

8 Source: www.wosa.co.za/Wine-Tourism

9 Source: www.constellationcsr.com/sustainability/

10 Sources: E&J Gallo www.gallo.com/responsibility; The Wine Group https://thewinegroup.com/vision-and-values/; Foster's Group (Treasury Wine Estates) www.tweglobal.com/responsibility; Pernod Ricard www.pernod-ricard-winemakers.com/corporate-social-responsibility/sustainability

11 Source: H. Krige, 'Writing on the wall for haphazard finances: Deloitte benchmarking study', *Wineland*, Cape Town, July 2005.

12 Source: Mike Veseth, 'South Africa wine industry: Serious problems, lofty goals, progress update', *Wine Economist*, 14 February 2017. https://wineeconomist.com/category/south-africa/

13 Source: Janina Grabs, personal communication.

14 Similar results have been found for in-house standards applied by a regional supermarket in South Africa and related to environmental practices in fresh fruit, vegetable and flower production (Thorlakson et al., 2018).

15 Source: Janina Grabs, personal communication.

16 Source: Janina Grabs, personal communication.

Chapter 5: Orchestrating Sustainability

1 I use the terms international organization (IO) and intergovernmental organization (IGO) interchangeably. In some circumstances, IOs are relevant for orchestrating sustainability, but in others the relevant organizations are not strictly governmental in their membership.

2 Sources: www.eea.europa.eu/data-and-maps/figures/specific-co2-emissions-per-passenger-3 and www.eea.europa.eu/data-and-maps/figures/specific-co2-emissions-per-tonne-2

3 Source: http://renewablejetfuels.org/what-we-do/the-basics

4 Sources: www.biofuelsdigest.com/bdigest/2014/04/21/biofuels-in-aviation-to-fly-or-not-to-fly and www.iata.org/whatwedo/environment/Documents/technology-roadmap-2013.pdf

5 Source: www.biofuelsdigest.com/bdigest/2014/04/21/biofuels-in-aviation-to-fly-or-not-to-fly/

6 Sources: Gossling and Upham (2009), www.worldwatch.org/global-air-transport-continues-expand-o and www.iata.org/whatwedo/environment/Documents/technology-roadmap-2013.pdf

7 Aviation not only emits substantial amounts of CO_2; it also has a range of other environmental and health impacts – noise pollution, land degradation, disturbance of wildlife and biodiversity, and emission of other air pollutants. In the following discussion, to keep the discussion reasonably focused, I only analyse orchestration in relation to the abatement of CO_2 emissions.

8 Source: www.biojetmap.eu/#31080

9 Source: www.biofuelsdigest.com/bdigest/2018/02/26/aviation-biofuels-10-years-100000-flights-and-were-still-arguing-about-feedstock-why/

10 Source: www.icao.int/environmental-protection/Pages/A39_CORSIA_FAQ1.aspx

11 Source: Directive 2009/28/EC of the European Parliament and of the Council of 23/04/2009 on the promotion of the use of energy from renewable sources and amending and subsequently repealing Directives 2001/77/EC and 2003/30/EC, Article 17 Sustainability criteria for biofuels and bioliquids, at pp.L140/36-L140/38.

12 Source: Thomas Vilsack, US Secretary of Agriculture, conference presentation attended at ABLC, Washington, DC, 15 April 2013.

13 Sources: Julia Whitty, 'Full Green Ahead', *Mother Jones*, March/April 2013 and www.navy.mil/submit/display.asp?story_id=82044

14 Source: Julia Whitty, 'Full Green Ahead'.

15 Source: www.navy.mil/submit/display.asp?story_id=95398

16 Source: www.iata.org

17 Elsewhere, similar initiatives are present in Brazil (Abraba) and Australia (AiSAF).

18 Source: http://ec.europa.eu/energy/renewables/biofuels/doc/20130911_a_performing_biofuels_supply_chain.pdf

19 Sources: www.caafi.org, CAAFI presentations attended at ABLC, Washington, DC, 15 April 2013; interviews ABLC21 and ABLC26, 15 April 2013.

20 Source: COM (2011) 144 final of 28.03.2011, see http://ec.europa.eu/transport/strategies/2011_white_paper_en.htm

21 Source: http://ec.europa.eu/transport/modes/air/doc/flightpath2050.pdf

22 Source: COM (2013) 17, see http://cor.europa.eu/en/activities/stakeholders/Documents/com2013-17.pdf

23 Source: UNCTAD, 2014. Review of maritime transport 2014. Geneva: United Nations Conference on Trade and Development Publications.

24 The full environmental footprint of shipping relates to a broader set of issues, including oil spills, sulphur oxide and nitrogen oxide emissions, invasive species, disposal of hazardous material, and noise pollution. In this chapter, I focus on CO_2 emissions.

25 Source: www.imo.org/Pages/home.aspx

26 Source: Third IMO GHG Study 2014, International Maritime Organization.

27 Source: www.imo.org/en/MediaCentre/PressBriefings/Pages/06GHGinitialstrategy.aspx

28 Sources: European Commission, 2013. 'Time for International Action on CO_2 Emissions from Shipping', Brussels, and European Commission, 2015. 'Reducing Emissions from the Shipping Sector', Brussels, http://ec.europa.eu/clima/policies/transport/shipping/index_en.htm

29 Source: https://ec.europa.eu/info/law/better-regulation/initiatives/ares-2017-3112662_pl

30 Source: http://ssi2040.org

31 Issue visibility is much higher in relation to oil spills from tankers. However, the analysis of aviation and shipping in this book is focused on GHG emissions, CO_2 in particular.

32 Source: *The Economist*, 28 April 2018.

33 Source: Resolution OIV-CST 1/2004: Development of sustainable vitiviniculture, and Resolution OIV-CST 518/2016: OIV general principles of sustainable vitiviniculture – environmental – social – economic and cultural aspects. See www.oiv.int/en/techni cal-standards-and-documents/environment-and-vitiviniculture

34 Source: Resolution OIV-CST 431/2011: General principles of the OIV greenhouse gas accounting protocol for the vine and wine sector, and Resolution OIV-CST 503AB/2015: Greenhouse gases accounting in the vine and wine sector – recognised gases and inventory of emissions and sequestrations. See www.oiv.int/en/technical-standards-and-documents/environment-and-vitiviniculture

35 Source: www.ico.org/sustaindev_e.asp

36 Source: www.irena.org/aboutirena

Conclusion

1 The term refers to the work of British economist William Jevons, who showed that improvements in engine and furnace efficiency in the nineteenth century led to higher consumption of coal, thus actually increasing the rate of its depletion (see Jevons, 1906).

2 I owe this formulation to Lisa Ann Richey.

REFERENCES

ABBOTT, K. W., GENSCHEL, P., SNIDAL, D. & ZANGL, B. (eds.) 2015. *International Organizations as Orchestrators*. Cambridge: Cambridge University Press.

ABBOTT, K. W., GREEN, J. F. & KEOHANE, R. O. 2016. Organizational ecology and institutional change in global governance. *International Organization*, 70, 247–277.

ABBOTT, K. W., LEVI-FAUR, D. & SNIDAL, D. 2017. Theorizing regulatory intermediaries: The RIT model. *Annals of the American Academy of Political and Social Science*, early view, doi: 10.1177/0002716216688272.

ABBOTT, K. W. & SNIDAL, D. 2009a. The governance triangle: Regulatory standards institutions and the shadow of the state. In: MATTLI, W. & WOODS, N. (eds.) *The Politics of Global Regulation*. Princeton, NJ: Princeton University Press.

ABBOTT, K. W. & SNIDAL, D. 2009b. Strengthening international regulation through transmittal new governance: Overcoming the orchestration deficit. *Vanderbilt Journal of Transnational Law*, 42, 501.

ABBOTT, K. W. & SNIDAL, D. 2010. International regulation without international government: Improving IO performance through orchestration. *Review of International Organizations*, 5, 315–344.

ABBOTT, K. W. & SNIDAL, D. 2013. Taking responsive regulation transnational: Strategies for international organizations. *Regulation & Governance*, 7, 95–113.

ADGER, W. N. & JORDAN, A. (eds.) 2009. *Governing Sustainability*. Cambridge: Cambridge University Press.

AFIONIS, S. & STRINGER, L. C. 2012. European Union leadership in biofuels regulation: Europe as a normative power? *Journal of Cleaner Production*, 32, 114–123.

AGYEMAN, J. 2013. *Introducing Just Sustainabilities: Policy, Planning and Practice*. London: Zed Books.

AGYEMAN, J., BULLARD, R. D. & EVANS, B. (eds.) 2003. *Just Sustainabilities: Development in an Unequal World*. Cambridge, MA: MIT Press.

AHI, P. & SEARCY, C. 2013. A comparative literature analysis of definitions for green and sustainable supply chain management. *Journal of Cleaner Production*, 52, 329–341.

AHI, P. & SEARCY, C. 2015. An analysis of metrics used to measure performance in green and sustainable supply chains. *Journal of Cleaner Production*, 86, 360–377.

AKOYI, K. T. & MAERTENS, M. 2017. Walk the talk: Private sustainability standards in the Ugandan coffee sector. *Journal of Development Studies*, 54, 1792–1818.

ALBAREDA, L. 2008. Corporate responsibility, governance and accountability: From self-regulation to co-regulation. *Corporate Governance*, 8, 430–439.

ALI-YRKKÖ, J. & ROUVINEN, P. 2015. Slicing up global value chains: A micro view. *Journal of Industry, Competition and Trade*, 15, 69–85.

ALTER, K. J. & MEUNIER, S. 2009. The politics of international regime complexity. *Perspectives on Politics*, 7, 13–24.

ALVAREZ, G., PILBEAM, C. & WILDING, R. 2010. Nestlé Nespresso AAA Sustainable Quality Program: An investigation into the governance dynamics in a multi-stakeholder supply chain network. *Supply Chain Management*, 15, 165–182.

ANDERSON, K. 2004. *The World's Wine Markets: Globalization at Work.* Cheltenham: Edward Elgar.

ANDERSON, K. & NELGEN, S. 2011. *Global Wine Markets: A Statistical Compendium, 1961–2009.* Adelaide: University of Adelaide Press.

ANDONOVA, L. B. 2010. Public–private partnerships for the earth: Politics and patterns of hybrid authority in the multilateral system. *Global Environmental Politics*, 10, 25–53.

ANDONOVA, L. B., BETSILL, M. M. & BULKELEY, H. 2009. Transnational climate governance. *Global Environmental Politics*, 9, 52–73.

ASIYANBI, A. P. 2018. Financialisation in the green economy: Material connections, markets-in-the-making and Foucauldian organising actions. *Environment and Planning*, 50, 531–548.

ATKIN, T., GILINSKY JR, A. & NEWTON, S. K. 2012. Environmental strategy: Does it lead to competitive advantage in the US wine industry? *International Journal of Wine Business Research*, 24, 115–133.

AULD, G. 2014. *Constructing Private Governance: The Rise and Evolution of Forest, Coffee, and Fisheries Certification.* New Haven, CT: Yale University Press.

AULD, G. & GULBRANDSEN, L. H. 2010. Transparency in nonstate certification: Consequences for accountability and legitimacy. *Global Environmental Politics*, 10, 97–119.

AULD, G. & RENCKENS, S. 2017. Rule-making feedbacks through intermediation and evaluation in transnational private governance. *The ANNALS of the American Academy of Political and Social Science*, 670, 93–111.

AVANT, D. D., FINNEMORE, M. & SELL, S. K. (eds.) 2010. *Who Governs the Globe?* Cambridge: Cambridge University Press.

AYERS, I. & BRAITHWAITE, J. 1992. *Responsive Regulation: Transcending the Deregulation Debate.* Oxford: Oxford University Press.

BÄCKSTRAND, K. 2006. Multi-stakeholder partnerships for sustainable development: Rethinking legitimacy, accountability and effectiveness. *European Environment*, 16, 290–306.

BÄCKSTRAND, K. 2008. Accountability of networked climate governance: The rise of transnational climate partnerships. *Global Environmental Politics*, 8, 74–102.

BÄCKSTRAND, K. & KRONSELL, A. 2015. *Rethinking the Green State: Environmental Governance towards Climate and Sustainability Transitions.* London: Routledge.

BAGLIONI, E. & CAMPLING, L. 2017. Natural resource industries as global value chains: Frontiers, fetishism, labour and the state. *Environment and Planning A*, 49, 2437–2456.

BAIR, J. 2005. Global capitalism and commodity chains: Looking back, going forward. *Competition & Change*, 9, 153–180.

BAIR, J. (ed.) 2009a. *Frontiers of Commodity Chain Research.* Stanford, CA: Stanford University Press.

BAIR, J. 2009b. Global commodity chains. In: BAIR, J. (ed.) *Frontiers of Commodity Chain Research.* Stanford, CA: Stanford University Press.

BAIR, J. 2017. Contextualising compliance: Hybrid governance in global value chains. *New Political Economy*, 22, 169–185.

BAIR, J., BERNDT, C., BOECKLER, M. & WERNER, M. 2013. Dis/articulating producers, markets, and regions: New directions in critical studies of commodity chains. *Environment and Planning A*, 45, 2544–2552.

BAIR, J. & GEREFFI, G. 2001. Local clusters in global chains: The causes and consequences of export dynamism in Torreon's blue jeans industry. *World Development*, 29, 1885–1903.

BAIR, J. & GEREFFI, G. 2003. Upgrading, uneven development, and jobs in the North American apparel industry. *Global Networks*, 3, 143–169.

BAIR, J. & PALPACUER, F. 2012. From varieties of capitalism to varieties of activism: The antisweatshop movement in comparative perspective. *Social Problems*, 59, 522–543.

BAIR, J. & PALPACUER, F. 2015. CSR beyond the corporation: Contested governance in global value chains. *Global Networks*, 15, S1–S19.

BAIR, J. & WERNER, M. 2011a. Commodity chains and the uneven geographies of global capitalism: A disarticulations perspective. *Environment and Planning A*, 43, 988–997.

BAIR, J. & WERNER, M. 2011b. The place of disarticulations: Global commodity production in La Laguna, Mexico. *Environment and Planning A*, 43, 998–1015.

BALDWIN, R. 2013. Global supply chains: Why they emerged, why they matter, and where they are going. In: ELMS, D. K. & LOW, P. (eds.) *Global Value Chains in a Changing World*. Geneva: WTO.

BALDWIN, R. 2016. *The Great Convergence: Information Technology and the New Globalization*. Cambridge, MA: Harvard University Press.

BARRIENTOS, S., GEREFFI, G. & ROSSI, A. 2010. Economic and social upgrading in global production networks: Developing a framework for analysis. *International Labor Review*, 150, 319–340.

BARRIENTOS, S. & SMITH, S. 2007. Do workers benefit from ethical trade? Assessing codes of labour practice in global production systems. *Third World Quarterly*, 28, 713–729.

BARRIENTOS, S. & VISSER, M. 2013. South African horticulture: Opportunities and challenges for economic and social upgrading in value chains. *Capturing the Gains Working Paper* 12. Manchester: University of Manchester.

BARTLEY, T. 2003. Certifying forests and factories: States, social movements, and the rise of private regulation in the apparel and forest products fields. *Politics & Society*, 31, 433–464.

BARTLEY, T. 2007. Institutional emergence in an era of globalization: The rise of transnational private regulation of labor and environmental conditions. *American Journal of Sociology*, 113, 297–351.

BARTLEY, T. 2014. Transnational governance and the re-centered state: Sustainability or legality? *Regulation & Governance*, 8, 93–109.

BARTLEY, T. 2018. *Rules without Rights: Land, Labor, and Private Authority in the Global Economy*. Oxford: Oxford University Press.

BATES, R. H. 1999. *Open-Economy Politics: The Political Economy of the World Coffee Trade*. Princeton, NJ: Princeton University Press.

BEK, D., MCEWAN, C. & BEK, K. 2007. Ethical trading and socioeconomic transformation: Critical reflections on the South African wine industry. *Environment and Planning A*, 39, 301–319.

BELGHITAR, Y., CLARK, E. & DESHMUKH, N. 2014. Does it pay to be ethical? Evidence from the FTSE4Good. *Journal of Banking & Finance*, 47, 54–62.

BENJAMINSEN, T. A. & BRYCESON, I. 2012. Conservation, green/blue grabbing and accumulation by dispossession in Tanzania. *Journal of Peasant Studies*, 39, 335–355.

BERNDT, C. & BOECKLER, M. 2011. Performative regional (dis)integration: Transnational markets, mobile commodities, and bordered North–South differences. *Environment and Planning A*, 43, 1057–1078.

BERNHARDT, T. & MILBERG, W. 2012. Economic and social upgrading in global value chains: Analysis of horticulture, apparel, tourism and mobile telephones. *Capturing the Gains Working Paper* 6. Manchester: University of Manchester.

BERNHARDT, T. & POLLAK, R. 2016. Economic and social upgrading dynamics in global manufacturing value chains: A comparative analysis. *Environment and Planning A*, 48, 1220–1243.

BERNSTEIN, S. 2011. Legitimacy in intergovernmental and non-state global governance. *Review of International Political Economy*, 18, 17–51.

BERNSTEIN, S. 2012. *The Compromise of Liberal Environmentalism*. New York: Columbia University Press.

BERNSTEIN, S. & CASHORE, B. 2007. Can non-state global governance be legitimate? An analytical framework. *Regulation & Governance*, 1, 347–371.

BIERMANN, F. 2014. *Earth System Governance*. Cambridge, MA: MIT Press.

BIERMANN, F., PATTBERG, P., VAN ASSELT, H. & ZELLI, F. 2009. The fragmentation of global governance architectures: A framework for analysis. *Global Environmental Politics*, 9, 14–40.

BITZER, V., FRANCKEN, M. & GLASBERGEN, P. 2008. Intersectoral partnerships for a sustainable coffee chain: Really addressing sustainability or just picking (coffee) cherries? *Global Environmental Change*, 18, 271–284.

BLACK, J. 2003. Enrolling actors in regulatory systems: Examples from UK financial services regulation. *Public Law*, 2003, 63–91.

BLACK, J. 2008. Constructing and contesting legitimacy and accountability in polycentric regulatory regimes. *Regulation & Governance*, 2, 137–164.

BLACKMAN, A. & NARANJO, M. A. 2012. Does eco-certification have environmental benefits? Organic coffee in Costa Rica. *Ecological Economics*, 83, 58–66.

BLAŽEK, J. 2015. Towards a typology of repositioning strategies of GVC/GPN suppliers: The case of functional upgrading and downgrading. *Journal of Economic Geography*, 16, 849–869.

BLOOMFIELD, M. J. 2012. Is forest certification a hegemonic force? The FSC and its challengers. *Journal of Environment & Development*, 21, 391–413.

BLOOMFIELD, M. J. 2014. Shame campaigns and environmental justice: Corporate shaming as activist strategy. *Environmental Politics*, 23, 263–281.

BLOOMFIELD, M. J. 2017a. *Dirty Gold: How Activism Transformed the Jewelry Industry*. Cambridge, MA: MIT Press.

BLOOMFIELD, M. J. 2017b. Global production networks and activism: Can activists change mining practices by targeting brands? *New Political Economy*, 22, 727–742.

BLOOMFIELD, M. J. & SCHLEIFER, P. 2017. Tracing failure of coral reef protection in non-state market-driven governance. *Global Environmental Politics*, 7, 127–146.

BOLTANSKI, L. & CHIAPELLO, E. 2000. *Le nouvel esprit du capitalisme*. Paris: Gallimard.

BOLTANSKI, L. & THÉVENOT, L. 1991. *De la justification. Les économies de la grandeur*. Paris: Gallimard.

BOLWIG, S., GIBBON, P. & JONES, S. 2009. The economics of smallholder organic contract farming in tropical Africa. *World Development*, 37, 1094–1104.

BOLWIG, S., PONTE, S., DU TOIT, A., RIISGAARD, L. & HALBERG, N. 2010. Integrating poverty and environmental concerns into value-chain analysis: A conceptual framework. *Development Policy Review*, 28, 173–194.

BORRAS JR, S. M., MCMICHAEL, P. & SCOONES, I. 2010. The politics of biofuels, land and agrarian change: Editors' introduction. *Journal of Peasant Studies*, 37, 575–592.

BORRELLA, I., MATAIX, C. & CARRASCO-GALLEGO, R. 2015. Smallholder farmers in the speciality coffee industry: Opportunities, constraints and the businesses that are making it possible. *IDS Bulletin*, 46, 29–44.

BORSELLINO, V., MIGLIORE, G., D'ACQUISTO, M., DI FRANCO, C. P., ASCIUTO, A. & SCHIMMENTI, E. 2016. 'Green' wine through a responsible and efficient production: A case study of a sustainable Sicilian wine producer. *Agriculture and Agricultural Science Procedia*, 8, 186–192.

BOSTRÖM, M., JÖNSSON, A. M., LOCKIE, S., MOL, A. P. J. & OOSTERVEER, P. 2015. Sustainable and responsible supply chain governance: Challenges and opportunities. *Journal of Cleaner Production*, 107, 1–7.

BOWEN, F. 2014. *After Greenwashing: Symbolic Corporate Environmentalism and Society*. Cambridge: Cambridge University Press.

BRACKING, S. 2012. How do investors value environmental harm/care? Private equity funds, development finance institutions and the partial financialization of nature-based industries. *Development and Change*, 43, 271–293.

BRAITHWAITE, J. & DRAHOS, P. 2000. *Global Business Regulation*. Cambridge: Cambridge University Press.

BRANDI, C. A. 2017. Sustainability standards and sustainable development: Synergies and trade-offs of transnational governance. *Sustainable Development*, 25, 25–34.

BREGMAN, R. 2017. *Utopia for Realists: And How We Can Get There*. London: Bloomsbury Publishing.

BREWER, B. D. 2011. Global commodity chains and world income inequalities: The missing link of inequality and the upgrading paradox. *Journal of World-Systems Research*, 17, 308–327.

BROCKINGTON, D. 2002. *Fortress Conservation: The Preservation of the Mkomazi Game Reserve, Tanzania*. Bloomington, IN: Indiana University Press.

BROCKINGTON, D., DUFFY, R. & IGOE, J. 2012. *Nature Unbound: Conservation, Capitalism and the Future of Protected Areas*. London: Routledge.

BROCKINGTON, D. & PONTE, S. 2015. The green economy in the Global South: Experiences, redistributions and resistance. *Third World Quarterly*, 36, 2197–2206.

BRUNDTLAND COMMISSION. 1987. *Our Common Future: Report of the World Commission on Environment and Development*. New York: United Nations.

BRUWER, J. 2003. South African wine routes: Some perspectives on the wine tourism industry's structural dimensions and wine tourism product. *Tourism Management*, 24, 423–435.

BRYSON, J. & DANIELS, P. 2010. Service worlds: The 'services duality' and the rise of manuservice economy. In: MAGLIO, P., KIELISZEWSKI, S. & SPOHRER, J. (eds.) *Handbook of Service Science*. New York: Springer.

BULKELEY, H., ANDONOVA, L., BÄCKSTRAND, K., BETSILL, M., COMPAGNON, D., DUFFY, R., KOLK, A., HOFFMANN, M., LEVY, D. & NEWELL, P. 2012. Governing climate change transnationally: Assessing the evidence from a database of sixty initiatives. *Environment and Planning C*, 30, 591–612.

BUSCH, L. 2011. *Standards: Recipes for Reality*. Cambridge, MA: MIT Press.

BÜSCHER, B., DRESSLER, W. & FLETCHER, R. (eds.) 2014. *Nature Inc.: Environmental Conservation in the Neoliberal Age*. Tucson, AZ: University of Arizona Press.

BÜSCHER, B., SULLIVAN, S., NEVES, K., IGOE, J. & BROCKINGTON, D. 2012. Towards a synthesized critique of neoliberal biodiversity conservation. *Capitalism Nature Socialism*, 23, 4–30.

BUSH, S. R., BELTON, B., HALL, D., VANDERGEEST, P., MURRAY, F. J., PONTE, S., OOSTERVEER, P., ISLAM, M. S., MOL, A. P. J. & HATANAKA, M. 2013. Certify sustainable agriculture? *Science*, 341, 1067–1068.

BUSH, S. R. & OSTERVEER, P. 2019. *Governing Sustainable Seafood*. London: Routledge.

BUSH, S. R., OOSTERVEER, P., BAILEY, C. & MOL, A. P. J. 2015. Sustainability governance of chains and networks: A review and future outlook. *Journal of Cleaner Production*, 107, 8–19.

BÜTHE, T. 2010. Private regulation in the global economy: A (P)review. *Business and Politics*, 12, 1–38.

BÜTHE, T. & MATTLI, W. 2011. *The New Global Rulers: The Privatization of Regulation in the World Economy*. Princeton, NJ: Princeton University Press.

CASHORE, B. 2002. Legitimacy and the privatization of environmental governance: How non-state market-driven (NSMD) governance systems gain rule-making authority. *Governance*, 15, 503–529.

CASHORE, B., AULD, G. & NEWSOM, D. 2004. *Governing through Markets: Forest Certification and the Emergence of Non-State Authority*. New Haven, CT: Yale University Press.

CASHORE, B. & BERNSTEIN, S. 2018. *The Tragedy of the Diffusion of the Commons Metaphor: Bringing the Environment Back in to Environmental Studies*. Presented at the International Studies Association Annual Meeting, San Francisco, 3–7 April.

CASHORE, B. & STONE, M. W. 2014. Does California need Delaware? Explaining Indonesian, Chinese, and United States support for legality compliance of internationally traded products. *Regulation & Governance*, 8, 49–73.

CATTANEO, O., GEREFFI, G. & STARITZ, C. (eds.) 2010. *Global Value Chains in a Postcrisis World: A Development Perspective*. Washington, DC: World Bank Publications.

CERNY, P. G. 2010. *Rethinking World Politics: A Theory of Transnational Neopluralism*. Oxford: Oxford University Press.

CHEYNS, E. 2011. Multi-stakeholder initiatives for sustainable agriculture: Limits of the 'inclusiveness' paradigm. In: PONTE, S., GIBBON, P. & VESTERGAARD, J. (eds.) *Governing through Standards: Origins, Drivers and Limitations*. Basingstoke: Palgrave Macmillan.

CHEYNS, E. 2014. Making 'minority voices' heard in transnational roundtables: The role of local NGOs in reintroducing justice and attachments. *Agriculture and Human Values*, 31, 439–453.

CHIPUTWA, B., SPIELMAN, D. J. & QAIM, M. 2015. Food standards, certification, and poverty among coffee farmers in Uganda. *World Development*, 66, 400–412.

CLAPP, J. & DAUVERGNE, P. 2011. *Paths to a Green World: The Political Economy of the Global Environment*. Cambridge, MA: MIT Press.

CLAPP, J. & HELLEINER, E. 2012. International political economy and the environment: Back to the basics? *International Affairs*, 88, 485–501.

CLARK, P. & HUSSEY, I. 2016. Fair trade certification as oversight: An analysis of fair trade international and the small producers' symbol. *New Political Economy*, 21, 220–237.

COE, N. M., DICKEN, P. & HESS, M. 2008. Global production networks: Realizing the potential. *Journal of Economic Geography*, 8, 271–295.

COE, N. M. & HESS, M. 2013. Global production networks, labour and development. *Geoforum*, 44, 4–9.

COE, N. M. & YEUNG, H. W.-C. 2015. *Global Production Networks: Theorizing Economic Development in an Interconnected World*. Oxford: Oxford University Press.

COFFEY, B. 2016. Unpacking the politics of natural capital and economic metaphors in environmental policy discourse. *Environmental Politics*, 25, 203–222.

COLMAN, T. 2008. *Wine Politics: How Governments, Environmentalists, Mobsters, and Critics Influence the Wines We Drink*. Berkeley, CA: University of California Press.

CONROY, M. E. 2007. *Branded! How the 'Certification Revolution' Is Transforming Global Corporations*. Gabriola Island, BC: New Society Publishers.

CORBERA, E., SOBERANIS, C. G. & BROWN, K. 2009. Institutional dimensions of payments for ecosystem services: An analysis of Mexico's carbon forestry programme. *Ecological Economics*, 68, 743–761.

COSA. 2013. *The COSA Measuring Sustainability Report: Coffee and Cocoa in 12 Countries*. Philadelphia, PA: Committee on Sustainability Assessment.

CRUTZEN, P. J. & STOERMER, E. F. 2000. The Anthropocene. *IGBP Global Change Newsletter*, 41, 17–18.

CUTLER, A. C., HAUFLER, V. & PORTER, T. (eds.) 1999. *Private Authority and International Affairs*. Albany, NY: SUNY Press.

D'ALISA, G., DEMARIA, F. & KALLIS, G. 2014. *Degrowth: A Vocabulary for a New Era*. London: Routledge.

DALE, G., MATHAI, M. V. & DE OLIVEIRA, J. A. P. (eds.) 2016. *Green Growth: Ideology, Political Economy and the Alternatives*. London: Zed Books.

DALLAS, M. 2014. Cloth without a weaver: Power, emergence and institutions across global value chains. *Economy and Society*, 43, 315–345.

DALLAS, M., PONTE, S. & STURGEON, T. 2017. A typology of power in global value chains. *Working Paper in Business and Politics* 92. Copenhagen: Copenhagen Business School.

DALLAS, M., PONTE, S. & STURGEON, T. 2019. Power in global value chains. *Review of International Political Economy*, forthcoming.

DARNALL, N., JI, H. & POTOSKI, M. 2017. Institutional design of ecolabels: Sponsorship signals rule strength. *Regulation & Governance*, 11, 438–450.

DAUVERGNE, P. 2016. *Environmentalism of the Rich*. Cambridge, MA: MIT Press.

DAUVERGNE, P. 2017. Is the power of brand-focused activism rising? The case of tropical deforestation. *Journal of Environment & Development*, 26, 135–155.

DAUVERGNE, P. & LISTER, J. 2013. *Eco-Business: A Big-Brand Takeover of Sustainability*. Cambridge, MA: MIT Press.

DAUVERGNE, P. & NEVILLE, K. J. 2009. The changing North–South and South–South political economy of biofuels. *Third World Quarterly*, 30, 1087–1102.

DAUVERGNE, P. & NEVILLE, K. J. 2010. Forests, food, and fuel in the tropics: The uneven social and ecological consequences of the emerging political economy of biofuels. *Journal of Peasant Studies*, 37, 631–660.

DAVIRON, B. & PONTE, S. 2005. *The Coffee Paradox: Global Markets, Commodity Trade and the Elusive Promise of Development*. London: Zed Books.

DAVIS, D., KAPLINSKY, R. & MORRIS, M. 2017. Rents, power and governance in global value chains. *Journal of World-Systems Research*, 24, 43–71.

DE BAKKER, F., RASCHE, A. & PONTE, S. 2019. Multi-stakeholder initiatives on sustainability: A cross-disciplinary review and research agenda. *Business Ethics Quarterly*, forthcoming.

DE MARCHI, V., DI MARIA, E. & GEREFFI, G. (eds.) 2017. *Local Clusters in Global Value Chains: Linking Actors and Territories through Manufacturing and Innovation.* London: Routledge.

DE MARCHI, V., DI MARIA, E. & MICELLI, S. 2013a. Environmental strategies, upgrading and competitive advantage in global value chains. *Business Strategy and the Environment*, 22, 62–72.

DE MARCHI, V., DI MARIA, E. & PONTE, S. 2013b. The greening of global value chains: Insights from the furniture industry. *Competition & Change*, 17, 299–318.

DE MARCHI, V. & GRANDINETTI, R. 2013. Knowledge strategies for environmental innovations: The case of Italian manufacturing firms. *Journal of Knowledge Management*, 17, 569–582.

DEATH, C. 2015. Four discourses of the green economy in the Global South. *Third World Quarterly*, 36, 2207–2224.

DEATH, C. 2016a. *The Green State in Africa.* New Haven, CT: Yale University Press.

DEATH, C. 2016b. Green states in Africa: Beyond the usual suspects. *Environmental Politics*, 25, 116–135.

DEFRIES, R. S., FANZO, J., MONDAL, P., REMANS, R. & WOOD, S. A. 2017. Is voluntary certification of tropical agricultural commodities achieving sustainability goals for small-scale producers? A review of the evidence. *Environmental Research Letters*, 12, 033001.

DELLA PORTA, D. & MATTONI, A. 1999. *Social Movements.* Chichester: Wiley.

DELMAS, M. & BLASS, V. D. 2010. Measuring corporate environmental performance: The trade-offs of sustainability ratings. *Business Strategy and the Environment*, 19, 245–260.

DELMAS, M. A. & YOUNG, O. R. (eds.) 2009. *Governance for the Environment: New Perspectives.* Cambridge: Cambridge University Press.

DEMPSEY, J. 2016. *Enterprising Nature: Economics, Markets, and Finance in Global Biodiversity Politics.* Chichester: Wiley.

DEN HOND, F. & DE BAKKER, F. G. 2007. Ideologically motivated activism: How activist groups influence corporate social change activities. *Academy of Management Review*, 32, 901–924.

DERKX, B. & GLASBERGEN, P. 2014. Elaborating global private meta-governance: An inventory in the realm of voluntary sustainability standards. *Global Environmental Change*, 27, 41–50.

DESOMBRE, E. R. 2006. *Flagging Standards: Globalization and Environmental, Safety, and Labor Regulations at Sea.* Cambridge, MA: MIT Press.

DICKEN, P. 2007. *Global Shift: Reshaping the Global Economic Map in the 21st Century.* Thousand Oaks, CA: Sage.

DINGWERTH, K. & PATTBERG, P. 2006. Global governance as a perspective on world politics. *Global Governance*, 12, 185–203.

DINGWERTH, K. & PATTBERG, P. 2009. World politics and organizational fields: The case of transnational sustainability governance. *European Journal of International Relations*, 15, 707–743.

DU TOIT, A., KRUGER, S. & PONTE, S. 2008. Deracializing exploitation? 'Black Economic Empowerment' in the South African wine industry. *Journal of Agrarian Change*, 8, 6–32.

EBERLEIN, B., ABBOTT, K. W., BLACK, J., MEIDINGER, E. & WOOD, S. 2014. Transnational business governance interactions: Conceptualization and framework for analysis. *Regulation & Governance*, 8, 1–21.

ECKERSLEY, R. 2004. *The Green State: Rethinking Democracy and Sovereignty*. Cambridge, MA: MIT Press.

ELDER, S. D., LISTER, J. & DAUVERGNE, P. 2014. Big retail and sustainable coffee: A new development studies research agenda. *Progress in Development Studies*, 14, 77–90.

ELGERT, L. 2012. Certified discourse? The politics of developing soy certification standards. *Geoforum*, 43, 295–304.

ENGELEN, E. 2008. The case for financialization. *Competition & Change*, 12, 111–119.

EPSTEIN, M. J. & BUHOVAC, A. R. 2014. *Making Sustainability Work: Best Practices in Managing and Measuring Corporate Social, Environmental, and Economic Impacts*. Oakland, CA: Berrett-Koehler Publishers.

ESTY, D. & WINSTON, A. 2009. *Green to Gold: How Smart Companies Use Environmental Strategy to Innovate, Create Value, and Build Competitive Advantage*. Chichester: Wiley.

EYMARD-DUVERNAY, F. 1989. Conventions de qualité et formes de coordination. *Revue Economique*, 40, 329–359.

EYMARD-DUVERNAY, F. (ed.) 2006. *L'économie des conventions, methodes et resultats*. Paris: La Découverte.

FAIRHEAD, J., LEACH, M. & SCOONES, I. 2012. Green grabbing: A new appropriation of nature? *Journal of Peasant Studies*, 39, 237–261.

FEENSTRA, R. C. & HAMILTON, G. G. 2006. *Emergent Economies, Divergent Paths: Economic Organization and International Trade in South Korea and Taiwan*. Cambridge: Cambridge University Press.

FENTON, P. 2017. The role of port cities and transnational municipal networks in efforts to reduce greenhouse gas emissions on land and at sea from shipping: An assessment of the World Ports Climate Initiative. *Marine Policy*, 75, 271–277.

FERREIRA, S. L. & HUNTER, C. A. 2017. Wine tourism development in South Africa: A geographical analysis. *Tourism Geographies*, 19, 676–698.

FILOSO, S., DO CARMO, J. B., MARDEGAN, S. F., LINS, S. R. M., GOMES, T. F. & MARTINELLI, L. A. 2015. Reassessing the environmental impacts of sugarcane ethanol production in Brazil to help meet sustainability goals. *Renewable and Sustainable Energy Reviews*, 52, 1847–1856.

FINE, B. 2002. *The World of Consumption: The Material and Cultural Revisited*. London: Routledge.

FINNVEDEN, G., HAUSCHILD, M. Z., EKVALL, T., GUINÉE, J., HEIJUNGS, R., HELLWEG, S., KOEHLER, A., PENNINGTON, D. & SUH, S. 2009. Recent developments in life cycle assessment. *Journal of Environmental Management*, 91, 1–21.

FITTER, R. & KAPLINSKY, R. 2001a. Can an agricultural 'commodity' be de-commodified, and if so who is to gain? *IDS Discussion Paper* 380. Institute of Development Studies, University of Sussex.

FITTER, R. & KAPLINSKY, R. 2001b. Who gains from product rents as the coffee market becomes more differentiated? A value-chain analysis. *IDS Bulletin*, 32, 69–82.

FLINT, D. J., GOLICIC, S. L. & SIGNORI, P. 2016. *Contemporary Wine Marketing and Supply Chain Management: A Global Perspective*. New York: Springer.

FOLD, N. 2002. Lead firms and competition in 'bi-polar' commodity chains: Grinders and branders in the global cocoa-chocolate industry. *Journal of Agrarian Change*, 2, 228–247.

FOLEY, P. 2013. National government responses to Marine Stewardship Council (MSC) fisheries certification: Insights from Atlantic Canada. *New Political Economy*, 18, 284–307.

FORTIN, E. 2013. Transnational multi-stakeholder sustainability standards and biofuels: Understanding standards processes. *Journal of Peasant Studies*, 40, 563–587.

FORTIN, E. & RICHARDSON, B. 2013. Certification schemes and the governance of land: Enforcing standards or enabling scrutiny? *Globalizations*, 10, 141–159.

FOUILLEUX, E. & LOCONTO, A. 2017. Voluntary standards, certification, and accreditation in the global organic agriculture field: A tripartite model of techno-politics. *Agriculture and Human Values*, 34, 1–14.

FRANSEN, L. 2011. Why do private governance organizations not converge? A political-institutional analysis of transnational labor standards regulation. *Governance*, 24, 359–387.

FRANSEN, L. 2012. Multi-stakeholder governance and voluntary programme interactions: Legitimation politics in the institutional design of corporate social responsibility. *Socio-Economic Review*, 10, 163–192.

FRANSEN, L. 2015. The politics of meta-governance in transnational private sustainability governance. *Policy Sciences*, 48, 293–317.

FRANSEN, L. 2018. Beyond regulatory governance? On the evolutionary trajectory of transnational private sustainability governance. *Ecological Economics*, 146, 772–777.

FRANSEN, L. & BURGOON, B. 2014. Privatizing or socializing corporate responsibility: Business participation in voluntary programs. *Business & Society*, 53, 583–619.

FRANSEN, L. & KOLK, A. 2007. Global rule-setting for business: A critical analysis of multi-stakeholder standards. *Organization*, 14, 667–684.

FRANSEN, L., SCHALK, J. & AULD, G. 2016. Work ties beget community? Assessing interactions among transnational private governance organizations in sustainable agriculture. *Global Networks*, 16, 45–67.

FRANSEN, L., SCHALK, J. & AULD, G. 2018. Community structure and the behavior of transnational sustainability governors: Toward a multi-relational approach. *Regulation & Governance*, early view, doi: 10.1111/rego/12185.

FREIDBERG, S. 2013. Calculating sustainability in supply chain capitalism. *Economy and Society*, 42, 571–596.

FREIDBERG, S. 2014. Footprint technopolitics. *Geoforum*, 55, 178–189.

FREIDBERG, S. 2017. Trading in the secretive commodity. *Economy and Society*, 46, 499–521.

FRIEDMAN, T. L. 2009. *Hot, Flat, and Crowded 2.0: Why We Need a Green Revolution – and How It Can Renew America*. London: Picador.

FROUD, J., HASLAM, C., JOHAL, S. & WILLIAMS, K. 2000. Shareholder value and financialization: Consultancy promises, management moves. *Economy and Society*, 29, 80–110.

FUCHS, D., KALFAGIANNI, A. & HAVINGA, T. 2011. Actors in private food governance: The legitimacy of retail standards and multistakeholder initiatives with civil society participation. *Agriculture and Human Values*, 28, 353–367.

GALE, F. 2014. Four models of interest mediation in global environmental governance. *Global Policy*, 5, 10–22.

GALE, F. & HAWARD, M. 2011. *Global Commodity Governance: State Responses to Sustainable Forest and Fisheries Certification*. Basingstoke: Palgrave Macmillan.

GARCÍA-LÓPEZ, G. A. & ARIZPE, N. 2010. Participatory processes in the soy conflicts in Paraguay and Argentina. *Ecological Economics*, 70, 196–206.

GARWOOD, S. 2011. *Advocacy across Borders: NGOs, Anti-Sweatshop Activism and the Global Garment Industry.* Sterling, VA: Kumarian Press Sterling.

GEREFFI, G. 1994. The organization of buyer-driven global commodity chains: How US retailers shape overseas production networks. In: GEREFFI, G. & KORZENIEWICZ, M. (eds.) *Commodity Chains and Global Capitalism.* Westport, CT: Praeger.

GEREFFI, G. 1999. International trade and industrial upgrading in the apparel commodity chain. *Journal of International Economics*, 48, 37–70.

GEREFFI, G. 2014. Global value chains in a post-Washington Consensus world. *Review of International Political Economy*, 21, 9–37.

GEREFFI, G. 2019. *Global Value Chains and Development: Redefining the Contours of 21st Century Capitalism.* Cambridge: Cambridge University Press.

GEREFFI, G., HUMPHREY, J. & STURGEON, T. 2005. The governance of global value chains. *Review of International Political Economy*, 12, 78–104.

GEREFFI, G. & LEE, J. 2012. Why the world suddenly cares about global supply chains. *Journal of Supply Chain Management*, 48, 24–32.

GEREFFI, G. & LEE, J. 2016. Economic and social upgrading in global value chains and industrial clusters: Why governance matters. *Journal of Business Ethics*, 133, 25–38.

GIBBON, P. 2001. Upgrading primary production: A global commodity chain approach. *World Development*, 29, 345–363.

GIBBON, P. 2008. Governance, entry barriers, upgrading: A re-interpretation of some GVC concepts from the experience of African clothing exports. *Competition & Change*, 12, 29–48.

GIBBON, P., BAIR, J. & PONTE, S. 2008. Governing global value chains: An introduction. *Economy and Society*, 37, 315–338.

GIBBON, P. & PONTE, S. 2005. *Trading Down: Africa, Value Chains, and the Global Economy.* Philadelphia, PA: Temple University Press.

GIBBON, P. & PONTE, S. 2008. Global value chains: From governance to governmentality? *Economy and Society*, 37, 365–392.

GIBBON, P., PONTE, S. & LAZARO, E. (eds.) 2010. *Global Agro-Food Trade and Standards: Challenges for Africa.* Basingstoke: Palgrave Macmillan.

GIBBS, D., RIGOT-MULLER, P., MANGAN, J. & LALWANI, C. 2014. The role of sea ports in end-to-end maritime transport chain emissions. *Energy Policy*, 64, 337–348.

GIBSON, C. C., MCKEAN, M. A. & OSTROM, E. (eds.) 2000. *People and Forests: Communities, Institutions, and Governance.* Cambridge, MA: MIT Press.

GIBSON-GRAHAM, J. K. 2006. *A Postcapitalist Politics.* Minneapolis, MN: University of Minnesota Press.

GIBSON-GRAHAM, J. K., CAMERON, J. & HEALY, S. 2013. *Take Back the Economy: An Ethical Guide for Transforming our Communities.* Minneapolis, MN: University of Minnesota Press.

GILBERT, D. U., RASCHE, A. & WADDOCK, S. 2011. Accountability in a global economy: The emergence of international accountability standards. *Business Ethics Quarterly*, 21, 23–44.

GILINSKY JR, A., NEWTON, S. K., ATKIN, T. S., SANTINI, C., CAVICCHI, A., CASAS, A. R. & HUERTAS, R. 2015. Perceived efficacy of sustainability strategies in the US, Italian, and Spanish wine industries: a comparative study. *International Journal of Wine Business Research*, 27, 164–181.

GILLON, S. 2010. Fields of dreams: Negotiating an ethanol agenda in the Midwest United States. *The Journal of Peasant Studies*, 37, 723–748.

GIOVANNUCCI, D., BYERS, A. & LIU, P. 2008. *Adding Value: Certified Coffee Trade in North America.* Rome: FAO.

GIOVANNUCCI, D. & PONTE, S. 2005. Standards as a new form of social contract? Sustainability initiatives in the coffee industry. *Food Policy*, 30, 284–301.

GIULIANI, E., CIRAVEGNA, L., VEZZULLI, A. & KILIAN, B. 2017. Decoupling standards from practice: The impact of in-house certifications on coffee farms' environmental and social conduct. *World Development*, 96, 294–314.

GIULIANI, E., MORRISON, A., PIETROBELLI, C. & RABELLOTTI, R. 2010. Who are the researchers that are collaborating with industry? An analysis of the wine sectors in Chile, South Africa and Italy. *Research Policy*, 39, 748–761.

GIULIANI, E., MORRISON, A. & RABELLOTTI, R. (eds.) 2011. *Innovation and Technological Catch-Up: The Changing Geography of Wine Production.* Cheltenham: Edward Elgar.

GIULIANI, E., PIETROBELLI, C. & RABELLOTTI, R. 2005. Upgrading in global value chains: Lessons from Latin American clusters. *World Development*, 33, 549–573.

GLÜCKLER, J. & PANITZ, R. 2016. Relational upgrading in global value networks. *Journal of Economic Geography*, 16, 1161–1185.

GOGER, A. 2013. The making of a 'business case'for environmental upgrading: Sri Lanka's eco-factories. *Geoforum*, 47, 73–83.

GOLD, S., SEURING, S. & BESKE, P. 2010. Sustainable supply chain management and inter-organizational resources: A literature review. *Corporate Social Responsibility and Environmental Management*, 17, 230–245.

GOSSLING, S. & UPHAM, P. (eds.) 2009. *Climate Change and Aviation.* London: Earthscan.

GRABS, J. 2017. The rise of buyer-driven sustainability governance: Emerging trends in the global coffee sector. *SSRN Scholarly Paper* ID 3015166. Rochester, NY: Social Science Research Network.

GRABS, J. 2018. Assessing the institutionalization of private sustainability governance in a changing coffee sector. *Regulation & Governance*, early view, doi: 10.1111/rego.12212.

GRABS, J. 2019. *The Effectiveness of Market-Driven Regulatory Sustainability Governance: Assessing the Design of Private Sustainability Standards and Their Impacts on Latin American Coffee Farmers' Production Practices.* PhD thesis, Westfälische Wilhelms-Universität Münster.

GRABS, J., KILIAN, B., HERNÁNDEZ, D. C. & DIETZ, T. 2016. Understanding coffee certification dynamics: A spatial analysis of voluntary sustainability standard proliferation. *International Food & Agribusiness Management Review*, 19, 31–55.

GRAHAM, E. R. & THOMPSON, E. 2015. Efficient orchestration? The Global Environmental Facility in the governance of climate adaptation. In: ABBOTT, K. W., GENSCHEL, P., SNIDAL, D. & ZANGL, B. (eds.) *International Organizations as Orchestrators.* Cambridge: Cambridge University Press.

GREEN, J. F. 2013. *Rethinking Private Authority: Agents and Entrepreneurs in Global Environmental Governance.* Princeton, NJ: Princeton University Press.

GREEN, J. F. 2017a. Policy entrepreneurship in climate governance: Toward a comparative approach. *Environment and Planning C*, 35, 1471–1482.

GREEN, J. F. 2017b. Transnational delegation in global environmental governance: When do non-state actors govern? *Regulation & Governance*, early view, doi: 10.1111/rego.12141.

GULBRANDSEN, L. H. 2008. Accountability arrangements in non-state standards organizations: Instrumental design and imitation. *Organization*, 15, 563–583.

GULBRANDSEN, L. H. 2009. The emergence and effectiveness of the Marine Stewardship Council. *Marine Policy*, 33, 654–660.

GULBRANDSEN, L. H. 2010. *Transnational Environmental Governance: The Emergence and Effects of the Certification of Forest and Fisheries*. Cheltenham: Edward Elgar.

GULBRANDSEN, L. H. 2014. Dynamic governance interactions: Evolutionary effects of state responses to non-state certification programs. *Regulation & Governance*, 8, 74–92.

GUNNINGHAM, N. 2002. Reconfiguring environmental regulation: The future public policy agenda. In: GUNNINGHAM, N. & SINCLAIR, D. (eds.) *Leaders and Laggards: Next Generation Environmental Regulation*. Sheffield: Greenleaf.

GUNNINGHAM, N. 2009. Environment law, regulation and governance: Shifting architectures. *Journal of Environmental Law*, 21, 179–212.

GUNNINGHAM, N., GRABOSKY, P. & SINCLAIR, N. 1998. *Smart Regulation: Designing Environmental Regulation*. Oxford: Oxford University Press.

GUNNINGHAM, N., KAGAN, R. A. & THORNTON, D. 2003. *Shades of Green: Business, Regulation, and Environment*. Stanford, CA: Stanford University Press.

GUTHMAN, J. 2014. *Agrarian Dreams: The Paradox of Organic Farming in California*. Berkeley, CA: University of California Press.

HAAS, P. M. 2004. Addressing the global governance deficit. *Global Environmental Politics*, 4, 1–15.

HACKMANN, B. 2012. Analysis of the governance architecture to regulate GHG emissions from international shipping. *International Environmental Agreements: Politics, Law and Economics*, 12, 85–103.

HALE, T. & ROGER, C. 2014. Orchestration and transnational climate governance. *Review of International Organizations*, 9, 59–82.

HALL, R. B. & BIERSTEKER, T. J. (eds.) 2002. *The Emergence of Private Authority in Global Governance*. Cambridge: Cambridge University Press.

HANSEN, U. E., FOLD, N. & HANSEN, T. 2014. Upgrading to lead firm position via international acquisition: Learning from the global biomass power plant industry. *Journal of Economic Geography*, 16, 131–153.

HARAWAY, D. 2015. Anthropocene, Capitalocene, Plantationocene, Chthulucene: Making kin. *Environmental Humanities*, 6, 159–165.

HARVEY, D. 2004. The 'new' imperialism: Accumulation by dispossession. *Socialist Register*, 40, 63–87.

HASSAN, A. & LUND-THOMSEN, P. 2016. Multi-stakeholder initiatives and corporate social responsibility in global value chains. In: JAMALI, D. (ed.) *Comparative Perspectives on Global Corporate Social Responsibility*. Hershey, PA: IGI Global Editors.

HATANAKA, M. 2010. Certification, partnership, and morality in an organic shrimp network: Rethinking transnational alternative agrifood networks. *World Development*, 38, 706–716.

HAVICE, E. & CAMPLING, L. 2013. Articulating upgrading: Island developing states and canned tuna production. *Environment and Planning A*, 45, 2610–2627.

HAVICE, E. & CAMPLING, L. 2017. Where chain governance and environmental governance meet: Interfirm strategies in the canned tuna global value chain. *Economic Geography*, 93, 292–313.

HAVNEVIK, K. & HAALAND, H. 2011. Biofuel, land and environmental issues: The case of SEKAB's biofuel plans in Tanzania. In: MATONDI, P. B., HAVNEVIK, K. & BEYENE, A. (eds.) *Biofuels, Land Grabbing and Food Security in Africa*. London: Zed Books.

HELMSING, A. & VELLEMA, S. (eds.) 2011. *Value Chains, Social Inclusion and Economic Development: Contrasting Theories and Realities*. London: Routledge.

HENDERSON, J., DICKEN, P., HESS, M., COE, N. & YEUNG, H. W.-C. 2002. Global production networks and the analysis of economic development. *Review of International Political Economy*, 9, 436–464.

HENRIKSEN, L. F. 2015. The global network of biofuel sustainability standards-setters. *Environmental Politics*, 24, 115–137.

HENRIKSEN, L. F. & PONTE, S. 2018. Public orchestration, social networks and transnational environmental governance: Lessons from the aviation industry. *Regulation & Governance*, early view, doi: 10.1111/rego.12151.

HENRIKSEN, L. F. & SEABROOKE, L. 2016. Transnational organizing: Issue professionals in environmental sustainability networks. *Organization*, 23, 722–741.

HÉRITIER, A. & ECKERT, S. 2008. New modes of governance in the shadow of hierarchy: Self-regulation by industry in Europe. *Journal of Public Policy*, 28, 113–138.

HESS, M. & YEUNG, H. W.-C. 2006. Whither global production networks in economic geography? Past, present, and future. *Environment and Planning A*, 38, 1193–1204.

HIGGS, K. 2014. *Collision Course: Endless Growth on a Finite Planet*. Cambridge, MA: MIT Press.

HILL, A. 2017. Blue grabbing: Reviewing marine conservation in Redang Island Marine Park, Malaysia. *Geoforum*, 79, 97–100.

HIRA, A. (ed.) 2013. *What Makes Clusters Competitive: Cases from the Global Wine Industry*. Montreal: McGill-Queen's University Press.

HOFFMANN, M. J. 2011. *Climate Governance at the Crossroads: Experimenting with a Global Response after Kyoto*. Oxford: Oxford University Press.

HOLLEY, C. GUNNINGHAM, N. & SHEARING, C. D. 2013. *The New Environmental Governance*. London: Routledge.

HOOGHE, L., MARKS, G. & MARKS, G. W. 2001. *Multi-Level Governance and European Integration*. Lanham, MD: Rowman & Littlefield.

HORNER, R. 2013. Strategic decoupling, recoupling and global production networks: India's pharmaceutical industry. *Journal of Economic Geography*, 14, 1117–1140.

HORNER, R. 2017. Beyond facilitator? State roles in global value chains and global production networks. *Geography Compass*, 11, early view, doi: 10.1111/gec3.12307.

HORNER, R. & NADVI, K. 2018. Global value chains and the rise of the Global South: Unpacking twenty-first century polycentric trade. *Global Networks*, 18, 207–237.

HOSPES, O., VAN DER VALK, O. & VAN DER MHEEN-SLUIJER, J. 2012. Parallel development of five partnerships to promote sustainable soy in Brazil: Solution or part of wicked problems? *International Food and Agribusiness Management Review*, 15, 29–52.

HUMES, E. 2011. *Force of Nature: The Unlikely Story of Wal-Mart's Green Revolution*. New York: Harper Business.

HUMPHREY, J. & NAVAS-ALEMÁN, L. 2010. Value chains, donor interventions and poverty reduction: A review of donor practice. *IDS Research Reports* 2010: 63. Institute of Development Studies, University of Sussex.

HUMPHREY, J. & SCHMITZ, H. 2001. Governance in global value chains. *IDS Bulletin*, 32, 19–29.

HUMPHREY, J. & SCHMITZ, H. 2002. How does insertion in global value chains affect upgrading in industrial clusters? *Regional Studies*, 36, 1017–1027.

HUMPHREY, J. & SCHMITZ, H. 2004. Local enterprises in the global economy: Issues of governance and upgrading. In: SCHMITZ, H. (ed.) *Local Enterprises in the Global Economy: Issues of Governance and Upgrading*. Cheltenham: Edward Elgar.

HUSAIN, A. 2017. *The Sentient Machine: The Coming Age of Artificial Intelligence*. New York: Simon & Schuster.

IBANEZ, M. & BLACKMAN, A. 2016. Is eco-certification a win–win for developing country agriculture? Organic coffee certification in Colombia. *World Development*, 82, 14–27.

IGOE, J. 2017. *The Nature of Spectacle: On Images, Money, and Conserving Capitalism*. Tucson, AZ: University of Arizona Press.

IMAI, K. & SHIU, J. M. 2011. Value chain creation and reorganization: The growth path of China's mobile phone handset industry. In: KAWAKAMI, M. & STURGEON, T. J. (eds.) *The Dynamics of Local Learning in Global Value Chains*. Basingstoke: Palgrave Macmillan.

INTERNATIONAL TRADE CENTRE. 2017. *The State of Sustainability Markets 2017: Statistics and Emerging Trends*. Geneva: ITC.

IPW. 2004. *The South African System of Integrated Production of Wine (IPW)*. Stellenbosch: IPW.

ISLAM, M. S. 2008. From pond to plate: Towards a twin-driven commodity chain in Bangladesh shrimp aquaculture. *Food Policy*, 33, 209–223.

ITÇAINA, X., ROGER, A. & SMITH, A. 2016. *Varietals of Capitalism: A Political Economy of the Changing Wine Industry*. Ithaca, NY: Cornell University Press.

IVARSSON, I. & ALVSTAM, C. G. 2010. Supplier upgrading in the home-furnishing value chain: An empirical study of IKEA's sourcing in China and South East Asia. *World Development*, 38, 1575–1587.

IVARSSON, I. & ALVSTAM, C. G. 2011. Upgrading in global value-chains: A case study of technology-learning among IKEA-suppliers in China and Southeast Asia. *Journal of Economic Geography*, 11, 731–752.

JACKSON, T. 2009. *Prosperity without Growth: Economics for a Finite Planet*. London: Routledge.

JAGD, S. 2011. Pragmatic sociology and competing orders of worth in organizations. *European Journal of Social Theory*, 14, 343–359.

JENA, P. R., STELLMACHER, T. & GROTE, U. 2017. Can coffee certification schemes increase incomes of smallholder farmers? Evidence from Jinotega, Nicaragua. *Environment, Development and Sustainability*, 19, 45–66.

JEPPESEN, S. & HANSEN, M. W. 2004. Environmental upgrading of Third World enterprises through linkages to transnational corporations: Theoretical perspectives and preliminary evidence. *Business Strategy and the Environment*, 13, 261–274.

JESPERSEN, K. S., KELLING, I., PONTE, S. & KRUIJSSEN, F. 2014. What shapes food value chains? Lessons from aquaculture in Asia. *Food Policy*, 49, 228–240.

JEVONS, W. S. 1906. *The Coal Question: An Inquiry Concerning the Progress of the Nation, and the Probable Exhaustion of Our Coal-Mines*. Basingstoke: Macmillan.

JUROWETZKI, R., LEMA, R. & LUNDVALL, B.-Å. 2018. Combining innovation systems and global value chains for development: Towards a research agenda. *European Journal of Development Research*, 30, 364–388.

KAPLINSKY, R. 2004. Spreading the gains from globalization: What can be learned from value-chain analysis? *IDS Working Paper* 110. Institute of Development Studies, University of Sussex.

KAPLINSKY, R. 2005. *Globalization, Inequality, and Poverty: Between a Rock and a Hard Place*. London: Polity.

KAWAKAMI, M. 2011. Inter-firm dynamics in notebook PC value chains and the rise of Taiwanese original design manufacturing firms. In: KAWAKAMI, M. & STURGEON, T. J. (eds.) *The Dynamics of Local Learning in Global Value Chains*. Basingstoke: Palgrave Macmillan.

KECK, M. E. & SIKKINK, K. 1998. Transnational advocacy networks in the movement society. In: MEYER, D. S. & TARROW, S. G. (eds.) *The Social Movement Society: Contentious Politics for a New Century*. Lanham, MD: Rowman & Littlefield.

KENDRA, P.-L. 2012. *Green Washed: Why We Can't Buy Our Way to a Green Planet*. New York: Ig Publishing.

KENIS, A. & LIEVENS, M. 2015. *The Limits of the Green Economy: From Re-Inventing Capitalism to Re-Politicising the Present*. London: Routledge.

KEOHANE, R. O. & VICTOR, D. G. 2011. The regime complex for climate change. *Perspectives on Politics*, 9, 7–23.

KHATTAK, A. & STRINGER, C. 2017. Environmental upgrading in Pakistan's sporting goods industry in global value chains: A question of progress? *Business & Economic Review*, 9, 43–64.

KHATTAK, A., STRINGER, C., BENSON-REA, M. & HAWORTH, N. 2015. Environmental upgrading of apparel firms in global value chains: Evidence from Sri Lanka. *Competition & Change*, 19, 317–335.

KLOOSTER, D. 2010. Standardizing sustainable development? The Forest Stewardship Council's plantation policy review process as neoliberal environmental governance. *Geoforum*, 41, 117–129.

KOLK, A. 2005. Corporate social responsibility in the coffee sector: The dynamics of MNC responses and code development. *European Management Journal*, 23, 228–236.

KOLK, A. 2012. Towards a sustainable coffee market: Paradoxes faced by a multinational company. *Corporate Social Responsibility and Environmental Management*, 19, 79–89.

KOLK, A. 2013. Mainstreaming sustainable coffee. *Sustainable Development*, 21, 324–337.

KOVEL, J. 2007. *The Enemy of Nature: The End of Capitalism or the End of the World?* London: Zed Books.

KRISHNAN, A. 2017a. The origin and expansion of regional value chains: The case of Kenyan horticulture. *Global Networks*, early view, doi: 10.1111/glob.12162.

KRISHNAN, A. 2017b. *Re-Thinking the Environmental Dimensions of Upgrading and Embeddedness in Production Networks: The Case of Kenyan Horticulture Farmers*. PhD thesis, University of Manchester.

KUIT, M., VAN RIJN, F. & JANSEN, D. 2010. *Assessing 4C Implementation among Small-Scale Producers: An Evaluation of the Effects of 4C Implementation in Vietnam, Uganda and Nicaragua*. Wageningen: Wageningen University.

LABRUTO, N. 2014. Experimental biofuel governance: Historicizing social certification in Brazilian ethanol production. *Geoforum*, 54, 272–281.

LAGENDIJK, A. 2004. Global 'lifeworlds' versus local 'systemworlds': How flying winemakers produce global wines in interconnected locales. *Tijdschrift voor Economische en Sociale Geografie*, 95, 511–526.

LAPLUME, A. O., PETERSEN, B. & PEARCE, J. M. 2016. Global value chains from a 3D printing perspective. *Journal of International Business Studies*, 47, 595–609.

LARSEN, M. 2016. Sustaining upgrading in agricultural value chains? State-led value chain interventions and emerging bifurcation of the South Indian smallholder tea sector. *Sustainability*, 8, 1102.

LEACH, M. & SCOONES, I. (eds.) 2015. *Carbon Conflicts and Forest Landscapes in Africa*. London: Routledge.

LEACH, M., SCOONES, I. & STIRLING, A. 2010. *Dynamic Sustainabilities: Technology, Environment, Social Justice*. London: Earthscan.

LEAKEY, R. E. 1996. *The Sixth Extinction: Patterns of Life and the Future of Humankind*. New York: Anchor.

LEHRER, N. 2010. (Bio) fueling farm policy: The biofuels boom and the 2008 Farm Bill. *Agriculture and Human Values*, 27, 427–444.

LERNOUD, J., POTTS, J., SAMPSON, G., VOORA, V., WILLER, H. & WOZNIAK, J. 2016. *The State of Sustainable Markets-Statistics and Emerging Trends 2015*. Winnipeg: International Institute for Sustainable Development.

LEVIDOW, L. & PAUL, H. 2010. Global agrofuel crops as contested sustainability, part I: Sustaining what development? *Capitalism Nature Socialism*, 21, 64–86.

LEVY, D. L. 2008. Political contestation in global production networks. *Academy of Management Review*, 33, 943–963.

LEVY, D. L. & NEWELL, P. J. (eds.) 2005. *The Business of Global Environmental Governance*. Cambridge, MA: MIT Press.

LEVY, D. L., REINECKE, J. & MANNING, S. 2014. Political dynamics of sustainable coffee and contested value regimes. *Academy of Management Proceedings*, early view, doi: 10.5465/ambpp.2014.281.

LEVY, D. L., REINECKE, J. & MANNING, S. 2016. The political dynamics of sustainable coffee: Contested value regimes and the transformation of sustainability. *Journal of Management Studies*, 53, 364–401.

LINDGREEN, A., MAON, F., VANHAMME, J. & SEN, S. (eds.) 2013. *Sustainable Value Chain Management*. Farnham: Gower.

LISTER, J. 2015. Green shipping: Governing sustainable maritime transport. *Global Policy*, 6, 118–129.

LISTER, J., POULSEN, R. T. & PONTE, S. 2015. Orchestrating transnational environmental governance in maritime shipping. *Global Environmental Change*, 34, 185–195.

LIU, Y. 2017. The dynamics of local upgrading in globalizing latecomer regions: A geographical analysis. *Regional Studies*, 51, 880–893.

LOCKE, R. M., AMENGUAL, M. & MANGLA, A. 2009. Virtue out of necessity? Compliance, commitment, and the improvement of labor conditions in global supply chains. *Politics & Society*, 37, 319–351.

LOCKE, R. M., RISSING, B. A. & PAL, T. 2013. Complements or substitutes? Private codes, state regulation and the enforcement of labour standards in global supply chains. *British Journal of Industrial Relations*, 51, 519–552.

LOVINS, L. H., LOVINS, A. & HAWKEN, P. 2007. *Natural Capitalism: Creating the Next Industrial Revolution*. New York: Little, Brown & Company.

LOW, P. 2013. The role of services in global value chains. In: ELMS, D. K. & LOW, P. (eds.) *Global Value Chains in a Changing World*. Geneva: WTO.

LUCIER, R. L. 1988. *The International Political Economy of Coffee: From Juan Valdez to Yank's Diner*. New York: Praeger.

LUNA, F. & WILSON, P. N. 2015. An economic exploration of smallholder value chains: Coffee transactions in Chiapas, Mexico. *International Food and Agribusiness Management Review*, 18, 85–106.

LUND-THOMSEN, P. & LINDGREEN, A. 2014. Corporate social responsibility in global value chains: Where are we now and where are we going? *Journal of Business Ethics*, 123, 11–22.

LUND-THOMSEN, P. & LINDGREEN, A. 2018. Is there a sweet spot in ethical trade? A critical appraisal of the potential for aligning buyer, supplier and worker interests in global production networks. *Geoforum*, 90, 84–90.

LUND-THOMSEN, P. & NADVI, K. 2010. Global value chains, local collective action and corporate social responsibility: A review of empirical evidence. *Business Strategy and the Environment*, 19, 1–13.

LUNDVALL, B.-Å. 2010. *National Systems of Innovation: Toward a Theory of Innovation and Interactive Learning*. London: Anthem Press.

LUTTINGER, N. & DICUM, G. 2011. *The Coffee Book: Anatomy of an Industry from Crop to the Last Drop*. New York: The New Press.

LYON, T. P. & MAXWELL, J. W. 2004. *Corporate Environmentalism and Public Policy*. Cambridge: Cambridge University Press.

MACGREGOR, F., RAMASAR, V. & NICHOLAS, K. A. 2017. Problems with firm-led voluntary sustainability schemes: The case of direct trade coffee. *Sustainability*, 9, 651.

MACKINNON, D. 2011. Beyond strategic coupling: Reassessing the firm-region nexus in global production networks. *Journal of Economic Geography*, 12, 227–245.

MANNING, S., BOONS, F., VON HAGEN, O. & REINECKE, J. 2012. National contexts matter: The co-evolution of sustainability standards in global value chains. *Ecological Economics*, 83, 197–209.

MANNING, S. & REINECKE, J. 2016. A modular governance architecture in-the-making: How transnational standard-setters govern sustainability transitions. *Research Policy*, 45, 618–633.

MARTINEZ-ALIER, J. 2003. *The Environmentalism of the Poor: A Study of Ecological Conflicts and Valuation*. Cheltenham: Edward Elgar.

MARX, A. 2008. Limits to non-state market regulation: A qualitative comparative analysis of the international sport footwear industry and the Fair Labor Association. *Regulation & Governance*, 2, 253–273.

MATTEN, D. & MOON, J. 2004. Corporate social responsibility. *Journal of Business Ethics*, 54, 323–337.

MATTEN, D. & MOON, J. 2008. 'Implicit' and 'explicit' CSR: A conceptual framework for a comparative understanding of corporate social responsibility. *Academy of Management Review*, 33, 404–424.

MAYER, F. & GEREFFI, G. 2010. Regulation and economic globalization: Prospects and limits of private governance. *Business and Politics*, 12, 1–25.

MAYER, F. W. & PHILLIPS, N. 2017. Outsourcing governance: States and the politics of a 'global value chain world'. *New Political Economy*, 22, 134–152.

MAZZUCATO, M. 2015a. *The Entrepreneurial State: Debunking Public vs. Private Sector Myths*. London: Anthem Press.

MAZZUCATO, M. 2015b. The green enterpreneurial state. In: SCOONES, I., LEACH, M. & NEWELL, P. (eds.) *The Politics of Green Transformations*. London: Routledge.

MCAFEE, A. & BRYNJOLFSSON, E. 2017. *Machine, Platform, Crowd: Harnessing Our Digital Future*. New York: W. W. Norton & Company.

MCCARTHY, J. F. 2012. Certifying in contested spaces: Private regulation in Indonesian forestry and palm oil. *Third World Quarterly*, 33, 1871–1888.

MCCOY, E. 2005. *The Emperor of Wine: The Rise of Robert M. Parker, Jr., and the Reign of American Taste*. New York: Ecco.

MCDONOUGH, W. & BRAUNGART, M. 2010. *Cradle to Cradle: Remaking the Way We Make Things*. London: Vintage.

MCEWAN, C. & BEK, D. 2009. The political economy of alternative trade: Social and environmental certification in the South African wine industry. *Journal of Rural Studies*, 25, 255–266.

MCNEILL, J. R. & ENGELKE, P. 2016. *The Great Acceleration*. Cambridge, MA: Harvard University Press.

MCWILLIAMS, A., SIEGEL, D. S. & WRIGHT, P. M. 2006. Corporate social responsibility: Strategic implications. *Journal of Management Studies*, 43, 1–18.

MECKLING, J. 2015. Oppose, support, or hedge? Distributional effects, regulatory pressure, and business strategy in environmental politics. *Global Environmental Politics*, 15, 19–37.

MENA, S. & PALAZZO, G. 2012. Input and output legitimacy of multi-stakeholder initiatives. *Business Ethics Quarterly*, 22, 527–556.

MEYER, A. & HOHMANN, P. 2000. Other thoughts; other results? Remei's Biore organic cotton on its way to the mass market. *Greener Management International*, 31, 59–70.

MILAN, S. 2013. *Social Movements and Their Technologies: Wiring Social Change*. Basingtsoke: Palgrave Macmillan.

MILANOVIC, B. 2016. *Global Inequality*. Cambridge, MA: Harvard University Press.

MILBERG, W. 2008. Shifting sources and uses of profits: Sustaining US financialization with global value chains. *Economy and Society*, 37, 420–451.

MILBERG, W. & WINKLER, D. 2011. Economic and social upgrading in global production networks: Problems of theory and measurement. *International Labour Review*, 150, 341–365.

MILBERG, W. & WINKLER, D. 2013. *Outsourcing Economics: Global Value Chains in Capitalist Development*. Cambridge: Cambridge University Press.

MILLARD, E. 2017. Still brewing: Fostering sustainable coffee production. *World Development Perspectives*, 7, 32–42.

MILLER, A. M. M. & BUSH, S. R. 2015. Authority without credibility? Competition and conflict between ecolabels in tuna fisheries. *Journal of Cleaner Production*, 107, 137–145.

MILLS, R. W. 2016. The interaction of private and public regulatory governance: The case of association-led voluntary aviation safety programs. *Policy and Society*, 35, 43–55.

MINTEN, B., DEREJE, M., ENGIDA, E. & KUMA, T. 2018a. Coffee value chains on the move: Evidence on Ethiopia. *Food Policy*, early view, doi: 10.1016/j.foodpol.2017.07.012.

MINTEN, B., DEREJE, M., ENGIDA, E. & TAMRU, S. 2018b. Tracking the quality premium of certified coffee: Evidence from Ethiopia. *World Development*, 101, 119–132.

MITCHELL, J. & COLES, C. 2011. *Markets and Rural Poverty: Upgrading in Value Chains*. London: Earthscan.

MOL, A. P. 2003. *Globalization and Environmental Reform: The Ecological Modernization of the Global Economy*. Cambridge, MA: MIT Press.

MOL, A. P. 2007. Boundless biofuels? Between environmental sustainability and vulnerability. *Sociologia Ruralis*, 47, 297–315.

MOL, A. P. 2015. Transparency and value chain sustainability. *Journal of Cleaner Production*, 107, 154–161.

MOOG, S., SPICER, A. & BÖHM, S. 2015. The politics of multi-stakeholder initiatives: The crisis of the Forest Stewardship Council. *Journal of Business Ethics*, 128, 469–493.

MOORE, J. W. 2015. *Capitalism in the Web of Life: Ecology and the Accumulation of Capital*. London: Verso.

MOORE, J. W. (ed.) 2016. *Anthropocene or Capitalocene? Nature, History, and the Crisis of Capitalism*. Oakland, CA: PM Press.

MORRIS, M. & STARITZ, C. 2014. Industrialization trajectories in Madagascar's export apparel industry: Ownership, embeddedness, markets and upgrading. *World Development*, 56, 243–257.

MORRISON, A., PIETROBELLI, C. & RABELLOTTI, R. 2008. Global value chains and technological capabilities: A framework to study learning and innovation in developing countries. *Oxford Development Studies*, 36, 39–58.

MOSER, C., HILDEBRANDT, T. & BAILIS, R. 2014. International sustainability standards and certification. In: SOLOMON, B. D. & BAILIS, R. (eds.) *Sustainable Development of Biofuels in Latin America and the Caribbean*. New York: Springer.

MURADIAN, R. & PELUPESSY, W. 2005. Governing the coffee chain: The role of voluntary regulatory systems. *World Development*, 33, 2029–2044.

MURPHY, J. T. 2007. The challenge of upgrading in African industries: Socio-spatial factors and the urban environment in Mwanza, Tanzania. *World Development*, 35, 1754–1778.

NADVI, K. 2008. Global standards, global governance and the organization of global value chains. *Journal of Economic Geography*, 8, 323–343.

NADVI, K. & RAJ-REICHERT, G. 2015. Governing health and safety at lower tiers of the computer industry global value chain. *Regulation & Governance*, 9, 243–258.

NAVAS-ALEMÁN, L. 2011. The impact of operating in multiple value chains for upgrading: The case of the Brazilian furniture and footwear industries. *World Development*, 39, 1386–1397.

NEILSON, J. & PRITCHARD, B. 2007. Green coffee? The contradictions of global sustainability initiatives from an Indian perspective. *Development Policy Review*, 25, 311–331.

NEILSON, J. & PRITCHARD, B. 2011. *Value Chain Struggles: Institutions and Governance in the Plantation Districts of South India*. Chichester: Wiley.

NEILSON, J. & SHONK, F. 2014. Chained to development? Livelihoods and global value chains in the coffee-producing Toraja region of Indonesia. *Australian Geographer*, 45, 269–288.

NEILSON, J., WRIGHT, J. & AKLIMAWATI, L. 2018. Geographical indications and value capture in the Indonesian coffee sector. *Journal of Rural Studies*, 59, 35–48.

NEIMARK, B., MAHANTY, S. & DRESSLER, W. 2016. Mapping value in a 'green' commodity frontier: Revisiting commodity chain analysis. *Development and Change*, 47, 240–265.

NEWELL, P. 2008. Civil society, corporate accountability and the politics of climate change. *Global Environmental Politics*, 8, 122–153.

NEWELL, P. 2012. *Globalization and the Environment: Capitalism, Ecology and Power*. Chichester: Wiley.

NEWELL, P. & PATERSON, M. 2010. *Climate Capitalism: Global Warming and the Transformation of the Global Economy*. Cambridge: Cambridge University Press.

NGUYEN, G. N. & SARKER, T. 2018. Sustainable coffee supply chain management: A case study in Buon Me Thuot City, Daklak, Vietnam. *International Journal of Corporate Social Responsibility*, 3, early view, doi: 10.1186/s40991-017-0024-x.

NICKOW, A. 2015. Growing in value: NGOs, social movements and the cultivation of developmental value chains in Uttarakhand, India. *Global Networks*, 15, S45–S64.

O'ROURKE, D. 2005. Market movements: Nongovernmental organization strategies to influence global production and consumption. *Journal of Industrial Ecology*, 9, 115–128.

O'ROURKE, D. 2006. Multi-stakeholder regulation: Privatizing or socializing global labor standards? *World Development*, 34, 899–918.

ORSATO, R. 2009. *Sustainable Strategies: When Does It Pay to Be Green?* Cheltenham: Palgrave Macmillan.

ÖSTERBLOM, H., JOUFFRAY, J.-B., FOLKE, C., CRONA, B., TROELL, M., MERRIE, A. & ROCKSTRÖM, J. 2015. Transnational corporations as 'keystone actors' in marine eco-systems. *PLOS ONE*, 10, e0127533.

OUMA, S. 2010. Global standards, local realities: Private agrifood governance and the restructuring of the Kenyan horticulture industry. *Economic Geography*, 86, 197–222.

OUMA, S., JOHNSON, L. & BIGGER, P. 2018. Rethinking the financialization of 'nature'. *Environment and Planning A*, early view, doi: 10.1177/0308518X18755748.

OVERDEVEST, C. 2010. Comparing forest certification schemes: The case of ratcheting standards in the forest sector. *Socio-Economic Review*, 8, 47–76.

OVERDEVEST, C. & ZEITLIN, J. 2014. Assembling an experimentalist regime: Transnational governance interactions in the forest sector. *Regulation & Governance*, 8, 22–48.

OVERDEVEST, C. & ZEITLIN, J. 2018. Experimentalism in transnational forest governance: Implementing European Union Forest Law Enforcement, Governance and Trade (FLEGT) voluntary partnership agreements in Indonesia and Ghana. *Regulation & Governance*, 12, 64–87.

PANHUYSEN, S. & PIERROT, J. 2014. *Coffee barometer 2014*. Hivos, IUCN Nederland, Oxfam Novib, Solidaridad, WWF.

PANICHELLI, L., DAURIAT, A. & GNANSOUNOU, E. 2009. Life cycle assessment of soybean-based biodiesel in Argentina for export. *International Journal of Life Cycle Assessment*, 14, 144–159.

PARENTI, C. 2016. Environment-making in the Capitalocene. In: MOORE, J. (ed.) *Anthropocene or Capitalocene? Nature, History and the Crisis of Capitalism*. Oakland, CA: PM Press.

PARR, A. 2012. *Hijacking Sustainability*. Cambridge, MA: MIT Press.

PARTZSCH, L. 2011. The legitimacy of biofuel certification. *Agriculture and Human Values*, 28, 413–425.

PATEL-CAMPILLO, A. 2011. Transforming global commodity chains: Actor strategies, regulation, and competitive relations in the Dutch cut flower sector. *Economic Geography*, 87, 79–99.

PATTBERG, P. H. 2005. The Forest Stewardship Council: Risk and potential of private forest governance. *Journal of Environment & Development*, 14, 356–374.

PATTBERG, P. H. 2006. Private governance and the South: Lessons from global forest politics. *Third World Quarterly*, 27, 579–593.

PATTBERG, P. H. 2007. *Private Institutions and Global Governance: The New Politics of Environmental Sustainability*. Cheltenham: Edward Elgar.

PEARCE, D. W., MARKANDYA, A. & BARBIER, E. 1989. *Blueprint for a Green Economy*. London: Earthscan.

PEET, R., ROBBINS, P. & WATTS, M. (eds.) 2010. *Global Political Ecology*. London: Routledge.

PEGELS, A. 2014. *Green Industrial Policy in Emerging Countries*. London: Routledge.

PEGLER, L. 2015. Peasant inclusion in global value chains: Economic upgrading but social downgrading in labour processes? *Journal of Peasant Studies*, 42, 929–956.

PELUPESSY, W. 1999. *Coffee in Cote d'Ivoire and Costa Rica: National and Global Aspects of Competitiveness*. Wageningen: Wageningen University.

PENDERGRAST, M. 2010. *Uncommon Grounds: The History of Coffee and How It Transformed Our World*. New York: Basic Books.

PEREZ, O. 2011. Private environmental governance as ensemble regulation: A critical exploration of sustainability indexes and the new ensemble politics. *Theoretical Inquiries in Law*, 12, 543–579.

PHILLIPS, N. 2011. Informality, global production networks and the dynamics of 'adverse incorporation'. *Global Networks*, 11, 380–397.

PICHLER, M. 2013. 'People, planet & profit': Consumer-oriented hegemony and power relations in palm oil and agrofuel certification. *Journal of Environment & Development*, 22, 370–390.

PICKLES, J., SMITH, A., BUČEK, M., ROUKOVA, P. & BEGG, R. 2006. Upgrading, changing competitive pressures, and diverse practices in the East and Central European apparel industry. *Environment and Planning A*, 38, 2305–2324.

PIMENTEL, D., MARKLEIN, A., TOTH, M., KARPOFF, M., PAUL, G., MCCORMACK, R., KYRIAZIS, J. & KRUEGER, T. 2010. Why we should not be using biofuels. In: ROSILLO-CALLE, F. & JOHNSON, F. X. (eds.) *Food versus Fuel: An Informed Introduction to Biofuels*. London: Zed Books.

PIORE, M. J. & SABEL, C. F. 1985. *The Second Industrial Divide: Possibilities for Prosperity*. New York: Basic Books.

POLETTI, A. & SICURELLI, D. 2016. The European Union, preferential trade agreements, and the international regulation of sustainable biofuels. *JCMS: Journal of Common Market Studies*, 54, 249–266.

PONTE, S. 2002a. Brewing a bitter cup? Deregulation, quality and the re-organization of coffee marketing in East Africa. *Journal of Agrarian Change*, 2, 248–272.

PONTE, S. 2002b. The 'latte revolution'? Regulation, markets and consumption in the global coffee chain. *World Development*, 30, 1099–1122.

PONTE, S. 2004. *Standards and Sustainability in the Coffee Sector*. Winnipeg: International Institute for Sustainable Development.

PONTE, S. 2007a. Bans, tests, and alchemy: Food safety regulation and the Uganda fish export industry. *Agriculture and Human Values*, 24, 179–193.

PONTE, S. 2007b. Governance in the value chain for South African wine. *TRALAC Working Paper* 2007/9. Stellenbosch: Trade Law Centre for Southern Africa.

PONTE, S. 2008. Greener than thou: The political economy of fish ecolabeling and its local manifestations in South Africa. *World Development*, 36, 159–175.

PONTE, S. 2009. Governing through quality: Conventions and supply relations in the value chain for South African wine. *Sociologia Ruralis*, 49, 236–257.

PONTE, S. 2012. The Marine Stewardship Council (MSC) and the making of a market for 'sustainable fish'. *Journal of Agrarian Change*, 12, 300–315.

PONTE, S. 2014a. The evolutionary dynamics of biofuel value chains: From unipolar and government-driven to multipolar governance. *Environment and Planning A*, 46, 353–372.

PONTE, S. 2014b. 'Roundtabling' sustainability: Lessons from the biofuel industry. *Geoforum*, 54, 261–271.

PONTE, S. 2016. Convention theory in the anglophone agro-food literature: Past, present and future. *Journal of Rural Studies*, 44, 12–23.

PONTE, S. & CHEYNS, E. 2013. Voluntary standards, expert knowledge and the governance of sustainability networks. *Global Networks*, 13, 459–477.

PONTE, S. & DAUGBJERG, C. 2015. Biofuel sustainability and the formation of transnational hybrid governance. *Environmental Politics*, 24, 96–114.

PONTE, S. & EWERT, J. 2007. South African wine: An industry in ferment. *TRALAC Working Paper* 2007/8. Stellenbosch: Trade Law Centre for Southern Africa.

PONTE, S. & EWERT, J. 2009. Which way is 'up' in upgrading? Trajectories of change in the value chain for South African wine. *World Development*, 37, 1637–1650.

PONTE, S., GEREFFI, G. & RAJ-REICHERT, G. (Eds) 2019. *Handbook on Global Value Chains*. Cheltenham: Edward Elgar.

PONTE, S. & GIBBON, P. 2005. Quality standards, conventions and the governance of global value chains. *Economy and Society*, 34, 1–31.

PONTE, S., GIBBON, P. & VESTERGAARD, J. (eds.) 2011. *Governing through Standards: Origins, Drivers and Limitations*. Basingstoke: Palgrave Macmillan.

PONTE, S., KELLING, I., JESPERSEN, K. S. & KRUIJSSEN, F. 2014. The blue revolution in Asia: Upgrading and governance in aquaculture value chains. *World Development*, 64, 52–64.

PONTE, S. & STURGEON, T. 2014. Explaining governance in global value chains: A modular theory-building effort. *Review of International Political Economy*, 21, 195–223.

PORTER, M. E. & KRAMER, M. R. 2011. The big idea: Creating shared value. *Harvard Business Review*, 89, 62–77.

POSTHUMA, A. 2010. Beyond 'regulatory enclaves': Challenges and opportunities to promote decent work in global production networks. In: NATHAN, D. (ed.) *Labour in Global Production Networks in India*. Oxford: Oxford University Press.

POTTS, J., LYNCH, M., WILKINGS, A., HUPPÉ, G. A., CUNNINGHAM, M. & VOORA, V. A. 2014. *The State of Sustainability Initiatives Review 2014: Standards and the Green Economy*. Winnipeg: International Institute for Sustainable Development.

POULSEN, R. T., PONTE, S. & LISTER, J. 2016. Buyer-driven greening? Cargo-owners and environmental upgrading in maritime shipping. *Geoforum*, 68, 57–68.

POULSEN, R. T., PONTE, S. & SORNN-FRIESE, H. 2018. Environmental upgrading in global value chains: The potential and limitations of ports in the greening of maritime transport. *Geoforum*, 89, 83–95.

QUACK, S. 2009. Law, expertise and legitimacy in transnational economic governance: An introduction. *Socio-Economic Review*, 8, 3–16.

QUENTIN, D. & CAMPLING, L. 2018. Global inequality chains: Integrating mechanisms of value distribution into analyses of global production. *Global Networks*, 18, 33–56.

RAJ-REICHERT, G. 2015. Exercising power over labour governance in the electronics industry. *Geoforum*, 67, 89–92.

RASCHE, A., WADDOCK, S. & MCINTOSH, M. 2013. The United Nations global compact: Retrospect and prospect. *Business & Society*, 52, 6–30.

RAWORTH, K. 2012. A safe and just space for humanity: Can we live within the doughnut? *Oxfam Policy and Practice: Climate Change and Resilience*, 8, 1–26.

RAYNOLDS, L. T. 2009. Mainstreaming fair trade coffee: From partnership to traceability. *World Development*, 37, 1083–1093.

REHNBERG, M. & PONTE, S. 2017. From smiling to smirking? 3D printing, upgrading and the restructuring of global value chains. *Global Networks*, 18, 57–80.

REINECKE, J., MANNING, S. & VON HAGEN, O. 2012. The emergence of a standards market: Multiplicity of sustainability standards in the global coffee industry. *Organization Studies*, 33, 791–814.

RENCKENS, S., SKOGSTAD, G. & MONDOU, M. 2017. When normative and market power interact: The European Union and global biofuels governance. *JCMS: Journal of Common Market Studies*, 55, 1432–1448.

RENNINGS, K. 2000. Redefining innovation: Eco-innovation research and the contribution from ecological economics. *Ecological Economics*, 32, 319–332.

RICHEY, L. A. & PONTE, S. 2008. Better (Red)™ than dead? Celebrities, consumption and international aid. *Third World Quarterly*, 29, 711–729.

RICHEY, L. A. & PONTE, S. 2011. *Brand Aid: Shopping Well to Save the World*. Minneapolis, MN: University of Minnesota Press.

RICHEY, L. A. & PONTE, S. 2014. New actors and alliances in development. *Third World Quarterly*, 35, 1–21.

RIISGAARD, L. 2011. Towards more stringent sustainability standards? Trends in the cut flower industry. *Review of African Political Economy*, 38, 435–453.

RIISGAARD, L., BOLWIG, S., PONTE, S., DU TOIT, A., HALBERG, N. & MATOSE, F. 2010. Integrating poverty and environmental concerns into value-chain analysis: A strategic framework and practical guide. *Development Policy Review*, 28, 195–216.

ROCKSTRÖM, J., STEFFEN, W., NOONE, K., PERSSON, Å., CHAPIN, F. S., LAMBIN, E. F., LENTON, T. M., SCHEFFER, M., FOLKE, C. & SCHELLNHUBER, H. J. 2009a. A safe operating space for humanity. *Nature*, 461, 472–475.

ROCKSTRÖM, J., STEFFEN, W., NOONE, K., PERSSON, Å., CHAPIN III, F. S., LAMBIN, E., LENTON, T. M., SCHEFFER, M., FOLKE, C. & SCHELLNHUBER, H. J. 2009b. Planetary boundaries: Exploring the safe operating space for humanity. *Ecology and Society*, 14, 2, Art 32.

RODRIK, D. 2014. Green industrial policy. *Oxford Review of Economic Policy*, 30, 469–491.

ROE, M. 2012. *Maritime Governance and Policy-Making*. New York: Springer.

ROGERS, H. 2013. *Green Gone Wrong: Dispatches from the Front Lines of Eco-Capitalism*. London: Verso Books.

ROSILLO-CALLE, F. & JOHNSON, F. X. (eds.) 2010. *Food versus Fuel: An Informed Introduction*. London: Zed Books.

ROSSI, A. 2013. Does economic upgrading lead to social upgrading in global production networks? Evidence from Morocco. *World Development*, 46, 223–233.

RUEDA, X., THOMAS, N. E. & LAMBIN, E. F. 2015. Eco-certification and coffee cultivation enhance tree cover and forest connectivity in the Colombian coffee landscapes. *Regional Environmental Change*, 15, 25–33.

SAKO, M. & ZYLBERBERG, E. 2017. Supplier strategy in global value chains: Shaping governance and profiting from upgrading. *Socio-Economic Review*, early view, doi: 10.1093/ser/mwx049.

SASSER, E. N., PRAKASH, A., CASHORE, B. & AULD, G. 2006. Direct targeting as an NGO political strategy: Examining private authority regimes in the forestry sector. *Business and Politics*, 8, 1–32.

SCARLAT, N. & DALLEMAND, J.-F. 2011. Recent developments of biofuels/bioenergy sustainability certification: A global overview. *Energy Policy*, 39, 1630–1646.

SCHEPERS, D. H. 2010. Challenges to legitimacy at the Forest Stewardship Council. *Journal of Business Ethics*, 92, 279–290.

SCHLEIFER, P. 2013. Orchestrating sustainability: The case of European Union biofuel governance. *Regulation & Governance*, 7, 533–546.

SCHLEIFER, P. & SUN, Y. 2018. Emerging markets and private governance: The political economy of sustainable palm oil in China and India. *Review of International Political Economy*, 25, 190–214.

SCHMITZ, H. (ed.) 2004. *Local Enterprises in the Global Economy*. Chichester: Edward Elgar.

SCHMITZ, H. 2006. Learning and earning in global garment and footwear chains. *European Journal of Development Research*, 18, 546–571.

SCHMITZ, H. & KNORRINGA, P. 2000. Learning from global buyers. *Journal of Development Studies*, 37, 177–205.

SCHOUTEN, G., LEROY, P. & GLASBERGEN, P. 2012. On the deliberative capacity of private multi-stakeholder governance: The roundtables on responsible soy and sustainable palm oil. *Ecological Economics*, 83, 42–50.

SCHROEDER, S. 2015. *When Ethics Are Good for Business: A Case Study on the Strategic Importance of Direct Trade for Three Speciality Coffee Roasters in Copenhagen*. MSc thesis, Copenhagen Business School.

SCHURMAN, R. 2004. Fighting 'Frankenfoods': Industry opportunity structures and the efficacy of the anti-biotech movement in Western Europe. *Social Problems*, 51, 243–268.

SCHURMAN, R. & MUNRO, W. 2009. Targeting capital: A cultural economy approach to understanding the efficacy of two anti-genetic engineering movements. *American Journal of Sociology*, 115, 155–202.

SCHWAB, K. 2017. *The Fourth Industrial Revolution*. Geneva: World Economic Forum.

SCHWAB, K. 2018. *Shaping the Fourth Industrial Revolution*. Geneva: World Economic Forum.

SCOONES, I. 2016. The politics of sustainability and development. *Annual Review of Environment and Resources*, 41, 293–319.

SCOONES, I., LEACH, M. & NEWELL, P. (eds.) 2015. *The Politics of Green Transformations*. London: Routledge.

SEABROOKE, L. & HENRIKSEN, L. F. (eds.) 2017. *Professional Networks in Transnational Governance*. Cambridge: Cambridge University Press.

SEABROOKE, L. & WIGAN, D. 2014. Global wealth chains in the international political economy. *Review of International Political Economy*, 21, 257–263.

SEABROOKE, L. & WIGAN, D. 2017. The governance of global wealth chains. *Review of International Political Economy*, 24, 1–29.

SEARCHINGER, T., EDWARDS, R., MULLIGAN, D., HEIMLICH, R. & PLEVIN, R. 2015. Do biofuel policies seek to cut emissions by cutting food? *Science*, 347, 1420–1422.

SELFA, T., BAIN, C. & MORENO, R. 2014. Depoliticizing land and water 'grabs' in Colombia: The limits of Bonsucro certification for enhancing sustainable biofuel practices. *Agriculture and Human Values*, 31, 455–468.

SELWYN, B. 2011. Beyond firm-centrism: Re-integrating labour and capitalism into global commodity chain analysis. *Journal of Economic Geography*, 12, 205–226.

SELWYN, B. 2013. Social upgrading and labour in global production networks: A critique and an alternative conception. *Competition & Change*, 17, 75–90.

SEURING, S. 2004. Integrated chain management and supply chain management: Comparative analysis and illustrative cases. *Journal of Cleaner Production*, 12, 1059–1071.

SEURING, S. & GOLD, S. 2013. Sustainability management beyond corporate boundaries: From stakeholders to performance. *Journal of Cleaner Production*, 56, 1–6.

SEURING, S. & MÜLLER, M. 2008. From a literature review to a conceptual framework for sustainable supply chain management. *Journal of Cleaner Production*, 16, 1699–1710.

SEURING, S., SARKIS, J., MÜLLER, M. & RAO, P. 2008. Sustainability and supply chain management: An introduction to the special issue. *Journal of Cleaner Production*, 16, 1545–1551.

SHEARING, C. D., GUNNINGHAM, N. & HOLLEY, C. 2013. *The New Environmental Governance*. London: Routledge.

SHIN, N., KRAEMER, K. L. & DEDRICK, J. 2012. Value capture in the global electronics industry: Empirical evidence for the 'smiling curve' concept. *Industry and Innovation*, 19, 89–107.

SHIVA, V. 2016. *Earth Democracy: Justice, Sustainability and Peace*. London: Zed Books.

SINCLAIR, D. 1997. Self-regulation versus command and control? Beyond false dichotomies. *Law & Policy*, 19, 529–559.

SLATER, D. 1997. *Consumer Culture and Modernity*. Chichester: Wiley.

SMITH, J. 2010. *Biofuels and the Globalization of Risk: The Biggest Change in North-South Relationships since Colonialism?* London: Zed Books.

SOGARI, G., MORA, C. & MENOZZI, D. 2016a. Factors driving sustainable choice: The case of wine. *British Food Journal*, 118, 632–646.

SOGARI, G., MORA, C. & MENOZZI, D. 2016b. Sustainable wine labeling: A framework for definition and consumers' perception. *Agriculture and Agricultural Science Procedia*, 8, 58–64.

SOLÉR, C., SANDSTRÖM, C. & SKOOG, H. 2017. How can high-biodiversity coffee make it to the mainstream market? The performativity of voluntary sustainability standards and outcomes for coffee diversification. *Environmental Management*, 59, 230–248.

STARICCO, J. I. & PONTE, S. 2015. Quality regimes in agro-food industries: A regulation theory reading of fair trade wine in Argentina. *Journal of Rural Studies*, 38, 65–76.

STARITZ, C., WHITFIELD, L., MELESE, A. T. & MULANGU, F. M. 2017. What is required for African-owned firms to enter new export sectors? Conceptualizing technological capabilities within global value chains. *CAE Working Paper* 2017: 1. Roskilde: Center of African Economies, Roskilde University.

STAROSTA, G. 2010. The outsourcing of manufacturing and the rise of giant global contractors: A Marxian approach to some recent transformations of global value chains. *New Political Economy*, 15, 543–563.

STATTMAN, S. L., HOSPES, O. & MOL, A. P. 2013. Governing biofuels in Brazil: A comparison of ethanol and biodiesel policies. *Energy Policy*, 61, 22–30.

STEFFEN, W., CRUTZEN, P. J. & MCNEILL, J. R. 2007. The Anthropocene: Are humans now overwhelming the great forces of nature? *AMBIO*, 36, 614–621.

STEFFEN, W., RICHARDSON, K., ROCKSTRÖM, J., CORNELL, S. E., FETZER, I., BENNETT, E. M., BIGGS, R., CARPENTER, S. R., DE VRIES, W. & DE WIT, C. A. 2015. Planetary boundaries: Guiding human development on a changing planet. *Science*, 347, 1259855.

STERN, D. I. 2004. The rise and fall of the environmental Kuznets curve. *World Development*, 32, 1419–1439.

STURGEON, T. J. 2002. Modular production networks: A new American model of industrial organization. *Industrial and Corporate Change*, 11, 451–496.

STURGEON, T. J. 2009. From commodity chains to value chains: Interdisciplinary theory building in an age of globalization. In: BAIR, J. (ed.) *Frontiers of Commodity Chain Research.* Stanford, CA: Stanford University Press.

STURGEON, T., VAN BIESEBROECK, J. & GEREFFI, G. 2008. Value chain networks and clusters: Reframing the global automotive industry. *Journal of Economic Geography,* 8, 297–321.

SULLIVAN, S. 2013. Banking nature? The spectacular financialisation of environmental conservation. *Antipode,* 45, 198–217.

SUNSTEIN, C. R. 2014. *Why Nudge? The Politics of Libertarian Paternalism.* New Haven, CT: Yale University Press.

SZOLNOKI, G., THACH, L. & KOLB, D. 2016. *Successful Social Media and E-Commerce Strategies in the Wine Industry.* Basingtsoke: Palgrave Macmillan.

TAGLIONI, D. & WINKLER, D. 2016. *Making Global Value Chains Work for Development.* Washington, DC: World Bank Publications.

TAKAHASHI, R. & TODO, Y. 2013. The impact of a shade coffee certification program on forest conservation: A case study from a wild coffee forest in Ethiopia. *Journal of Environmental Management,* 130, 48–54.

TALBOT, J. M. 1997. Where does your coffee dollar go? The division of income and surplus along the coffee commodity chain. *Studies in Comparative International Development,* 32, 56–91.

TALBOT, J. M. 2004. *Grounds for Agreement: The Political Economy of the Coffee Commodity Chain.* Lanham, MD: Rowman & Littlefield.

TAMM HALLSTRÖM, K. & BOSTRÖM, M. 2010. *Transnational Multi-Stakeholder Standardization: Organizing Fragile Non-State Authority.* Cheltenham: Edward Elgar.

TAMPE, M. 2016. Leveraging the vertical: The contested dynamics of sustainability standards and labour in global production networks. *British Journal of Industrial Relations,* 56, 43–74.

TAPSCOTT, D. & TAPSCOTT, A. 2016. *Blockchain Revolution: How the Technology Behind Bitcoin Is Changing Money, Business, and the World.* New York: Penguin.

TEWARI, M. 1999. Successful adjustment in Indian industry: The case of Ludhiana's woolen knitwear cluster. *World Development,* 27, 1651–1671.

TEWARI, M. 2006. Adjustment in India's textile and apparel industry: Reworking historical legacies in a post-MFA world. *Environment and Planning A,* 38, 2325–2344.

TEWARI, M. & PILLAI, P. 2005. Global standards and the dynamics of environmental compliance in India's leather industry. *Oxford Development Studies,* 33, 245–267.

THÉVENOT, L. 1995. Des marchés aux normes. In: ALLAIRE, G. & BOYER, R. (eds.) *La grande transformation de l'agriculture: Lectures conventionnalistes et regulation-nistes.* Paris: INRA-Economica.

THORLAKSON, T., HAINMUELLER, J. & LAMBIN, E. F. 2018. Improving environmental practices in agricultural supply chains: The role of company-led standards. *Global Environmental Change,* 48, 32–42.

TOKATLI, N. 2007. Networks, firms and upgrading within the blue-jeans industry: Evidence from Turkey. *Global Networks,* 7, 51–68.

TOKATLI, N. 2012. Toward a better understanding of the apparel industry: A critique of the upgrading literature. *Journal of Economic Geography,* 13, 993–1011.

TOKATLI, N., WRIGLEY, N. & KIZILGÜN, Ö. 2008. Shifting global supply networks and fast fashion: Made in Turkey for Marks & Spencer. *Global Networks,* 8, 261–280.

TURCOTTE, M.-F., REINECKE, J. & DEN HOND, F. 2014. Explaining variation in the multiplicity of private social and environmental regulation: A multi-case integration across the coffee, forestry and textile sectors. *Business and Politics*, 16, 151–189.

TURNER, B. L., KASPERSON, R. E., MATSON, P. A., MCCARTHY, J. J., CORELL, R. W., CHRISTENSEN, L., ECKLEY, N., KASPERSON, J. X., LUERS, A. & MARTELLO, M. L. 2003. A framework for vulnerability analysis in sustainability science. *Proceedings of the National Academy of Sciences*, 100, 8074–8079.

UNWIN, T. 2005. *Wine and the Vine: An Historical Geography of Viticulture and the Wine Trade*. London: Routledge.

VAN DER VEN, H. 2014. Socializing the C-suite: Why some big-box retailers are 'greener' than others. *Business and Politics*, 16, 31–63.

VAN LEEUWEN, J. 2010. *Who Greens the Waves? Changing Authority in the Environmental Governance of Shipping and Offshore Oil and Gas Production*. Wageningen: Wageningen Academic Publishers.

VANDERGEEST, P., PONTE, S. & BUSH, S. 2015. Assembling sustainable territories: space, subjects, objects, and expertise in seafood certification. *Environment and Planning A*, 47, 1907–1925.

VANDERMERWE, S. & RADA, J. 1988. Servitization of business: Adding value by adding services. *European Management Journal*, 6, 314–324.

VELLEMA, S. & VAN WIJK, J. 2015. Partnerships intervening in global food chains: The emergence of co-creation in standard-setting and certification. *Journal of Cleaner Production*, 107, 105–113.

VERBRUGGEN, P. 2013. Gorillas in the closet? Public and private actors in the enforcement of transnational private regulation. *Regulation & Governance*, 7, 512–532.

VERHOEVEN, P. 2010. A review of port authority functions: Towards a renaissance? *Maritime Policy & Management*, 37, 247–270.

VERMEULEN, S. & COTULA, L. 2010. Over the heads of local people: Consultation, consent, and recompense in large-scale land deals for biofuels projects in Africa. *Journal of Peasant Studies*, 37, 899–916.

VICOL, M., NEILSON, J., HARTATRI, D. F. S. & COOPER, P. 2018. Upgrading for whom? Relationship coffee, value chain interventions and rural development in Indonesia. *World Development*, 110, 26–37.

VOGEL, D. 2008. Private global business regulation. *Annual Review of Political Science*, 11, 261–282.

VON GEIBLER, J. 2013. Market-based governance for sustainability in value chains: Conditions for successful standard setting in the palm oil sector. *Journal of Cleaner Production*, 56, 39–53.

VURRO, C., RUSSO, A. & PERRINI, F. 2010. Shaping sustainable value chains: Network determinants of supply chain governance models. *Journal of Business Ethics*, 90, 607–621.

WAHL, A. & BULL, G. Q. 2014. Mapping research topics and theories in private regulation for sustainability in global value chains. *Journal of Business Ethics*, 124, 585–608.

WANG, M., HAN, J., DUNN, J. B., CAI, H. & ELGOWAINY, A. 2012. Well-to-wheels energy use and greenhouse gas emissions of ethanol from corn, sugarcane and cellulosic biomass for US use. *Environmental Research Letters*, 7, 045905.

WATTS, M. & PELUSO, N. 2014. Resource violence. In: DEATH, C. (ed.) *Critical Environmental Politics*. London: Routledge.

WERNER, M. 2016. Global production networks and uneven development: Exploring geographies of devaluation, disinvestment, and exclusion. *Geography Compass*, 10, 457–469.

WHITE, B. & DASGUPTA, A. 2010. Agrofuels capitalism: A view from political economy. *Journal of Peasant Studies*, 37, 593–607.

WHITFIELD, L., THERKILDSEN, O., BUUR, L. & KJÆR, A. M. 2015. *The Politics of African Industrial Policy: A Comparative Perspective*. Cambridge: Cambridge University Press.

WHITLEY, R. 1999. *Divergent Capitalisms: The Social Structuring and Change of Business Systems*. Oxford: Oxford University Press.

WIJEN, F. 2014. Means versus ends in opaque institutional fields: Trading off compliance and achievement in sustainability standard adoption. *Academy of Management Review*, 39, 302–323.

WILKINSON, J. 1997. A new paradigm for economic analysis? *Economy and Society*, 26, 305–339.

WILKINSON, R. G., PICKETT, K. E. & DE VOGLI, R. 2010. Equality, sustainability, and quality of life. *BMJ*, 341, c5816.

WILSON, A. P. & WILSON, N. L. 2014. The economics of quality in the specialty coffee industry: Insights from the Cup of Excellence auction programs. *Agricultural Economics*, 45, 91–105.

WOLLNI, M. & ZELLER, M. 2007. Do farmers benefit from participating in specialty markets and cooperatives? The case of coffee marketing in Costa Rica. *Agricultural Economics*, 37, 243–248.

YEUNG, H. W.-C. 2016. *Strategic Coupling: East Asian Industrial Transformation in the New Global Economy*. Ithaca, NY: Cornell University Press.

YEUNG, H. W.-C. & COE, N. 2015. Toward a dynamic theory of global production networks. *Economic Geography*, 91, 29–58.

ZELLI, F. & VAN ASSELT, H. 2013. The institutional fragmentation of global environmental governance: Causes, consequences, and responses. *Global Environmental Politics*, 13, 1–13.

INDEX

ZED

Zed is a platform for marginalised voices across the globe.

It is the world's largest publishing collective and a world leading example of alternative, non-hierarchical business practice.

It has no CEO, no MD and no bosses and is owned and managed by its workers who are all on equal pay.

It makes its content available in as many languages as possible.

It publishes content critical of oppressive power structures and regimes.

It publishes content that changes its readers' thinking.

It publishes content that other publishers won't and that the establishment finds threatening.

It has been subject to repeated acts of censorship by states and corporations.

It fights all forms of censorship.

It is financially and ideologically independent of any party, corporation, state or individual.

Its books are shared all over the world.

www.zedbooks.net
@ZedBooks